D1108491

GROWTH IN THE BRITISH ECONOMY

P E P is an independent research body, financed from private sources. Its objects are to study questions on which public thought and discussion are needed, and to present both the facts themselves, and the conclusions to which they seem to point, in an objective and readable way.

The aim is to provide a clear and accurate account of all the main elements of the problem and to draw attention to the likely consequences of possible lines of action as a basis for recommendations on policy. The results are published either in major reports or as broadsheets containing shorter studies in pamphlet form.

The method of work is to bring together as a group people professionally concerned with one or other aspect of the problem under discussion, together with a few non-specialists who can ask the fundamental questions which sometimes escape the experts. This technique enables P E P to bring to bear on a problem the combined experience of men and women working in such different spheres as business, politics, the Government and local authority services, and the universities. The groups are assisted by the paid research staff, who act as their secretaries and drafters.

A leaflet giving full details of the work of P E P will be sent on application to:

The Director,
P E P (Political and Economic Planning),
16 Queen Anne's Gate,
London, S.W.1.
Telephone: WHItehall 7245–47

GROWTH IN THE BRITISH ECONOMY

A Study of Economic Problems and Policies in Contemporary Britain

1960

London

POLITICAL AND ECONOMIC PLANNING

16 QUEEN ANNE'S GATE, S.W.1

GEORGE ALLEN & UNWIN LTD

40 MUSEUM STREET, W.C.1

FIRST PUBLISHED IN 1960
SECOND IMPRESSION 1962

Made and printed in England by
STAPLES PRINTERS LIMITED
at their Rochester, Kent, establishment

CONTENTS

ACKNOWLEDGEMENTS

THIS report is the work of a Research Group which has met regularly at P E P over the past three years. In carrying out its work the Group has received help from a variety of sources and particular thanks are due to a number of individuals who have read drafts and given advice on particular sections of the report.

The Group wishes to acknowledge the help it has received throughout its existence from Mr. G. R. Denton, the Research Officer in charge of the project, and Mrs. S. Trench, the Research Assistant, who were responsible for drafting the report.

INTRODUCTION

IN examining British economic problems and policies in this report one major assumption has been employed: namely, that economic growth is desirable, that Britain should look forward to a continuous and fairly rapid advance in material standards of life. The report is based on the assumption, essential to any study of Britain's economic problems, that economic progress is a proper object of policy, and no apology is made for this here.

Attention is sometimes drawn, however, to the social upheaval caused by economic progress. There are indeed social limitations on the rate of economic growth, but economic stagnation can also give rise to social stresses, for which a moderate advance of living standards can then be a useful palliative. Raising the national income has always had more aggregate social value than its redistribution.

If economic growth is pressed too fast the social and political requirements may of course be unacceptable. The best illustration of this is the contrast between the Soviet economic system and those of the Western powers. There is much talk of economic competition with the Soviets, but the West is probably not prepared to put itself on equal terms in such competition by adopting political and social systems that will facilitate economic growth, at the expense of other aims. If it is true that the Soviet system permits more rapid economic growth than the democratic mixed economies of the West, Britain then in particular, may not in fact wish to accept the political and social consequences of successful economic competition with the Russians. The existing political system, to which great value is attached in the West independently of its economic performance, may permit a rate of growth of, say, 4 to 5 per cent per annum, but may be destroyed if the attempt is made to achieve 8 to 10 per cent.

This study therefore limits itself to considering the conditions for achieving a rate of economic growth comparable with that achieved in other Western industrial nations. This does not mean that the question of trying to compete with the Soviet bloc is dismissed as being unrealistic. It is rather that it must remain outside the scope of this report, as being a matter which concerns the whole economic strategy of the Western world. This study is limited to the narrower question of achieving a rate of growth as rapid as that of other Western industrial nations. In discussing the reasons and the possible remedies for this comparative failure P E P will be tackling the first and clearest problem, and others may take the matter further from the point where this report concludes by using more rigorous criteria of economic success.

The report intentionally refrains from any discussion of social attitudes. Yet these, of course, lie at the root of many of the problems of the British economy and it is perhaps necessary to say a few words about them here.

In a society where material progress is highly regarded, the attitude of managers to their work, and the attitude of the rest of society, and especially workers, to managers, is more conducive to the growth of productivity than in a society where other ends are given priority. Many observers have noted fundamental differences in this respect between this country and the United States. In the United States management as a career earns not only considerable wealth but also great social respect. Industry is seen as the foundation of the national life and the main hope of future progress. In Britain management appears to enjoy much less public esteem. The social prestige of being an administrator in the civil service is greater than that attached to being an administrator in industry. To be directly concerned with making money is still sometimes regarded as inferior to being one, or preferably more, stages removed from industry or trade. These attitudes, which derive from aristocratic traditions and the class structure, have been breaking down in recent years, but their influence is still significant, and removes from industry that zest and drive which complete confidence in the importance of its task could bring. Compared with America, and most Continental countries, the class structure in Britain is still relatively rigid. This tends to reduce mobility between economic groups, limiting the opportunities of talent for social and economic advancement and thus to some extent reducing the incentive to effort.

Without having attained the wealth of the United States, Britain appears to have developed, or more probably retained, much more strongly the disrespect for the pursuit of greater material wealth that is sometimes thought to underlie even current American attitudes: the desire for security, and for social ends which may not be consistent with the absolute maximum production of goods and services. This is not necessarily something to regret, indeed it may be considered a most heartening sign of a healthy civilisation. But if the real reason why the British economy does not grow as fast as some other economies is that the British people would rather strive for other aims, it would be good to see this recognised and incorporated into the philosophy of British life. Until it is, the suspicion remains that some other less desirable traits of the national character may be responsible for the slower economic progress.

It is probably true that the chief impediment to a faster growth of the British economy is that we do not want it enough. Both management and labour and, more widely, people in general, do not attach such a priority to material progress as might lead them to great enough efforts to achieve the economic results for example of the United States, or Western Germany, or the Soviet countries. This pervading attitude towards industry is something that cannot be criticised in itself: if men prefer leisure and security or just idleness to more motor cars or television sets they can neither be praised nor blamed by economists. But, whether the motives for these attitudes to industry are high or low, the economist has the right to point out that such attitudes are not consistent with as rapid a rate of economic advance as has been achieved in other countries.

This is not to say, of course, that the British do not want more material goods: that they are giving themselves over to asceticism, or even that they feel enough is enough. Far from it. The British worker is as persistent in his demands for higher wages as workers in any other country. But the crux is that he is not so prepared, for example as the American is, to take risks, move to a new job, and fight for advancement. If the prospect of more wealth is held out to him, but at the risk of unsettling his established pattern of life, perhaps being separated from his family for a period, then he is inclined to settle for security and things as they are. Similarly for the British businessman: the aggressive, dynamic, restless spirit is not so much in evidence as the desire for an easy life and small but safe profits.

If, however, these natural desires for security can in some way be met, then they need not constitute a barrier to economic progress. The solution is neither to condemn nor to ignore them, but to face up to them as valid human needs, which may limit the pace of technological advance, and the rate of growth of the national product, just as much as do the physical limitations on man's control over his environment, and which are equally susceptible to deliberate measures to overcome them. A compromise with the non-economic human motivations need not always be assumed to mean a sacrifice of economic ends, for men are often more efficient in the production of goods if attention is paid to their other needs.

CHAPTER I

SUMMARY

PRODUCTIVITY, INVESTMENT AND LABOUR[1]

BRITAIN is a wealthy country and in comparison with most nations of the world has no economic problem. In Europe, it is the wealthiest major industrial power. Outside Europe, its economic achievement is exceeded only by that of the United States and of some parts of the white Commonwealth—areas with special advantages in land and resources that have enabled them rapidly to acquire even greater wealth than Britain enjoys. Much has been made of the superior economic achievements of the United States, quite naturally in view of the fact that the British national product per head is only about two-thirds that of the United States, but the reasons for this superiority are not very relevant to any critique of Britain's post-war economic policies. American superiority appears to have come about historically, mainly through superior endowment with resources and in the present century through more favourable experience in the two world wars. In fact, in the period since the second world war the growth of the American economy has not been significantly faster than that of the United Kingdom.

However, many other countries have in the post-war years greatly surpassed, in their rates of growth of production and productivity, both the United States and the United Kingdom. This in itself is not surprising. Although Britain suffered greatly in the second world war, its losses were as nothing beside the devastation and disruption in countries like Russia, Germany and Japan. Any country which has the background of education and science and administrative ability and the social environment that makes for efficient economic organisation can increase its production at a very rapid rate while it is occupied in rebuilding industries and restoring economic activity. It was inevitable and natural, and therefore no cause for concern, that for some years after the war countries that had suffered more than Britain should enjoy a faster rate of economic growth. In the case of France there

[1] See Chapter 2.

were in addition special historical reasons why the economy should have grown very rapidly. A fairly complacent view of the slower rate of growth of output in Britain was therefore justified, but only so long as other countries were regaining the same economic position in relation to this country that they had held before the war. However, it may be that reconstruction has given these countries an impetus to progress or that their economies have been better directed, for, whatever the reasons, it is plain from the statistics quoted in Chapter 2 that their superior rate of growth has continued beyond the stage of merely regaining the relative position they had held before the war. To put the matter differently, the rate of growth of the British economy has been unduly slow when compared with that of these other countries, and, although Britain may at the moment be a comparatively wealthy country, the continuation into the 1960's of this relatively poor economic performance would, within a few years, leave Britain with a lower standard of living in relation to other countries.

Now this may not matter much, for it is quite feasible to give economic growth a low priority and, in particular, to hold that the performance of the British economy in relation to that of other countries is unimportant. If it is assumed, however, that economic progress does matter and that Britain should be able to maintain a rate of growth comparable to that achieved by other countries at similar stages of development, it becomes of no little interest to try to understand the reasons why the British economy has expanded so slowly since the second world war.

The role of capital in economic growth has long been considered by economists to be decisive. It is particularly vital, of course, in the early stages of industrial development, and interest in the significance of investment has been stimulated by the achievements of the Socialist countries, especially the USSR, and by the problems of underdeveloped territories in Asia, Africa and South America, where investment is clearly the chief requisite if hundreds of millions of people are to be raised above subsistence standards of living. This concern with investment has been carried over into discussions of economic performance in the more advanced industrial countries of the West and different rates of growth of product have been associated with different proportions of investment. The British rate of investment expressed as a percentage of the gross national product has been significantly low compared with that of most other countries in Western Europe, just as the rate of growth of production has been low, and it is possible that the low rate of investment in part explains the low rate of growth of output. But the relation between investment and output is by no means simple. Investment includes many items whose connection with production is, to say the least, very indirect, and many countries since the war have needed a high rate of investment in circumstances that did not suggest that this investment would necessarily lead to a high rate of growth of output. Perhaps the best example is the high rate of investment in housing needed in Western Germany in order to replace houses destroyed during the war. The importance of factors of this kind has led another school of economists to minimise the importance of investment, suggesting that there is some appropriate rate for each country in given circumstances and that perhaps the appropriate rate for Britain has been much lower than the appropriate rate for other countries. That there is some truth in this contention is clear if rates of population growth are related to the level of investment. The relatively low rate of investment in Britain as a percentage of the national product has none the less represented a relatively high rate of investment per head of the population. A country with a rapidly expanding population of working age, such as Western Germany in the 1950's, needs a great deal of investment merely to widen the capital structure and provide employment for all the extra workers who are joining the labour force. It must also provide the social capital which is needed for these extra people. The high rate of investment per head in Britain suggests that the yield on investment may not in fact have been as high since the war as that in other countries, and might have been lower still if the attempt had been made to invest much more than in fact was invested. Certainly factors in addition to investment appear to have played an important part in limiting the growth of productivity. There is statistical evidence, for example from the Norwegian economy, that where there has been an extremely high rate of investment per head since the war, the yield on that investment may have been rather low.

From all this, some observers conclude that Britain should not try to invest more. This conclusion is, however, invalid, unless it can be shown on other grounds that the reduced return which may be expected on the extra investment is in fact not worth while. Even though falling returns on the investment of more capital are expected, it may none the less be correct to increase investment if a high rate of growth of output is desired. The relevance of the arguments about investment is that they help to explain why the rate of growth of output in Britain has been relatively poor, rather than that they lead directly to any conclusions about what the rate of investment should be. Indeed, it would be possible to argue that the lower the yield on investment the more investment should be carried out in order to achieve a satisfactory rate of growth. This is a question of balancing future gains against present sacrifices.

One of the factors which has affected the rate of growth of production in Britain appears to have been the lack of growth of the working population. At first consideration the growth of population appears merely to be a burden which requires that the country should invest a great deal in order to provide employment at the existing levels of productivity, so that little capital is left over in order to increase productivity. Yet there are indications that a rapid increase in population, especially an increase brought about by the immigration of young, able-bodied men, gives the countries that experience it some advantages in raising their productivity. The building of new factories to employ the extra workers provides a stimulus to the economy which is not enjoyed when the labour force is stationary and improvements proceed on a piece-meal basis, continually hampered by the existence of older capacity. Of course, if a country with a stationary working population were to devote as much investment to replacing and modernising its older equipment as a country with an expanding population has to devote to widening its capital structure, then the country with the stationary population should have an advantage in increasing its productivity. The point is, however, that it is unlikely to have an urgent enough incentive to carry out this investment in greater efficiency, and its whole economy will be more sluggish and less responsive to change. This points to the need, in a country like Britain since 1945, with a very slowly increasing working population, for close attention to be paid to measures to replace the impetus to greater efficiency of an expanding population.

Even where population is not increasing, countries which are less industrially developed than the United Kingdom have an advantage in expanding their production deriving from the transfer of labour from industries where productivity is low into more modern industries where productivity is much higher. The most important example is, of course, the transfer of labour from agriculture into industry. In Britain, the agricultural population is now only about 4 per cent of the total working population, and agricultural productivity is probably almost as high as productivity in manufacturing industry. Even though a large proportion of the workers who were employed in agriculture at the end of the second world war have moved into industry in the past fifteen years, their number has not been great enough and cannot in the future be great enough to have much impact on the total of industrial manpower. In some other countries the situation is very different. In France more than one-quarter of the working population is employed in agriculture where productivity is much lower than in manufacturing, and there is room for continuing significant transfers of labour from agriculture into industry. This transfer of labour has been important in maintaining the growth of the French economy in the 1950's. It will continue to be important in the future in other countries as well as in France.

The general tightness of the labour situation, combined with the determination of the Government to maintain a high level of employment, has enabled the United Kingdom since the war to enjoy a greater degree of full employment than most other countries. In most respects this is admirable, but such a degree of full employment may not have been consistent with the optimum rate of economic growth. Too great a shortage of labour, expressed in terms of a considerable excess of jobs vacant over men unemployed, has resulted in a lack of flexibility in industry and in some wasteful hoarding and inefficient use of labour. In particular, severe shortages of certain kinds of skilled labour have seriously limited output. These shortages are, of course, partly related to the generally tight employment situation, but they are also very much bound up with provisions for education and training. Under full employment, also, the rigours of competition are reduced and it is possible for high-cost firms to continue to operate, whereas in more competitive conditions they would be driven out, to the advantage of the average level of productivity. There is evidence of long-standing excess capacity in some industries, suggesting that capital investment may have been pushed beyond the possibility of expanding the labour force to make use of all the capacity. This waste of investment resources could not have taken place if labour had moved more readily from the less efficient firms.

The British economy has remained on the whole very fully employed since 1945, although the stabilisation policies employed have had serious effects on the rate of growth of the economy. Full employment has induced some inflexibilities and waste of resources in itself, but when anti-inflationary measures have resulted in a fall in the level of employment, the inefficiencies have been, if anything, greater, for much of the mentality of the full employment years has continued, while labour has been either unemployed or employed on short time. Between 1956 and 1959, capacity was also widely unemployed, and this had a severe effect on the rate of growth.

THE DISTRIBUTION OF PUBLIC INVESTMENT[2]

While it is extremely difficult to draw conclusions from a consideration of the aggregate level of investment and its proportion of the national product, it is more feasible to examine investment in particular industries and particular sectors of the economy, and to assess whether investment opportunities in these areas have been fully utilised. The study of the distribution of investment can provide concrete and detailed evidence of areas of inadequate investment. Excessive expenditures in some sectors and failures to invest in others tend to reduce the overall return on investment, and in this way may help to explain the paradox pointed out above, namely, that while investment per head in Britain has been higher than in many other countries, the rate of growth of output has been lower. In addition, the study of the distribution of investment can throw light on the reasons for particular failures to invest. Since this report is concerned primarily with official policies affecting growth, consideration has been given mainly to the areas of the economy where governmental control operates most directly, that is, to social services and to the nationalised industries. The most notable feature of the distribution of gross investment is that housing and social service capital expenditure take almost one-third of the total. By far the

[2] See Chapter 3.

greater part of this goes to housing, and lesser amounts for school building, hospitals, and so on. In view of the continued shortage of houses and the need for replacing older houses, the overcrowding in the schools and the need for more schools and colleges, and the pitiable amounts spent on hospitals, it is not possible to assert that this social capital expenditure has been extravagant. It is more to the point to claim that it is not productive investment and therefore should not be used to inflate the figures for gross investment. But it has already been pointed out that other countries have also had high capital expenditures on housing and many have had much greater expenditure on public works in their post-war reconstruction. The proportion of aggregate investment which goes to social purposes has certainly not been excessive in relation to that in other countries. It is, in any case, doubtful whether social investment is in any true sense unproductive. Good and plentiful housing is an aid to the health, productivity and mobility of labour; education helps to provide the intelligent and skilled workers who are vital to modern industry; and the health service reduces the hours that are lost to industry through sickness. There is ground for concern at the number of scientists and technicians in this country, compared with other countries. Even if the annual output of trained people can be raised to a satisfactory level, it will still be many years before the total number available to industry is adequate. Provision of the necessary educational institutions is therefore an extremely urgent need. It may be concluded that social investment and particularly capital expenditure on education is among the most urgent calls on the investment resources available to the nation, for it is a hoary, but none the less still worth while, statement that Britain, lacking great indigenous natural resources, must rely on the skill and brain-power of the population if the standard of living is to be maintained and increased.

The basic fuel and power and transport sectors of the economy are mostly nationalised and account for another large proportion of aggregate investment. In some parts of this sector investment has been very heavy, and almost every part has been accused either of excessive or of inadequate investment or both. The investment records of the railways, the coal industry and the electricity industry are examined in some detail in Chapter 3. This investment has been determined largely on the basis of forecasts of the future demand for the products of these industries and not influenced greatly by the commercial considerations which would apply under free enterprise. The aim has been to ensure that adequate supplies of power and adequate transport facilities were available for the needs of the rest of industry. In the electricity industry, which has been rapidly expanding its output, this investment has gone hand-in-hand with greater efficiency. Each new power station has represented an advance on the one before it, and the real cost of generating electricity has been progressively reduced in favourable technical circumstances. In the coal industry, investment to maintain and to try to increase output of what has until recently been a scarce commodity, has proceeded to some extent at the expense of investment in greater efficiency. Now that the demand for coal is not so urgent there would appear to be a strong case for investment in greater efficiency so as to increase more rapidly the productivity, and so lower the cost, of coal mining. The railways were for many years deliberately starved of capital as a result of a decision to give more urgent needs a prior claim on the limited capital available. The railway system was adequate to cater for the needs of the nation and expansion was not necessary, but the neglect of investment was at the expense of efficiency and has now helped to create an awkward situation for the industry. It was, however, a deliberate measure of policy in view of the urgency of investment in other sectors and the limited total of resources available in the post-war years, and since 1955 something has been done to remedy the situation under the modernisation programme.

PRICING POLICIES IN NATIONALISED INDUSTRIES[3]

The examination of the investment histories of these nationalised industries since the second world war has revealed that although forecasts of the demand for the products of each industry have generally determined the level of capital spending, pricing policies have been an important factor leading to either inadequate or excessive investment. Pricing policies have also affected the efficiency of these industries and therefore the productivity of the capital that has been put into them. In the case of electricity supply, it is clear that the large sums invested, though on the

[3] See Chapter 4.

whole well justified by the need to expand output, need not have been quite so large if some method could have been devised to discriminate in the tariffs against consumers who use electricity at peak periods, when its cost in terms of capital investment is so high. Nuclear power stations are even more expensive in capital than conventional ones, and if in future a large proportion of the new generating capacity is to be nuclear, the urgency of adopting pricing policies that will minimise the amount of new capital required, without, of course, implying the refusal to supply any really urgent needs for power, becomes even more important. Now that there is a surplus of small coal, ideal for the generation of electricity in coal-fired stations, the immediate economic justification for building further expensive nuclear power stations becomes more doubtful still.

In the coal industry itself, much investment is capable, at the present prices, of yielding a return comparable to that which can be earned on investment in manufacturing industry. But much coal is still being mined in old and inefficient pits at considerable losses per ton. This may have been justified while the industry was still finding it difficult to maintain urgently needed supplies. For many years it was urged that the price of coal should be increased so as to reduce the marginal demand which kept these uneconomic pits in operation. But it is the long-run marginal cost of getting coal from new pits which should determine the price, rather than the cost of getting coal from the older pits. In an industry of small competing producers, the older pits would be forced to close. Within a nationalised industry, however, once the situation of shortage has ended, increasing the average efficiency of coal production and therefore reducing average costs by eliminating the extreme high-cost capacity, must be a matter for administrative arrangement. But it is important in the future that investment should be investment in efficiency rather than in volume of output, and the industry may be healthier if it is smaller.

The railways have not only suffered from lack of capital investment but also have been greatly hampered by restrictions on pricing and operating policies. These have prevented them from providing with the greatest efficiency those services which they are best suited to provide, leaving to the roads those services which the roads can provide more efficiently. The modernisation programme, which is attempting to catch up with the arrears of capital expenditure, has already run into great difficulties because the pricing and public service obligations of the railways have not yet been satisfactorily revised. The railways might possibly be operated as a commercial service without subsidy, if existing losses were written off, or they could be operated, partly at least, as a public service with subsidy. What is clear from the history of the past few years is that they cannot efficiently be operated as a semi-public service without subsidy. Until this is understood and acted upon, there is a grave risk that much of the investment which is being put into the railways will be misdirected and will not be allowed to yield the results that it could.

Some general issues relating to the pricing policies of the nationalised industries are of wider significance and perhaps really more important than the detailed position of each industry. One point concerns the financing of investment. Prices have been kept in general very low in relation to prices elsewhere in the economy, largely out of a desire to prevent increases in prices being passed on in an inflationary manner from these basic industries into other parts of the economy, and partly because workers were thought to be particularly sensitive to increases in the consumer prices for these products. The result has been that investments have had to be financed out of gilt-edged Government stocks at low rates of interest. Even so, the industries, at the ruling prices, have mostly failed to cover costs, so the yield on their investments has been much lower than in the private sector of the economy. Government financing of their investment programmes has been a major factor in the difficulties experienced in curbing inflation. It is, to say the least, doubtful whether keeping down the prices of particular products is of much assistance in preventing inflationary price increases throughout the economy, but it is clear that when this restraint of prices in the public sector has the effect of requiring the Government to finance their investment programmes by the issue, year by year, of more and more Government securities, there is a serious impediment in the way of policies to prevent inflation. Now that a more competitive situation exists in the fuel and the transport industries, it would be good to see prices adjusted to levels where a return is earned on capital invested which bears some relation to that which can be obtained in manufacturing industry (due allowance being made, of course, for the difference in the risk factor). It would also be better if the public industries financed a part of their capital requirements out of their own resources, and, where recourse to outside finance is justified, went to the market and competed for capital on equal terms with the rest of industry.

Within this general and rather unfortunate restraint of prices in the public sector, consumer prices had been held down much more than the prices charged to industry. The failure to charge the true cost of the peak demand for electricity is largely a failure to charge the domestic consumer the correct price, for the domestic consumer is particularly responsible for peak demand. In keeping down railway charges, the Transport Tribunal has been influenced by the desire of the Government to prevent inflation. Charges for bulk freights have been increased so that they are in real terms about the same as before the war. But passenger fares are in real terms much lower than before the war. In the coal industry large coal has been particularly scarce and small coal relatively plentiful, and yet the relative prices have not been adjusted so as to equate the demands for the different types of coal. Large coal is used particularly by the domestic consumer and small coal by industry and the power stations, so that in this way also the domestic consumer has been favoured. A comparison with European countries of the relative prices for domestic use and for industry of coal, gas, and electricity, and the relationship between railway tariffs per passenger mile and per ton mile, shows that the domestic consumer in relation to industry is much more favoured in Britain that he is on the Continent. This keeping consumer prices down at the expense of higher prices for industry and of harmful methods of financing the capital requirements of the public sector, appears to have been a particularly unfortunate result of pricing policies under public ownership. The result has been to stimulate consumption while increasing costs to industry, to increase unnecessarily the large investments needed in these industries, and in the final analysis to deflate the true cost of labour in relation to capital, with harmful effects on productivity.

THE IMPACT OF TAXATION[4]

A general example of this tendency to keep down consumer prices at the expense of industry, one which affects private as well

[4] See Chapter 5.

as public industry, is the method of financing the social services. On the Continent, most social service charges are applied as a tax on the wage bill which hits the employer as a part of the total cost of employing labour. In Britain, on the other hand, four-fifths of social service expenditure is financed out of taxation. By this method of financing, part of the real cost of labour appears to the firm in the guise of a general tax on profits instead of a specific charge related to labour. In this way the ratio of labour costs to capital costs is distorted in such a manner as to encourage the employment of more labour and to discourage the use of more capital instead of labour. It is impossible to say how important this influence may have been on the level of capital investment and many other factors have to be taken into account in assessing this effect. But in view of the inadequate growth of productivity it does seem to be an unnecessary loading of the dice against capital.

The level of investment, the distribution of investment, and the pricing policies of the nationalised industries are some of the factors that may help to explain the relatively poor economic progress of Britain in the post-war years. Another common suggestion has been that the level of taxation has been far too high and has had severe disincentive effects which have influenced the level and the distribution of investment and, more generally, that it has operated against enterprise and effort of all kinds. Particular taxes and related provisions for allowances have been the subject of much controversy and some of the detailed problems are discussed in Chapter 5. All too often it is assumed that the only effect of a tax or a method of taxation is a harmful one. It is important to realise that taxes and allowances can be used to stimulate investment and enterprise as well as to restrict it. Taxes can be, and are, used by the Government to take money away from private consumption and divert it to public investments, and when this happens the main effect of taxation on economic growth may be a favourable one. It is true, of course, that the situation would be much happier if the capital requirements of the nationalised industries were met out of their own prices or on the market, as suggested above, and were not financed by below-the-line expenditure. Taxation has obviously made a great contribution to economic growth in financing the development of atomic energy and the aircraft industry, and a great deal of Government-sponsored research and development work that would have taken much longer if left to private enterprise. It is important to bear these positive considerations in mind while discussing the particular defects or general results of the system of taxes.

For all the spate of comment on the evils of taxation, there is still insufficient evidence to support the more sweeping assertions that are made about the harmfulness of the system. The arguments on the subject of the effects of the general level of taxation are particularly badly supported despite the strong views that are held on this question. If it is to be assumed that the onus of proof lies on those who call for reforms and for a reduction in the total of taxation, then it must be concluded that their case fails for lack of sufficient evidence of the evils they allege. That wastes and distortions of the economy do arise out of heavy taxes is apparent —a prime example is the misuse of the business expense allowance —but this would appear to constitute a case for the tightening of the regulations regarding expenses rather than for the abolition of the taxes that leave room for these abuses. Admittedly, however tight the restrictions on expenses, there would still be abuse. Only a major reduction of income and surtax would sufficiently lessen the desirability of being paid expenses rather than personal income, and some abuses have to be accepted in view of the advantages of taxes, namely, that the Government can provide things which the private citizen and the firm cannot provide for themselves.

Although it is repeatedly asserted that the level of taxation has had a serious effect on investment, companies have been able, in the post-war period, to finance an unprecedented amount of development out of their own internal resources, and there is little evidence of severe shortages of finance for development. Moreover, the heavy rate at which profits are taxed has made it possible to operate investment incentives through the initial and investment allowance. These have operated as interest-free loans and, in the case of investment allowances, gifts of money conditional on their use for investment, and in the years when an increase of investment has been desired they have acted as a strong stimulus to expansion. Only because the positive burden of taxation has been so great have these concessions been able to operate so effectively. Whether they have been used wisely is another matter.

In relation to Continental firms, British industry has suffered in respect of allowances for the depreciation of capital assets. The British definition of expenditures which attract the allowance is usually more restricted than on the Continent and the allowances themselves are based on historical rather than on replacement cost, which makes them inadequate in a time of inflation. The initial and the investment allowances may be regarded as compensations for these relative disadvantages, and at the same time have provided a flexible method of controlling investment. Another aspect of the profits tax up to April 1958 which may have helped to make more funds available for industrial investment, though at the same time it hindered the mobility of capital, was the discrimination against distributed profits. This operated so as to encourage industry to retain profits instead of distributing them to the shareholders. In so far as some part of the distributed profits would have been spent, this discrimination acted to increase the capital available in industry. But in so far as profits distributed to shareholders are reinvested anyway, the effect of discrimination was merely to leave those firms that had been able to make profits with plenty of capital, and those that had not made profits, without capital. The latter category would include new firms and firms that were expanding rapidly, that is, those most in need of outside funds. From this point of view the change to an average rate in the 1958 Budget was beneficial.

The very heavy rates at which death duties are levied have led family firms to withdraw funds and hold them idle for many years in order to meet the possibility of death duties. The funds are therefore not available to finance improvements, thus restricting the expansion of the firm. The suggestion that the estate duty should be transformed into a legacy duty is not very helpful because it could succeed in reducing the total duty paid, and therefore the need to put funds aside for this purpose, only in so far as the ownership of the business was split up among a number of heirs rather than passed intact to one heir, and this division of ownership might itself impede the efficient running of a family business.

Changes in the level of purchase tax have been used primarily to influence the demand, and therefore the output, in a number of industries making consumer goods. When taxes are used in this way as the instruments of Government policies and not merely as a source of revenue, they cannot be judged in themselves as good or bad taxes. All that can be done is to judge the effectiveness of the policies of which these tax arrangements are the instrument, or the failings that have made these policies necessary. This is the case with regard to both depreciation allowances and purchase tax. If the purchase tax is used not primarily to raise revenue but deliberately to suppress the production of certain items, this cannot be held to be an example of a bad tax but only of a bad policy on the part of the Government in its regulation of the economy. So a lot of the criticism of the tax system is really misdirected. High rates of purchase tax have had severe effects on some industries, and the depreciation allowances given at times when initial and investment allowances have been suspended have probably been inadequate to allow for replacement costs. But both should be regarded not so much as taxes but rather as deliberate measures of economic control. It should also be noted that taxes used as economic controls do not invariably have unfavourable effects. If the variation of purchase tax can succeed in maintaining the stability of the economy then it can be an aid to the development and profitability of industry and not an impediment. If variations in purchase tax have in fact succeeded in keeping the demand, for example for motor cars, more steady from year to year, than it would otherwise have been, then, although any increase in the tax will meet with cries of protest, the tax must be held to have been helpful over the period to the industry as well as to the economy as a whole. Purchase tax was particularly harmful to a number of industries soon after the war when it was necessary to divert a lot of production from the home market into exports. But this was a price that had to be paid for one of the most effective and precise instruments of Government control over consumers' expenditure.

Two large claims on resources have sometimes been held responsible for strain in the economy and failure to expand production and productivity adequately since the war. The first is defence: Britain has undertaken as large a defence effort in relation to its national wealth as any other nation in the Western world. The second is the so-called Welfare State: Britain entered on the post-war era committed to a great extension of the coverage of social security and other welfare schemes.

DEFENCE[5]

This is not the place to discuss the political and strategic arguments about Britain's post-war defence policies. The economist has, however, the right, and the duty, to point out the economic effects of defence spending. For some years after the war criticisms of defence policies were usually political and strategic but since 1950 defence spending has been increasingly opposed because of its economic effects. It has been maintained that large defence efforts are either self-defeating because the economic crises they precipitate reduce Britain's military effectiveness just as much as the larger forces enhance it. It can also be objected that they prevent the deployment of the economic weapon of loans or gifts to the uncommitted nations, or that they impair long-run economic strength by cutting the rate of investment and growth in the home economy. It is the latter argument that is most relevant to this study. The level of defence spending in Britain since the war has represented as great an economic burden, in relation to the national wealth and to other commitments and problems, as that of any other member of the Western Alliance. At one time Britain was spending a larger proportion of the national income on defence even than the United States, and, though United States spending in the post-Korean armament drive exceeded the British as a percentage of the national income, it is questionable whether this represented a greater burden for a nation so much richer than Britain.

In 1951 and 1952 personal consumption was reduced in order to make room for heavier defence spending. This does not prove that in the absence of this defence effort these funds could have been channelled into productive investment, for such sacrifices of consumption may require a major international crisis, and not just an internal economic crisis, in order to be politically acceptable. The effect on investment and on the balance of payments of the adoption of a larger defence programme in 1951 is also brought out by the study of the financing of the post-Korean defence programme. The strain on physical resources, and consequent heavy imports of goods in short supply, was clearly marked, and investment programmes were cut. Even apart from the special effects of this acceleration of defence spending it is clear that

[5] See Chapter 6.

investment could have been higher and the balance of payments healthier throughout the post-war period if defence spending had been less or non-existent. And there is no doubt that the economy has been weaker as a result. But for the purpose of further discussion the existing level of defence expenditure has to be accepted as determined largely by non-economic factors.

SOCIAL SERVICES[6]

Social service expenditure lies in quite a different category from defence expenditure, for it is by no means correct to regard it as wasted from the economic point of view. Social service expenditure represents rather a transfer of the initiative in expenditure from individuals to Government departments. While this transfer may result in an increase in total consumption through extra spending, or through redistributive methods of financing, this increase is not measured by estimates of total social service expenditure, and indeed is very difficult to measure at all. A large proportion of social service expenditure is classified as capital expenditure and has good claim to be in the long run as vital to production as capital investment in industry. Much of the current spending also may be regarded in the light of essential "repairs and maintenance" to the human factor of production. In the absence of State provision these services would in large measure be bought by individuals out of their own pockets, and the statistics do not indicate that State provision is notably more generous than private provision. Expenditure has increased since the war, but so has the number of people in the "dependent" age groups who make most use of the social services.

The inflationary effect of redistribution of income via the social services consists only in the extent to which total consumption is thereby increased, without compensating effects on productive efficiency, and it must be emphasised again that this falls very far short of the figures of total social service expenditure. The real value of social service expenditure, even accounting for demographic changes, has increased at a faster rate since 1938 than the real value of consumers' expenditure. There is no evidence, however, to suggest that consumption is taking a larger share of national resources than it would if individuals were still making

[6] See Chapter 6.

their own provisions in place of the existing social services. Comparisons between the pre-war and post-war period show that the share of the national product taken by consumption and the social services together has fallen steadily since 1938. Whether the share of both forms of spending would have fallen faster in the absence of a high rate of social service expenditure is unverifiable. Contrary to a common misconception, British social services are certainly not excessive when compared with those of other wealthy nations. It may be concluded that the Welfare State has not constituted an unnecessary nor an excessive burden on the post-war economy. The reasons for the slow rate of growth must be sought elsewhere.

THE BALANCE OF PAYMENTS[7]

Inadequate investment and growth only become apparent after the lapse of several years. The problem which has been in the forefront of discussion since the war has been the balance of payments, and it is right that considerable attention should be paid to its connection with the question of economic growth. First, in what sense has there been a problem of exports? It was realised immediately after the war that a great expansion of exports would be needed if the country was to pay its way in the world, when it had lost overseas sources of income and had piled up debts overseas, and when it was facing worsened terms of trade. The targets fixed at that time were achieved and passed. To this extent the post-war export drive has been a great success. The increase which has already taken place in the volume of exports during the post-war period has been well in excess of the increase in the volume of imports. For many years after the war it was easy to export because of the immense backlog of demand all over the world, and the virtual absence from world markets of two main competitors, Western Germany and Japan. Since trading conditions became more normal, in the 1950's, the development of British exports in relation to those of other countries, especially Western Germany, has not been encouraging. Nevertheless, there are many good reasons why the German economy, and German exports, should have grown more rapidly than the British in this period. Moreover, it does not matter that Britain's share in world trade

[7] See Chapter 7.

should have fallen, for this is inevitable in a rapidly industrialising world, where other countries are experiencing a faster growth of population. The decline may be expected to proceed so long as industries are growing faster in other countries, either through the process of industrialisation or through a more rapid population increase in economies that are already industrialised. A decline in the British share does not matter so long as world markets are expanding and so long as the share in question represents a volume of exports that is sufficient to purchase the imports needed to maintain a satisfactory rate of growth of the national product. But the fact remains that balance of payments problems have been persistent and have inhibited economic development. Despite a quite considerable achievement, it has to be concluded that in so far as a balance of payments crisis can always be solved by increasing exports, exports have been inadequate.

At the same time the balance of payments problem has been aggravated by the addition of several items of overseas expenditure to the debit side. Some of these expenditures of foreign currency arise out of defence spending. Others have taken place as a result of a too ready acceptance of "traditional" commitments and responsibilities overseas. Notable among this type of expenditure is the export of capital, which has been at about the same level in post-war years as the surplus earned on current account transactions. If this capital had not been exported the surplus on current account could have gone to build up the reserves and might thus have prevented the recurrent crises, with their harmful effects on investment and growth. There are two sides to any balance of payments problem: a deficit may arise either out of too few credit items, or out of too many debit items. Some of the blame must be attached to over-spending, and not all to earning too little.

The sums in question when the export of capital from the United Kingdom is criticised are small in comparison with the total which is invested at home, and most is in any event in the form of the ploughing back of profits made on earlier foreign investment. The amount may, however, be quite significant in relation to the balance of payments. Overseas investment may help British exports indirectly by assisting the growth of future markets for exports of goods, but its importance in this respect is now much less than in the nineteenth century, and there is little direct help to British exports arising out of the establishment of manufacturing subsidiaries overseas. Britain could still gain by curtailing exports of capital from this country while other advanced countries continued to assist the process of industrialisation, but if all nations followed similar reasoning economic growth throughout the world would suffer.

The special arguments for reducing British long-term investment overseas do not then appear to be very strong. But this still leaves untouched the most immediate argument for their curtailment. This is simply that, however valuable overseas investment may be in the long run, it cannot be permitted to take place unless the country is earning a sufficient surplus on current account to finance it without running into payments crises. If the £200 million or so per annum of overseas investment is precisely the marginal amount by which exports have failed to finance all the unavoidable current outgoings, then the investment should be sacrificed in the interests of sounder short-term international finances. This is a powerful case, much more so than all the supporting arguments seeking to show that overseas investment anyway is not profitable for the country. However, it is always possible to argue that this expenditure is superior to consumption expenditure, and that if anything is cut it should be consumption. Britain is a rich country by contrast with many of the countries that so urgently need capital for their development, rich in comparison with the Soviet Union, which yet manages to support a greater defence and investment burden per head of the population. While the struggle against inflation has not been won, it could be argued that to cut overseas investment would only have the effect of increasing the resources devoted to satisfying the home consumer, and that no lasting improvement in the balance of payments would result. And even if such a cut could succeed in its object, it would appear to be inferior to a restraint at home that made it possible for Britain to be solvent without giving up a valuable international role.

As to the results of balance of payments difficulties, the most serious has been that investment has been cut back in attempts to cure payments crises. It has been true on one occasion, in 1955, that an upsurge of investment, too sudden and too great to be accommodated since it was superimposed on a boom in consumption, was itself the immediate cause of the payments troubles, so that investment cuts were an appropriate part of the remedy.

But in other years investment programmes that were by no means excessive have been cut or slowed down as a result of balance of payments crises. It is difficult to estimate the effect of these cuts on the total of post-war investment, but it must have been quite significant. Shortage of foreign currency reserves has reduced the level of investment, but perhaps more significantly it has reduced the total of output with the given productive capacity. This has been a matter for particular concern in the late 1950's. Investment since 1955 has in fact been well maintained, but a high rate of investment is of little value if the new industrial capacity that is installed is not allowed to increase the output of goods.

INFLATION AND THE ALLOCATION OF RESOURCES[8]

Increased production would be the most satisfactory way of solving Britain's economic problems, but in circumstances where production could not be immediately increased, the allocation of resources has been a vital matter. With defence spending that has been no more than has been necessary on political and military grounds, and social service expenditure that has not been greater than has been needed to maintain a healthy and well-educated population, then only one other item in the national accounts can logically be blamed for the failure to devote sufficient resources to investment and the strengthening of the foreign exchange reserves: personal consumption expenditure. If other cuts, in overseas investment, or in defence spending, or in the social services, were not acceptable, then the only possible conclusion is that personal consumption ought to have been restrained in order to put the economy into a more healthy position. But a vague appeal to "take in belts" is not good enough: it is necessary to be quite clear about what has happened to consumers' expenditure since the war, and what is involved in any proposal for restraint in the interests of more investment.

Comparisons with other countries show that consumption has been taking a higher share of the national income in Britain than in any other comparable country. At the same time a considerable measure of restraint of consumption has already taken place since

[8] See Chapter 8.

1938. Consumption in the United Kingdom has not advanced at as rapid a rate as production because of the extra calls that have been made on national resources in comparison with 1938. But it still takes a high proportion of the gross national product, not much lower than in 1938, which was by no means a model year. It has not been fully adjusted to the radically different circumstances of post-war years, and runs at a higher level than in most Western industrial nations. It is concluded that if all the other calls on resources are accepted, or at least recognised to offer only a limited scope for reduction, then consumption expenditure has not been restrained sufficiently to keep the economy in a healthy condition and to permit a satisfactory steady rate of growth.

What has prevented the Government from controlling consumption at a level that would have left room for the re-establishment of a surplus on the balance of payments, for defence programmes, overseas investment, and an adequate rate of investment at home? The answer is to be found in the failure to control sufficiently the pressures of demand in the economy, and to solve the problem of costs and prices continuing to rise even in years when the pressure of demand has not been high. The Government has available a whole armoury of monetary and fiscal measures for the regulation of demand, and some physical controls could also be used. The varying combinations of these measures that have been used in the last fourteen years have not succeeded in completely preventing strain on resources and consequent price increases and balance of payments crises. The policy of deflation, which can only succeed by reducing the level of employment and weakening the bargaining power of the unions, is bound to be regarded with disfavour in many sections of the community, and particularly among workers. Many people have therefore hoped for a policy that could cure inflation directly, by co-operation with the unions in ensuring that the average percentage wage increase did not exceed the average percentage increase in productivity.

Such a policy of co-operation need not be confined to preventing inflationary wage increases, but could be extended to positive efforts to achieve a faster rate of economic growth. Indeed, the best way to ensure that the percentage increase in wages does not in any year exceed the percentage rise in productivity is to increase more rapidly each year the level of output per head. In this way price stability can be achieved with a high rate of growth instead of by putting the economy into a straitjacket. Although this co-operative solution may be accepted as superior to the policies used in the post-war period, it would be idle to assume that having stated the ideal solution it can immediately be put into effect. All that can be proposed is that all efforts should be made, by the Government, by the employers, and by the unions, to increase co-operation in economic life. This process is bound, however, to be a slow one, having to overcome deep-seated prejudices and to break down institutional barriers, and it will be many years before it can make a significant contribution to the better functioning of the economy.

INTERNATIONAL COMPARISONS[9]

Comparisons of the post-war economic histories of France and Western Germany with that of the United Kingdom reinforce some of the conclusions arrived at by the independent study of events in Britain. There are three main features of German and French experience which are particularly relevant to the problems discussed in this report.

First, both Western Germany and France undoubtedly benefited in the 1950's from an easier labour supply for industry than Britain. The Western Germans began the 1950's with a large reserve of unemployed workers, and have in addition enjoyed a substantial influx of people, mainly young workers, from the East. France, like Britain, was not able to expand its total working population very rapidly, but with rising productivity in the still large agricultural sector of the French economy, substantial numbers of workers have been released for industry. France has also relieved the labour shortage by attracting foreign workers into French industries. Western Germany is now suffering from a lack of flexibility in the labour supply, being affected already by the low birth rates of the years immediately after the war and by a reduction in the inflow of refugees.

Secondly, growth in the French and German economies has not been limited so much as in Britain by balance of payments crises and the restrictions needed to alleviate them. Western Germany has for many years had large surpluses on foreign payments,

[9] See Chapter 9.

surpluses that have created their own problems, but problems that have not required the restriction of economic growth for their solution. France has been faced with balance of payments difficulties every bit as severe as the British: for instance, in 1957. But France has been both able and willing to press forward with policies for economic growth even at the expense of temporarily aggravating its international liquidity. This points two morals for Britain: first, that overseas obligations which cost foreign currency or expose the £ sterling to speculation should not be lightly undertaken, and, secondly, that perhaps Britain should not be quite so sensitive to payments crises, when they do arise, at least, not to the extent of sacrificing the growth of the economy in order to correct the immediate liquidity situation.

Thirdly, and lastly, France and Western Germany present contrasting histories so far as economic planning is concerned. Yet the German policies of incentives for private effort, and the French use of more *dirigiste* methods have this in common: that they have both had economic expansion as their central objective. Either of these policies might have been better for Britain than the vague and hesitant policies that have in fact been pursued, though the French example seems more relevant to the condition of the British economy in the 1950's than the German.

PLANNING FOR ECONOMIC GROWTH[10]

It is also suggested that a greater degree of planning, particularly of investment, could ensure that productivity would increase at a faster rate. Part of any bargain that might finally be reached with the trade union movement for a national wages policy would have to be a greater measure of control and planning of private industry. It certainly appears that one of the reasons for the inadequate rate of growth of the British economy since the second world war may have been that there has never been an objective of growth to aim at. The desirability of expansion has been alluded to from time to time, but there has never been a clear aim expressed in terms that could enlist the enthusiasm of all sections of the community towards its fulfilment. The mere publication of an estimate of the possible achievement of the economy for a few years ahead, if such an estimate has been

[10] See Chapter 10.

carefully drawn up with the co-operation of the people who will be responsible for its realisation, may in itself be a potent force making for success. For various reasons, that are outlined in Chapter 9, it is likely that the example of the French economy, where considerable use has been made of investment planning, is more relevant to British conditions than that of the German economy. It is therefore tempting to conclude that central investment planning is the answer to the problem of achieving a more rapid rate of growth. But, as in the case of union co-operation, little hope can be entertained of the success of such a policy if private industrialists retain their present desire for independent decision on development policy. It is improbable that agreement would be reached in many industries on a meaningful investment programme for several years ahead. Once more, progress can only be made slowly, and the scope of co-operation gradually extended. The Government could certainly make a start by publishing its plans for the public sector on a more regular and consistent basis, and this in itself would be a good indication of possibilities for the rest of private industry.

But just as important as the publication of programmes for investment and expansion as a guide to investment decisions and as an impulse towards a faster growth of output, is the testing of many other aspects of policy against the needs of economic expansion. The distribution of investment in the public sector, pricing policies, the methods of raising taxes, measures to solve crises in the balance of payments, should all be checked against the need for economic growth much more assiduously than has been done up to now. And, most important, a national objective for raising living standards and achieving other national aims is essential if the co-operation of the unions is to be secured in the solution of the problem of inflation, and more generally in the increase of productivity.

CHAPTER 2

PRODUCTIVITY, INVESTMENT AND LABOUR

PRODUCTIVITY

THE level of national product per head of the population gives a general indication of the historical achievement of the economy up to a particular year, while the rate of growth of the national product per head shows the speed at which the economy is currently growing. It may be that a country with a relatively high level of national product per head does not need as high an annual rate of growth as a country which has a lower level and which needs to grow faster in order to correct this. The level of British national product per head of the population, like that of other European countries, is well below that of the United States. A study by the Organisation for European Economic Co-operation,[1] published in 1958, gave indices of the levels of gross national product per head for the United States and for eight European countries. The calculations using United States price weights showed that seven of the eight European countries had national products per head in 1955 around two-thirds as great as the product per head in the United States. For the eighth country, Italy, the output per head was only 35 per cent of the American. Figures based on an average of European price weights showed that among the European countries the United Kingdom had by a narrow margin the highest income per head in 1950 and in 1955. These figures are shown in Table 1.

It would thus appear that so far as the level of the national product per head of the population of these countries and the United States is concerned, the main cause for worry is the poor situation of Britain in comparison with the United States, and this situation is shared with the other Western European countries. Other countries besides the United States have, however, surpassed the British level of national product per head, notably Sweden, New Zealand, Australia and Canada.

[1] Milton Gilbert and Associates, *Comparative National Products and Price Levels* (OEEC), 1958.

TABLE I

INDICES OF THE LEVEL OF GROSS NATIONAL PRODUCT PER HEAD IN THE UNITED KINGDOM AND SEVEN EUROPEAN COUNTRIES

(United States = 100)

	1950 *at* 1950 *prices*	1955 *at* 1955 *prices*
United Kingdom	49	51
Norway	47	50
Belgium	47	49
Denmark	49	46
Western Germany	32	44
France	40	43
Netherlands	39	42
Italy	21	24

Source: Comparative National Products and Price Levels (OEEC), 1958, p. 28, Table 4.

Discontent with industrial and economic progress in Britain in relation to that in the United States is not a phenomenon of the 1950's but dates back to the middle of the last century, though views differ as to the exact date at which British economic performance was surpassed by the Americans. Certainly British observers were beginning to worry about the greater American productivity in some sectors of manufacturing industry by the middle of the nineteenth century, and by the end of the century there was fairly widespread uneasiness at the relative inefficiency of several British industries. The faster rate of increase of American productivity has continued in the present century, and at such a rate as to widen the differential which already existed at the turn of the century. Dr. Rostas, in a pioneering study,[2] first provided measurements of the level and rate of increase of productivity in Britain and in the United States. He found that for thirty-one industries in 1935–39 output per worker was 116 per cent higher in the United States than in Britain, and output per man-hour 187 per cent higher. Comparing all factory trades he concluded that productivity was then two-and-a-quarter times higher in the United States than in the United Kingdom. Between 1907 and 1937 the growth in output per wage earner was 1·4 per cent per

[2] L. Rostas, *Comparative Productivity in British and American Industry*, National Institute of Economic and Social Research, Occasional Paper XIII (Cambridge University Press), 1948.

annum for the United Kingdom and 1·8 per cent per annum for the United States; and in output per man-hour, 1·7 per cent and 2·9 per cent respectively. These results have been confirmed and brought further up to date by a study of Professor Frankel.[3] Out of thirty-four industries chosen for their comparability and the availability of data, American labour productivity (output per man-hour) exceeded British labour productivity in thirty-three industries in 1948. The one exception, where British productivity exceeded American, was the manufactured ice industry. Among the other thirty-three industries, United States output per man-hour was over four times the British in seven industries; over three times the British in five; over twice the British in a further seven; and over one-and-a-half times in another nine industries.

Sir Donald MacDougall[4] has challenged the common view that United States economic superiority expressed itself in a higher rate of growth of productivity than that of the rest of the world in peace time in the present century, but his account leaves unchallenged the difference in the absolute level of productivity at the present time between the United States and the rest of the world. Briefly, whereas productivity in the United States has been if anything stimulated by the productive efforts of the two world wars, productivity in the rest of the world has fallen steadily in each of the wars. It has then risen more rapidly than American productivity for a period of five years or so to regain the pre-war level, and thereafter has risen at the same rate as the American, though at a lower level. The reason for the overall superiority of the Americans in increasing productivity has been that other economies in their post-war recoveries have not normally been able to make up for the loss of the increments of productivity that they should have had during the war years. From 1900 until the outbreak of the first world war in 1914, in the 1920's and the 1930's, and since the second world war, productivity in the rest of the world as a whole has risen as fast as in the United States. But as a result of the sharp declines suffered in the rest of the world outside the United States in the two world wars, physical output per head in the United States doubled between 1913 and 1955, whereas physical output per head in the rest of the world reached

[3] Marvin Frankel, "British and American Manufacturing Productivity", *University of Illinois Bulletin*, Vol. 54, No. 49, February 1957.

[4] *The World Dollar Problem* (Macmillan), 1957, Chapter 5.

by 1955 a level only 50 per cent higher than that of 1913.

However, what can be said about the rest of the world as a whole in comparison with the United States is not necessarily true for the United Kingdom, and indeed the chief implication of MacDougall's argument so far as this country is concerned is that the growth of output per head in Britain has in fact been less than the average for the world outside the United States. The rather reassuring things that can be said about economic growth in the rest of the world in peace time during the present century in relation to the United States cannot be said about the United Kingdom. In particular, they cannot be said about the United Kingdom in the period since the second world war. A good deal of statistical information exists for this period, and however one interprets the figures or questions their accuracy, they cannot but show a lower rate of growth for the United Kingdom in comparison with most other industrialised countries. The following table compares the growth in real national product between a pre-war year and 1957 for the United States, Western Germany, all OEEC member countries combined, and the United Kingdom. The United Kingdom has by far the lowest rate of growth, only 35 per cent, against an average of 59 per cent for the OEEC countries as a whole, 120 per cent for Western Germany, and 129 per cent for the United States. It may also be noted that the gross national product in the United States grew rapidly between 1938 and 1948,[5] while little growth was enjoyed in Europe. The indices show that the OEEC countries as a whole have grown faster since 1948 than the United States, but the British economy has grown at a slower rate than the United States.

TABLE 2

VOLUME INDICES OF GROSS NATIONAL PRODUCT AT MARKET PRICES

1938 = 100 (converted from base year 1953)*

Country	1948	1949	1950	1951	1952	1953	1954	1955	1956	1957
United States . .	165	165	179	194	200	208	204	221	227	229
Western Germany .	n.a.	n.a.	128	143	152	164	175	197	208	220
All OEEC countries .	100	107	116	122	125	132	138	146	153	159
United Kingdom .	106	110	113	117	116	120	127	130	133	135

Source: OEEC, *General Statistics*, 1959, No. 1, January, p. 99.

* Western Germany: 1936 = 100.

[5] This rate of growth may, however, have been affected by the depth of the US depression of 1938.

The growth of the gross national product is affected by outside events, such as changes in the terms of trade, but one of the main determinants of the growth of the gross national product is the growth of industrial production. The following table shows the different progress of industrial production in Western Europe and in the United States since 1950.

TABLE 3

INDICES OF INDUSTRIAL PRODUCTION

1950 = 100 (converted from base year 1953)

Country	1951	1952	1953	1954	1955	1956	1957	1958
Western Germany	118	126	139	156	179	193	204	211
France	111	110	112	122	131	144	156	165
Italy	114	117	128	140	153	164	177	181
Netherlands	103	103	114	125	134	140	143	143
Belgium	114	109	108	114	125	132	132	124
Luxembourg	122	122	112	116	130	139	142	136
The "Six"	115	118	125	138	153	165	175	180
All OEEC countries	109	109	116	127	138	145	152	155
United States	107	111	119	111	124	127	127	119
United Kingdom	104	101	106	115	121	121	123	121

Source: OEEC, *General Statistics*, 1959, No. 3, May, p. 7.

The most notable feature of these indices is that they show that the rise in industrial production in the United Kingdom was almost entirely achieved in the years 1953, 1954 and 1955, and since 1955 industrial production has been almost stationary. This was in contrast to events in the "Six", where the growth of industrial production was much more continuous from 1950 to 1957, but similar to the developments in the United States. Down to 1955 the growth of industrial production in the United Kingdom since 1950 did not seem too poor in relation to that in the Western European countries, though it was even then lower, partly because of a more serious check to growth in the years 1950–52. A large part of the explanation of the lower rate of growth of industrial production in the United Kingdom would therefore appear to lie in the discontinuity of growth. The problem of the checks to economic growth is discussed later in this chapter on page 49 and is also dealt with in detail in Chapter 7.

Different rates of growth of the population may account for a large part of the differences in the rates of growth of the gross national product. The population of the United Kingdom has been increasing relatively slowly, by only 9 per cent between 1938 and 1958, compared with an increase in Western Germany over the same period of 31 per cent, and in the United States of 34 per cent. Several other Western European countries had considerably larger rates of increase in their populations than the United Kingdom.[6] But if comparisons are made in terms of gross national product per head, which is a rough indication of the advance in the standard of living, the United Kingdom still shows a significantly lower rate of growth than the United States, Western Germany, and the average for all the OEEC member countries. Both Western Germany and the United States have increased their gross national product per head more than twice as fast as the United Kingdom in the last twenty years, and the OEEC countries as a whole have grown significantly faster.

TABLE 4

VOLUME INDICES OF GROSS NATIONAL PRODUCT PER HEAD

1938 = 100 (converted from base year 1953)*
1950 = 100 (converted from base year 1953)

Country	1938	1948	1949	1950	1951	1952	1953	1954	1955	1956	1957
United States .	100	146	142	153	163	164	169	164	175	175	175
				100	107	108	111	108	114	114	114
Western Germany .	n.a.	n.a.	n.a.	101	111	119	127	134	148	156	162
				100	110	118	125	133	146	154	160
All OEEC countries .	100	93	99	106	110	112	116	121	127	130	136
				100	104	105	110	114	120	123	129
United Kingdom .	100	100	103	107	109	108	112	117	120	122	125
				100	102	101	105	109	113	115	117

Source: OEEC, *General Statistics*, 1959, No. 1, January, p. 99.

* Western Germany: 1936 = 100.

While the better performance of the United States may be mainly attributed to the favourable economic effects of the second world war, the West German achievement has been concentrated in the post-war era. The United Kingdom has increased its gross national product per head as fast—or as slowly—as the United States since 1950. But Western Germany has increased its productivity three-and-a-half times as fast, though admittedly through special causes, which are discussed later in Chapter 9.

[6] See Table 8, p. 35.

The following table shows that even between 1953 and 1955, when Britain was enjoying the boom of the mid-1950's, the growth of industrial productivity over the two years was only 8 per cent, compared with 12 per cent for Western Germany and 17 per cent for France. Then by 1958, when the virtual stagnation of production in the United Kingdom, and the continuing growth in Western Germany and France, had taken effect, the British growth of productivity over the whole five years amounted to only 10 per cent, against 33 per cent for Western Germany and 40 per cent for France.

TABLE 5

INDICES OF PRODUCTION, EMPLOYMENT AND OUTPUT PER MAN-HOUR IN INDUSTRY

(1953 = 100)

	1953	1954	1955	1956	1957	1958
Production						
United Kingdom	100	108	114	114	116	114
Western Germany	100	112	128	138	147	151
France	100	110	120	133	145	154
Employment						
United Kingdom	100	102	105	105	105	105
Western Germany	100	105	114	121	124	124
France	100	100	101	103	106	108
Output per man-hour						
United Kingdom	100	105	108	108	110	110
Western Germany	100	105	112	116	126	133
France	100	108	117	126	132	140

Source: ECE, *Economic Survey of Europe in 1958*, Appendix A, Table VII.

There is no doubt therefore that Britain has had a most unsatisfactory economic record in the post-war years, and not only in connection with problems that might be thought to spring from special difficulties, for example on overseas payments, but also in respect of production and productivity, which are the basic tests of any economy. The remainder of this chapter seeks to amplify some of the features, and to elucidate the more general economic causes, of this inadequacy of production.

INVESTMENT

The superiority of capital equipment is one of the most favoured explanations of the success of the American economy, and was particularly stressed in the reports of the Anglo-American Productivity Committees in the late 1940's and early 1950's. It is commonly estimated that the amount of capital per worker in manufacturing industry in the United States, whether measured directly, or indirectly in terms of horse-power used per worker, is about two-and-a-half times as great as in the United Kingdom. The American worker in manufacturing industry in fact enjoys between two and two-and-a-half times as much mechanical assistance as his British counterpart, and this is precisely the difference in their relative productivity. The difference is not merely one of quantity of capital: it also expresses itself in quality, and in frequency of replacement. Emphasis on investment has also been carried over into the discussion of the problems of Western industrialised countries from the study of the startling progress of Soviet Russia, and from the discussions about the initiation of economic development in the underdeveloped countries. Capital is so self-evident a need in countries where land, natural resources, and labour are in such abundance, that a direct and simple relationship between the rate of investment and the rate of economic growth has often been assumed.

This kind of approach was quite common a few years ago, and since net investment was regarded as the key magnitude a "league table" was drawn up showing net investment as a percentage of net national product.[7] The United Kingdom usually came a very poor last at the bottom of the table, with a net investment rate of only 5 or 6 per cent of the net national product, compared with rates in other countries of Western Europe between 10 and 20 per cent, and in some even over 20 per cent. Since depreciation has taken a larger proportion of gross investment in the United Kingdom than in the countries with a higher rate of gross investment, the comparison of gross investment does not appear quite so unfavourable, although the United Kingdom remains at the bottom of the list. The following table shows gross domestic fixed capital formation as a percentage of the gross national product for various OEEC countries in 1938 and in 1948 to 1957, ranked in order of the proportions in 1957.

[7] See, for example, the ECE *Economic Survey of Europe in 1955*, p. 44, Table 22.

TABLE 6

GROSS DOMESTIC FIXED CAPITAL FORMATION AS A PERCENTAGE OF GROSS NATIONAL PRODUCT AT MARKET PRICES

Country	1938	1948	1949	1950	1951	1952	1953	1954	1955	1956	1957
Norway . .	18	27	29	28	24	26	29	29	30	27	27
Netherlands .	n.a.	21	20	20	19	19	21	21	23	25	25
Luxembourg .	n.a.	n.a.	23	24	17	18	24	23	22	20	24
Western Germany .	14*	n.a.	n.a.	19	19	19	20	21	23	23	22
Italy . .	16	19	17	18	18	19	19	20	20	21	22
Sweden . .	17†	18	17	18	18	19	20	21	20	20	20
France . .	n.a.	n.a.	17	15	16	16	16	16	17	18	18
Belgium . .	n.a.	n.a.	15	16	14	14	15	15	16	16	16
United Kingdom .	11	12	13	13	13	13	14	14	15	15	15
OEEC members combined .	13	16	16	16	16	17	17	18	18	19	19
United States .	13	16	16	17	16	16	16	16	17	17	17

Source: OEEC, *General Statistics*, 1959, No. 1, January, pp. 103 ff.

* 1936. † 1938–39.

Comparisons made over more recent periods paint a very unsatisfactory picture. The following table, adapted from the ECE *Economic Survey of Europe in 1958*, compares the average annual industrial investment in 1953–57 per employee in 1953 with the percentage increase in industrial employment and in output per man-hour in 1953–57. In the cases of Austria, Western Germany and Italy, a high average annual investment per employee may perhaps be attributed to the provision of more jobs. But no such explanation applies to the comparisons with Belgium, Denmark, France, Norway and Sweden. All these countries have had, with Britain, increases in industrial employment of around 5 per cent. And all have had considerably greater percentage increases in output per man-hour over the same period, with the exception of Denmark, which invested less per employee than the United Kingdom and shows a growth of output per man-hour only slightly greater.

These figures, it may be noted, relate to years when investment in the United Kingdom had been expanding rapidly, and when its share in the national product had considerably increased. Even in the years of the investment boom it appears that industrial investment has been low in relation to that in other countries.

TABLE 7

INDUSTRIAL INVESTMENT, EMPLOYMENT AND PRODUCTIVITY, 1953 TO 1957

	(a) *Average annual investment per employee in 1953 in dollars at 1954 prices*	(b) *Percentage increase in employment, 1953–57*	(c) *Percentage increase in output per man-hour, 1953–57*
Western Germany	650	24	26
Italy	620	10	29
Austria	430	21	20
Belgium	570	6	24
Norway	950	5	20
Sweden	590	4	15
United Kingdom	400	5	10
France	590	4	32
Denmark	310	5	13

Source: ECE, *Economic Survey of Europe in 1958*: (*a*) Chapter 11, p. 37, Chart 6; (*b*) Appendix A-10, Table VIII; (*c*) Appendix A-8, Table VII.

Population growth

One qualification to simple comparisons of investment rates is that some reference must be made to the much faster rates of growth of population in many other countries than in the United Kingdom since the second world war. The following table shows that Britain is near the bottom not only of the "investment league" but also of the "population league".

TABLE 8

INDICES OF THE GROWTH OF TOTAL POPULATION, 1938, 1950, 1957 AND 1958

Country	1938	1950	1957	1958
United States	100	117	132	134
Western Germany	100	121	130	131
Netherlands	100	117	127	129
Norway	100	111	119	120
Sweden	100	111	117	118
Italy	100	108	113	113
United Kingdom	100	106	109	109
Belgium	100	103	107	n.a.
France	100	101	107	108
Luxembourg	100	99	104	n.a.

Source: OEEC, *General Statistics*, 1959, No. 3, May, p. 50.

The significance of this slow rate of population growth is seen by considering the rate of increase of capital per worker. For manufacturing industry alone Dr. T. Barna has calculated that capital *per worker* rose between 1938 and 1956 by 25 per cent in the United States, by 30 per cent in Western Germany, but by no less than 70 per cent in the United Kingdom.[8] So whatever may be concluded about the adequacy of investment in Britain, it is necessary to try to find some explanation for the failure of the economy to grow rapidly despite the evidence of a relatively high rate of investment *per worker* in manufacturing industry over the last twenty years as a whole. Why, despite a higher rate of investment per worker than either Western Germany or the United States, has the United Kingdom yet had a lower rate of growth? The answer to this question must lie in the efficiency and productivity of the investment that has been carried out.

Types of investment

A general distinction, already used in this chapter, is commonly made between gross investment and net investment. A large proportion of the total expenditure on fixed capital must be devoted to maintaining the stock of capital which is already in existence. Expenditure on repairs and maintenance is not normally counted as capital expenditure, but as a running cost. The "depreciation" or capital consumption which is the difference between gross investment and net investment refers to money spent to provide new machines to replace those that are completely worn out. But machines are rarely replaced by identical units. Capital equipment for replacement purposes, like all new capital, will take advantage of the latest technical developments. So it is possible that even with zero net investment, as usually defined, that is, with a total gross investment only great enough to replace worn-out units in the existing capital stock, there may still be considerable progress through a gradual improvement in the quality of capital as replacements are made. Only subject to this qualification, may it be accepted as a general statement that major economic advances depend on net investment.

Net investment may be divided into two kinds. The first is that which merely adds further units to the existing types of capital,

[8] T. Barna, "Investment in Industry—has Britain lagged?", *The Banker*, April 1957, p. 229.

and is commonly referred to as "widening" the capital structure. The second, the net investment, called "deepening" the capital structure, depends on new techniques. Widening requires not only more capital but also more of the other factors of production, especially labour, in the same proportions as were previously being employed. Deepening the capital structure usually implies that more capital will be employed in relation to labour so that in the case of new capital which produces an existing product but uses a radical new process, an increase in labour productivity is usually expected. Of course these types of investment cannot be neatly distinguished in practice, but shade into each other. Widening investment, like replacement investment, will rarely involve using plant identical to that already in use, but will take advantage of the results of the latest technological improvements.

Capital and output

Historical estimates of the capital stock and the output of several countries have suggested a direct relationship between net investment and the growth of output. Such a relationship is understandable in theoretical terms, given the productivity of capital, and attempts have been made on the basis of this observed statistical relationship to estimate for the future the rates of growth that can be achieved with varying amounts of net investment. A simple calculation is sometimes made: net investment as a percentage of the gross national product, multiplied by the average percentage yield on investment, equals the percentage rate of growth of the gross national product. Subtracting the percentage rate of growth of the population, which is particularly important in some underdeveloped countries, leaves the percentage rate of increase in national product per head. For example, if the rate of net investment is 6 per cent, and the yield 25 per cent, the rate of growth of the gross national product will be 6 per cent multiplied by 25 per cent, which is 1·5 per cent, per annum. From such a calculation it is a short step to emphasise the value of net investment, and to plead for a cut in consumption that will allow it to be increased. Because such a large proportion of gross investment in industrialised countries has to go to depreciation, a small percentage increase in gross investment will make a large percentage increase in net investment, which means that a small "sacrifice" of current consumption will have a large influence on the rate of growth of the economy. For example, if the rate of gross investment is 15 per cent of the gross national product, and this results in the net investment rate of 6 per cent, a sacrifice of a mere 5 per cent of gross national product, which may be perhaps 7 per cent of the current total of consumption, will put up gross investment to 20 per cent, net investment say to 10 per cent, and the rate of growth of the economy to no less than 2·5 per cent per annum. But even this is not the end of the story. If the population is growing at a rate of 1 per cent per annum, the original rate of growth of 1·5 per cent in gross national product would have resulted in only 0·5 per cent per annum growth in the gross national product per head.[9] Whereas with the new rate of investment the gross national product per head will now grow at a rate of 1·5 per cent per annum. The growth of the economy will have been stepped up to no less than three times its previous rate by a temporary sacrifice of only 7 per cent of consumption. At the new rate of growth the cut in consumption will soon be made good, and the consumer can advance to undreamed-of levels of prosperity.

A Norwegian study

However, the similar observed ratios of capital to output in different countries and in different periods may be due not to a causal relationship between capital and output but to other factors not explained by such a formula. For example, the observed historical "yields" on net investment of 20 or 25 or 30 per cent include unspecified returns not from net investment but from the increase in the quality of capital as replacement takes place, and also from increases in the productivity of both labour and capital which result from work study and other methods of increasing efficiency which do not require significant amounts of net investment for their implementation. Other theories of the relationship between capital and output have attempted to account for this "technical factor" of growth arising out of replacement and out of improved methods which do not require net investment. For example, a Norwegian study[10] has given the technical factor a

[9] But see below, pp. 43–4, for a qualification of this relationship between the growth of population and the growth of output per head.

[10] Odd Aukrust and Juul Bjerke, "Real Capital in Norway, 1900–1956", *Income and Wealth*, Series VII, International Association for Research in Income and Wealth.

key role in the determination of the rate of growth of the Norwegian economy in the period since 1945.

Norway has been as high in the investment "league tables" as Britain has been low. But the Norwegians also have found a disproportion between the efforts devoted to investment since the second world war and the returns in the shape of production. The marginal capital output ratio for the whole economy is calculated to have risen from 2·9 in the period between 1946 and 1951 to 5·48 between 1951 and 1956. Or, to put it another way, the return on new capital has fallen from almost 35 per cent to under 20 per cent. This falling yield is thought to have been a result of the very high rate of investment. In face of these statistics showing diminishing returns to the use of more capital, the importance of the supply of labour as a determinant of economic growth is stressed.[11] It will be noted later in this chapter (in the section on "Manpower") that there is reason to believe that British productivity may have suffered in relation to other countries from the fact that the population has been almost stationary, and the working population only slowly expanding.

The yield on investment

What then has been the output yield on investment in the United Kingdom since the second world war? If only this question could be clearly answered, and in detail, it would be possible to be much more positive in the conclusions to this chapter. There is clearly an enormous range of output yields between various industries, while many investments, especially those of a social nature, may have no meaningful or measurable yield, even though they may be as important in the long run in increasing the national product as industrial investments with a clear and large return. Dr. Barna[12] has estimated the real depreciated value of fixed assets in thirty-eight manufacturing industries, and compared this with the value added in each industry in 1954. The result is a series of capital output ratios ranging from 1·0 in the tobacco industry to 7·9 in mineral oil refining; that is to say, yields ranging from 100 per cent down to 12·5 per cent. The average for all the thirty-eight industries is a capital

[11] See Appendix C for a fuller treatment of this example.

[12] "The Replacement Cost of Fixed Assets in British Manufacturing Industry in 1955", *Journal of the Royal Statistical Society*, Series A (General), Part I, 1957, Table 5.

output ratio of 2·2, or a yield of 45 per cent. But this is an average yield, on the written down value of past investments, for one year only. It tells us nothing about the return on *additional* investments. And this is only for manufacturing industry, where the yield must be expected to be much higher than for all investment in the whole economy.

With the statistics that are available at present, it is possible to calculate only from some broad national aggregates. Over the ten years from 1948 to 1957 the real gross domestic product increased by 30 per cent, or roughly 3 per cent per annum.[13] Over the same period, the net fixed capital formation at home averaged about 6 per cent of the gross domestic product every year. The output yield of this net investment must therefore be put at 50 per cent. But this increase in output must have resulted in part from the improvement factor in that part of gross investment that went to replace old equipment, so it may be more realistic to calculate the yield on gross investment. Gross investment averaged about 15 per cent of the gross domestic product between 1948 and 1957, which gives an output yield of 20 per cent.

With regard to the future, much hinges on whether diminishing returns must be expected as more capital is invested, and the Norwegians have estimated a fall from 33 per cent to 20 per cent in the yield on net investment since the war. One of the factors that affects the overall return on total capital investment in the whole economy is its distribution among the various openings for more capital that are available. If more capital is invested in the social sector, and less in manufacturing, it must be expected that the yield on investment will fall. But this is not to say that such investment is non-productive. Investment in more social capital, especially for example in more schools and technical colleges, may be vital for the productivity of future investments in industry. So, social investments, like necessary investments in public utilities such as power supplies, though their immediate return may be low, may be making a highly significant contribution to the yields that can later be obtained on industrial investment only if these basic investments have previously been made. Since all investment takes some time to fructify, it must also be expected that the apparent yield on investment will fall in a period when the total of investment is increasing. This indeed

[13] *National Income and Expenditure 1958* (HMSO).

may be an important explanation of such evidence as there is of falling yields. The solution in such a case is not to cut investment but to be patient and wait for the yield to be realised.

If it is expected that the yield on new investment in Britain will continue at much the same level as on past gross investment, that is, will continue at around 20 per cent, then raising the rate of investment from 15 per cent to 20 per cent would raise the rate of growth of the national product from 3 per cent to 4 per cent per annum. With population increasing at 0·5 per cent per annum, the rate of growth of the national product per head would be increased from 2·5 per cent to 3·5 per cent, an increase of 40 per cent. Unfortunately, it is impossible to be certain even about the yield on past investments, due to the vast difficulties in the measurement of capital. Much uncertainty surrounds even the estimate for the whole economy such as has been suggested above.

A natural rate of investment

The wide range of proportions of gross national products which are invested in various European countries argues that the investment rate in any one country is no sure guide to the optimum rate in another, and supports the idea of a "natural" rate of investment for each country. If there were in some sense a natural rate of investment for each country in particular economic circumstances, and if for Britain since 1945 it could be calculated to be lower than for most other Western nations, this might be held to justify a relatively low rate of investment. Professor Cairncross has supported the idea of what he calls an "appropriate" rate of investment, attacking the validity of international comparisons of investment, and particularly of net investment. He concluded that:

> International comparisons of investment cannot be made really satisfactorily on a "league table" basis: the rate of investment in one country is no sure guide to the rate appropriate in other countries. How much a country should invest must depend on the opportunities open to it, the arrears from which it is suffering, and the growth in the population which it has to house and employ. It is not the volume of investment, nor even the proportion of income saved and invested that matters, but the gains that would flow from *additional* investment.[14]

[14] A. K. Cairncross, "The Investment League", *Progress*, Vol. 46, No. 255, Summer 1957, p. 17. Also, "Reflections on the Growth of Capital", *The Scottish Journal of Political Economy*, June 1959.

This argument is correct as far as it goes: it may be recognised that there is a natural rate of investment, and that the gains from investment may be disappointing if this natural rate is exceeded. But this is not to say that the natural or appropriate rate is also a desirable rate. The whole point of discussing the rate of investment is to suggest policy that may be needed to adjust this level either upwards or downwards. If it were thought that natural forces entirely determined the rate of investment in the best manner, then there would be no point in discussing the rate of investment. The idea of a natural rate is one that is extremely useful in explaining the differences in the rates of investment in different countries, and sometimes in explaining why a high rate of investment in a particular country has not yielded the hoped-for returns. But this explanation cannot at the same time be a complete justification for either a higher or a lower rate of investment.

If some advocates of more investment perhaps take too optimistic a view of the relationship between capital and output, others are also incorrect to use the arguments that have been advanced in the preceding pages as a basis for recommending that the rate of investment should be reduced or at least not increased any further.[15] If there is a low or falling marginal productivity of capital in a developed country with little increase in the labour force, it is also more difficult to get increases in output from the use of more capital. But increases in labour productivity *are* possible, and greater, rather than less, use of capital may be justified by the difficulty of using other factors to increase production.[16] To conclude that investment should not be increased, or should even be reduced, would be defeatist. Equally, to press blindly ahead, recommending more investment irrespective of the kind or amount, would be flying in the face of the facts. Investment should be maintained and increased, but with a clear understanding that the returns may not be very great, and with some selection of emphasis in order to avoid pressing investment too far in areas where the returns may fall.

A special argument for pressing investment at home to the

[15] It may be correct to advocate on these grounds a cut in the rate of net investment when this is over 20 per cent of the national product, and sustained by borrowing from overseas, as in Norway, but not for Britain, with one of the lowest rates of net investment in Europe, and a substantial net exporter of capital.

[16] A fall in the productivity of capital may of course affect the attractiveness of investment overseas in relation to investment at home. (See Chapter 7.)

utmost even in the face of falling returns is that Britain is more dependent on international trade than any other country in the world, and must compete in export markets with countries that are enjoying the benefits of a rapid expansion of population. Only great determination in scrapping old plants and generally in investing in greater productivity will enable Britain to overcome the disadvantages, in the form of a lack of flexibility, that a static labour force can bring.

MANPOWER

Any country with an expanding population is under some obvious disadvantages in increasing its productivity in comparison with a country that has a stable population. Out of a given amount of investment, a greater proportion may well have to be used to provide jobs and homes and services for the extra population, and less capital will be available for deepening the capital structure. But the country with a rapidly expanding population also has certain advantages, though these are rather less obvious. These advantages will depend a great deal on the nature of the increase in population. If the increase is due to a falling death rate, it may mean merely that there are more old people to look after, and clearly this is an economic liability with few or no offsetting advantages. If the increase derives from a higher birth rate, there will be a period during which the existing adult population is burdened with the rearing and education of larger numbers of children. But when the larger generation of young people begins to be taken into the labour force, there will be considerable economic advantages in certain conditions. But the most favourable kind of population increase is that which results from the immigration of young people of working age. This may give the equivalent benefit of a higher birth rate, without the fifteen or so years' burden of a larger number of dependents.

But, however the increase is brought about, any country with a rapid increase in the number of workers has some advantages in increasing productivity over a country with a stable working population. Even though most of its capital investment is going to expand and widen the structure of industry and little may be left over for the modernisation of existing industrial capacity, nevertheless, productivity may increase quite rapidly through the averaging of a large amount of new plant that has a high rate of productivity. A few years of a high rate of investment can quickly reduce the average age of plants and increase the average level of productivity. This may be made clearer by a simple numerical example. If one assumes that the productivity of new plant during a period of expansion of population and industry is twice as great as that of older plant already in existence, and if population and the physical amount of capital both increase by, for example, 50 per cent, then even though physical capital *per worker* has not increased, the average level of productivity will have gone up by 33 per cent. This of course assumes that new plant that is installed during a period of expansion is much more productive than pre-existing plant, and it could be argued that the average level of productivity ought to increase even faster if the population were not expanding and all this capital used for widening the structure of industry could be used for replacing the older and less efficient plants. In the numerical example, for instance, if population did not increase but the same amount of investment was used to replace older plants, then the rise in average productivity would be not 33 per cent but 50 per cent.

For various reasons, however, it appears likely that a large amount of capital investment may result in a greater increase of average productivity if devoted to new plants employing new workers than if it is used for improvement schemes in existing factories. For when there is a rapid expansion of population and production, complete and integrated new plants tend to be built; whereas if it is a question of modernisation, the tendency is to work on a more piecemeal basis rather than to scrap older plants ruthlessly. A new plant can take advantage of all the latest innovations, whereas the existence of a mass of equipment and facilities from an earlier technological period holds up the modernisation of existing plants and reduces the yield that can be obtained on this kind of investment. Technological breakthroughs are much easier for a country that is expanding its population and more difficult for a country that has a stationary population.

The rapid expansion of population due both to natural increase and particularly to a constant flow of immigrants is one of the more general historical explanations of the superiority of the United States economy. The United States benefited from a rapidly rising population, and one moreover with a predominance of young and active men, which gave industry a plentiful and flexible supply of labour. In the years since the second world war also, Western Germany has benefited from an influx of young people. It seems likely that the increase in the number of workers has produced advantages which have offset the effects on the rate of investment per head.

This argument has been used in general terms in the *Economic Survey of Europe in 1958* published by ECE in March 1959. The slow growth of output and of productivity in the United Kingdom (and in Denmark) in the years 1953 to 1958 was attributed to low rates of industrial investment per worker combined with a small increase in employment, and the Survey continued:

> Since, when employment stagnates, a given volume of investment will raise the amount of capital per worker faster than when employment increases rapidly, one might have expected to find a tendency towards a more rapid rise in productivity in the countries where employment rose relatively slowly. It would appear, however, that the wider opportunities provided by a high level of gross investment for taking advantage of technical progress have been a more important influence on productivity than the slowing-down of the rise in capital per worker in consequence of a rapid rise in employment. Thus the rise in productivity has depended less upon the amount of investment per additional worker employed than upon the level of investment in relation to the total number of workers employed or to total output.[17]

In other words, although larger amounts of capital have been needed in some countries with a growing population, merely to keep up the average level of investment per worker, so that at first sight it seems unlikely that productivity would be increased, a built-in improvement factor, arising not out of replacement investment, but out of the size and scope of net widening investment, has had an important influence on productivity.

Of course, no simple correlation can be expected between the countries which have had the greatest increases in productivity and those that have had the greatest increases in population since the war, for many other factors besides the size of population are involved. One important consideration is that flexibility of labour, and in particular the movement of workers from industries with low productivity to those with higher productivity, can do a lot to offset the disadvantages of lack of growth in the total popu-

[17] ECE, *Economic Survey of Europe in 1958*, Chapter II, pp. 37–8.

lation. This structural point helps to explain why France in particular, with one of the lowest rates of population increase, has yet had one of the highest rates of increase of productivity. Another facet of the manpower situation is the effect of checks on the growth of the economy which are necessary from time to time in order to avoid the worst excesses of inflation. Third, there is the special problem of the shortage of particular classes of manpower, especially scientists and technicians, and skilled workers, that has held up progress. The remainder of this chapter examines these aspects of the influence of manpower on the growth of productivity.

Some expansion of the labour force in the United Kingdom has come about by the attraction into employment of a greater proportion of the total population since the war. In 1938 there were 9·5 per cent unemployed, but in the mid-1950's only around 2 per cent. The employment of more women has also been an important source of labour. In 1958 nearly 8 million out of the total working population of 24 million were women. These additions to the labour force have, however, been offset to some extent by the retirement of more old people as the age structure of the population changes.

One of the most important of the "internal" sources of labour for industry is the transfer of labour from other sectors of the economy. Expansion can take place, even with a stationary total labour force, if some sectors decline and release labour, or increase their productivity so fast that they need less labour, and this labour moves into sectors with scope for rapid growth. The table below shows the percentage of the total occupied labour force employed in the main sectors of the economies of the United Kingdom, Western Germany and France in 1957.

TABLE 9

OCCUPIED LABOUR FORCE BY SECTORS

(Percentages)

<table>
<tr><th></th><th>Agriculture</th><th>Industry</th><th>Building</th><th>Services</th></tr>
<tr><td>United Kingdom</td><td>4</td><td>45</td><td>6</td><td>45</td></tr>
<tr><td>Western Germany</td><td>17</td><td colspan="2">48</td><td>35</td></tr>
<tr><td>France</td><td>26</td><td>29</td><td>7</td><td>37</td></tr>
</table>

Source: ECE, *Economic Survey of Europe in 1958*, Appendix A-10, Table VIII.

The United Kingdom had a far higher proportion employed in services in 1957: 45 per cent, against 35 per cent for Western Germany and 37 per cent for France. It also had the largest proportion engaged in industry and building: 51 per cent against the German 48 per cent, and the French 36 per cent. Such high proportions in services and industry are possible only because the agricultural population has been reduced to an extremely low proportion of the total labour force: just over 4 per cent. France still has 26 per cent of its labour force on the land, and Western Germany 17 per cent. In the United Kingdom the scope for the release of labour to industry and services has been carried to about the limit. But in Germany and France, as also in many other European countries, there is still plenty of room for the transfer of labour from agriculture to other sectors, if agricultural efficiency can be increased.

Between the pre-war period and 1955 in the United Kingdom only 16 per cent of the total increase in the labour force in those industries that gained labour over the period came from "losing" sectors; and only 25 per cent of this labour was released from agriculture. The main part came from trade, and a small amount from mining. The productivity differences were too small for these movements to have much effect on average productivity. In Western Germany only 5 per cent of the total increase in the labour force in the gaining sector came by transfer from "losing" sectors. The significance of this factor was lessened in the vast increase resulting from immigration. But in France transfer of labour between sectors has been important: 59 per cent of the increase in employment in the gaining sectors came from "losing" sectors, and 97 per cent of the labour released came from agriculture. The transfer of labour from low productivity agriculture into high productivity industry has been one of the factors sustaining the boom of recent years.[18]

Between mid-1939 and the end of 1958[19] the gaining sectors of

[18] ECE, *Economic Survey of Europe in 1956*, Chapter VII, Table 12, p. 22.

[19] There is no continuous series of manpower figures over this period, since a new series, with considerable changes both of coverage and classification, began in 1948. The figures in this paragraph have been obtained by adding together the changes between 1939 and 1948 in the old manpower series, and the changes between 1948 and 1958 in the new series. The reader is referred to Table A1 in Appendix A for details of the changes in the total and in the distribution of manpower between 1939 and 1948, and between 1948 and 1958.

the British economy increased their labour force by a total of 2,458,000. Of this total, 2,017,000 came from the increase in the total of civil employment, and only 441,000, or 18 per cent, from the "losing" sectors, which were agriculture, mining, and the distributive trades. Only 5 per cent of the total increase of employment in the gaining sectors came from agriculture. In manufacturing industry, 1,394,000 out of the total increase in the labour force of 1,868,000 came from the increase in total employment in manufacturing, and only 474,000, or 25 per cent, from transfers within manufacturing industry between losing and gaining industries.

Excess demand for labour

There is no doubt that the expansion of the labour force, together with the wage restraint to which it contributed, has been an important factor operating against inflation in Western Germany. In this country, there have been periods of high levels of jobs vacant in relation to numbers employed, which is often expressed as an excess of vacancies over unemployment.[20] One harmful effect of a labour shortage which results in an "excess demand" for labour is that employers may have retained labour that they have not really needed because of the difficulty of recruiting more labour when it was needed again. There are of course often good reasons for wanting to "keep the team together", rather than disband a successful team just because of a temporary slackening of demand. This is a good reason for holding on to labour during a recession, but in times of high demand since 1945 it has been exaggerated to the point of hoarding. In other ways also labour tends to be used inefficiently when it is in great demand, though it is not easy to estimate how great this "wastage" of manpower may have been. More important perhaps has been the fact that measures designed to reduce this excess demand for labour, while they may help in some directions, in others lead to even more waste of labour resources.

The rate of increase of productivity was slowed down after 1955 because while production was held back and in some cases eventually reduced, labour was often retained in anticipation of a resumption of expansion. In some firms wasteful hoarding of labour may have been eliminated; but in others overtime was

[20] See Appendix B.

reduced, and a four-day week introduced. Even when labour was released, or recruitment discontinued, as in the coal industry, the increase in unemployment that resulted also lowered the overall productivity of the whole economy, even though productivity in individual industries may have been increased. It may be argued that this reduction in the effective use of labour was only a temporary phase of adjustment during the period of anti-inflationary measures and the 1958 recession and that when the economy is expanding healthily once more, labour will be effectively used. The evidence at the moment is, however, that in the periods when demand has been cut back in order to curb the inflation, labour has been even more inefficiently used because of the increase in unemployment and in short-time working. And this has not so far effected any permanent cure of inflation.

The serious effect on the average annual rise in production of the stagnation or cutting back of production in particular years can be seen from the following table, which shows the index of industrial production since 1948, from which the simple annual average rate of increase in production has been calculated in the second column. It can be seen that the effect of the 1952 recession was to reduce the annual average rate from a peak of 7·0 per cent in 1950 to a low of 3·5 per cent in 1952 (though the effect is exaggerated by the nearness to the base year). Similarly, the stagnation in industrial production since 1955 has reduced the

TABLE 10

INDUSTRIAL PRODUCTION, 1948–1958

	Index of industrial production		*Average percentage rise per annum*	
			(*a*) from 1948	(*b*) from 1954
1948	*100*			
1949	106		6·0	
1950	114		7·0	
1951	117		5·7	
1952	114		3·5	
1953	121		4·2	
1954	130	*100*	5·0	
1955	137	105	5·3	5·0
1956	138	106	4·8	3·0
1957	139	107	4·3	2·3
1958	138	106	3·8	1·5

annual average rate of increase from 5·3 per cent in 1955 to 3·8 per cent in 1958. The second column of figures based on 1954 = 100 shows the effect on the average rate of growth of production since 1954.

Shortage of skilled men

Another disadvantage arising out of the labour shortage is that the new capacity that has been installed since the war has not always been fully utilised through lack of labour. The shortage of labour has been most severe in the highly skilled grades, such as plant mechanics, electricians, skilled foundry workers, sheet-metal workers, tool makers, precision fitters and machine-tool setters. It is not clear how far this shortage of skilled workers has led to under-utilisation of industrial capacity, and how far it has itself delayed the installation of new capacity. The OEEC Engineering Report of 1958, which said that "on the whole the existing production capacity in the European engineering industries has been used to a higher degree", made a special exception in the case of the United Kingdom, and mentioned the long-standing shortages of skilled workers and technicians as an important limiting factor leading to under-employment of capacity, apart from the excess capacity caused by the restraints on demand.[21]

Excess capacity

The long-standing excess of productive capacity, not over demand but over the quantity of labour available to operate it, would explain partly, at least, why returns on capital have been disappointing. If faulty appreciations have been made of the possibility of getting more labour, then investment may too often have been of the "widening" variety. Statistics of the utilisation of capacity are a notable gap in the information available about the working of the economy since the war. If they were available they would enable this possible explanation of a low rate of growth of productivity to be confirmed and quantified.

Evidence about the current amount of excess capacity in the metal-using industries was obtained by the National Institute for Economic and Social Research in 1958. The Institute's enquiry into capacity and output showed that in July 1958 capacity was

[21] OEEC, *The Engineering Industries in Europe*, May 1958, pp. 55 and 57.

available in the metal-using industries to expand output by about 20 per cent.

> To achieve this extra 20 per cent of output in the metal-using industries, would require more labour in most firms. The average of the replies suggests a 7 per cent increase in numbers employed and a 3 per cent increase in average weekly hours. The increase in hours worked would be obtained by ending short time where it exists and by returning to an amount of overtime which would be regarded as perfectly normal both by management and labour; it probably implies a customary working week of 47 to 48 hours. A 7 per cent increase in employment implies the addition of 250–300,000 to the manpower of the metal-using industries. Had the trends in employment between 1954 and 1956 continued, manpower in the metal-using industries would be 225,000 higher today. The data obtained imply that with fuller use of plant there would be a sharp increase in output per man and in output per man-hour.[22]

The greater part of the excess capacity referred to here has resulted from the check to production since 1955, while investment continued to increase up to 1958. Whether this is regarded as the continuation and aggravation of a long-term tendency, or as a new feature of the economy, it is clear that for some time to come manpower, rather than capital, is going to be the chief obstacle to the expansion of output. Although in 1959 big increases of output, and of productivity, were achieved by reducing the number of unemployed, certain industries will apparently be hit again by labour shortage before all the excess capacity can be utilised.

A STATEMENT OF THE PROBLEMS

This chapter has ranged widely over the subjects of productivity, investment and manpower. A number of important conclusions stand out, and since these form the basis and starting point for the remainder of this report, it is worthwhile to summarise them in the following paragraphs.

First, Britain is a wealthy country and the level of the gross national product per head compares favourably with that of most European countries. But although the present level of the national income and of living standards compared with most of the rest of

[22] National Institute of Economic and Social Research, Press Statement, 6 August 1958.

the world may be high, there is cause for concern in that the British level has been surpassed by several other nations.

Second, moreover, the rate of growth of production and of productivity in the United Kingdom has been much slower since the second world war than in many other countries, and a continuation of this poor economic performance would leave Britain with a lower standard of living than several other European countries within a few years.

Third, a possible explanation of this low rate of growth is that there has not been sufficient investment, and indeed the proportion of the gross national product invested in the United Kingdom since 1945 has been lower than in most other Western European countries. Correspondingly, the proportion of the national product devoted to consumption has been higher.

Fourth, this low rate of investment has nevertheless represented quite a high rate of investment per head, because of the relatively slow rate of increase of the working population over the last twenty years. This suggests that the yield on investment may not have been so high as in other countries, and that factors in addition to investment may have played an important part in limiting the growth of productivity.

Fifth, other countries, especially the United States and Western Germany, have had much more rapid increases of population than has the United Kingdom, and this may have given them some advantages in increasing productivity, even though the need to provide social and industrial capital for these extra numbers must have reduced the finances available to increase the amount of capital per head.

Sixth, Britain has also reached a stage of much greater structural maturity in the economy than these other countries, and has therefore not been able to obtain significant increases in the industrial labour force by transfers from agriculture, as, for example, the French have been able to do.

Seventh, the United Kingdom has had throughout most of the post-war period a very high level of employment. The specific shortages of certain kinds of skilled labour have had a serious effect on the growth of output. In addition the country has suffered from the lack of flexibility that goes with very full employment of resources. There has been a lack of pressure on the inefficient firms to force them to give up resources to the more efficient, and labour itself has been used inefficiently and wastefully hoarded.

Eighth, the economy has also, within the general condition of pressure of demand, suffered from oscillations caused from time to time by policies designed to prevent the chronic inflation from getting out of hand. The loss of increments to production involved in these periods of anti-inflationary measures has had a serious effect on the rate of growth of the economy. There is evidence of long-standing excess capacity in some industries, suggesting that capital investment may have been pushed beyond the possibility of securing the labour to make use of all the new capacity. A more serious failure to use capital equipment to the full has been experienced in the late 1950's when the expansion of production was held back for several years in order to cure the excessive pressure of demand.

Survey of the report

It is then from these general conclusions about the performance of the British economy that the remaining chapters of this report take their starting point. Chapter 3 examines the distribution of investment, and Chapter 4 considers the influence on this of pricing policies in the public sector. Chapter 5 considers the impact of taxation on investment and enterprise and the desire to work. Chapter 6 is devoted to accounts of the particular burdens of two kinds of Government spending, on defence and on the social services. Chapter 7 turns to the influence of external events, and the special difficulties arising out of the balance of payments. Chapter 8 sums up the combined effect of many of the pressures described in previous chapters under the topic of inflation. Chapter 9 examines more systematically some of the international comparisons used earlier. Chapter 10 discusses the practicability of one suggested remedy for the British economic problem, planning.

CHAPTER 3

THE DISTRIBUTION OF PUBLIC INVESTMENT

IN both the public and private sectors, there have been two forces at work determining the amount of investment in particular industries since 1945. First, there have been long-range investment plans, influenced by the post-war problems of shortages of goods and deterioration of services, and the need to catch up with the general buoyant demand created by post-war reconstruction and expansion. Secondly, there have been recurring cuts or restraints on investment, arising primarily out of balance of payments crises. The interplay of these two opposing forces, the one positive and deliberate, the other negative and hasty, has largely determined the overall rate of investment and has also affected its distribution. They have affected the distribution as well as the total because whenever cuts have been made, even of the most general kind, some scale of priority has been applied. For example, in 1952 housing was specifically excluded from the impact of dearer money; in 1957 the road programme was excluded from the restraint on capital investment which was applied to other sectors, including atomic energy. Longer-term planning has also been affected by the consideration of the balance of payments, for the problem of combining solvency with expansion has been foremost in limiting the rate of growth which has been planned for the public and the controlled sectors of the economy.

Given that the rate of economic growth has been influenced in these ways, two important questions have to be considered. First, is it possible to devise some means of preventing a recurrence of the history of progressing by fits and starts, from which both the public and the private sectors of the economy have suffered? Would it be possible to achieve better short-term forecasts of the economic situation, so as to avoid crises and cuts in investment? This problem is discussed in Chapter 10. For the moment attention is confined to the second question: has the general distribution of investment been satisfactory?

Total investment in the United Kingdom may be divided into three main categories: social investment, investment in transport and public utilities, and investment in the private sector in manufacturing and distribution and services. Some of this investment is essentially unplanned, though influenced by various Government policies, but in the social sector and in public utilities and transport, which together comprise about half the total of investment, there is considerable scope for regulation of investment according to some overall plan. Investment has been motivated by the need to expand output in the nationalised industries, rather than by the desire to increase efficiency. In fact, however, investment in the public industries has not in this country been organised entirely according to a consistent set of objectives, but has resulted from a variety of pressures, many of them relics of past events. In particular, pricing policies, in some cases obligatory on account of past and obsolete legislation, in other instances resulting from the traditional practice of the industry, and in others arising from a desire on the part of the Government to avoid price increases that might be inflationary, have influenced the distribution of investment. The aim of the present chapter is to describe the general distribution of investment and then, in more detail, to discuss the adequacy of investment in the most important industries in the public sector. Chapter 4 then examines the influence which pricing policies have had on these investments. The special problems of the influence on investment and economic growth of the way in which the Government raises the money it needs for its general expenditure and for the social services, is held over to Chapter 5.

On the average, gross fixed capital formation in the years 1948–58 was about 22 per cent more in real terms than in 1938. Measured in 1954 prices, investment in 1938 was £1,993 million, and the annual average for 1948–58 was £2,431 million. By 1958 capital formation had reached £2,973 million at 1954 prices, a 49 per cent increase over 1938, and 59 per cent over 1948. In this total three main categories may be distinguished: housing and social services; public utilities and transport; and manufacturing, distribution and other services. The first category is not directly productive, though it plays an important part in ensuring the effectiveness of investment in other sectors; while the second yields only very low returns on the capital invested given the existing pricing policies. These first two sectors correspond roughly to the "public" sector. The third sector corresponds to the "private" sector of industry.

TABLE 11

GROSS FIXED CAPITAL FORMATION BY INDUSTRY GROUP AT 1945 PRICES

(£ million)

	1938	1948	1949	1950	1951	1952	1953	1954	1955	1956	1957	1958	*Total* 1948–58	*Average* 1948–58
Housing	599	425	416	408	399	477	622	644	579	561	539	507	5,577	507
Social services	109	59	81	99	103	102	105	110	113	131	150	153	1,206	110
Other public services	130	55	57	67	77	72	79	81	83	95	94	110	870	79
TOTAL	838	539	554	574	579	651	806	835	775	787	783	770	7,653	696
Mining and quarrying	23	37	45	41	40	48	62	79	82	82	87	88	691	63
Gas, electricity and water	184	175	215	239	241	241	262	303	325	305	313	331	2,950	268
Transport and communications*	268	281	289	267	238	218	258	270	274	326	381	384	3,186	290
TOTAL	475	493	549	547	519	507	582	652	681	713	781	803	6,827	621
Distribution and other services†	‡	206	243	256	256	249	272	328	413	428	440	473	3,564	324
Manufacturing	603‡	430	486	559	591	566	550	581	644	731	767	731	6,636	603
Agriculture, forestry and fishing	43	120	118	113	104	96	93	100	108	96	104	111	1,163	106
Building and contracting	‡	28	30	30	35	36	35	44	48	46	49	48	429	39
Legal fees, etc.	34	53	51	51	50	38	35	38	41	40	38	37	472	43
GRAND TOTAL	1,993	1,869	2,031	2,130	2,134	2,143	2,373	2,578	2,710	2,841	2,962	2,973	26,744	2,431

Source: National Income and Expenditure 1959 (HMSO), Table 52, and, for 1938 figures, *National Income and Expenditure 1958* (HMSO), Table 59. The 1959 Blue Book revised previous figures for the period 1948–57 in accordance with the New Standard Industrial Classification, 1958. The 1938 figures, taken from the 1958 Blue Book, are therefore not strictly comparable.

* Excludes road goods transport.
† Includes road goods transport.
‡ In 1938 fixed capital formation by building and contracting and by distribution and other services is included with manufacturing.

Table 11 analyses investment in broad industry groups between 1948 and 1958. All the figures are at 1954 prices. The shares of each category in the total investment over the ten-year period were as follows:

I. Housing, education and child care, health services, national assistance, sewerage and land drainage, other public services:
£7,653 million . . . . . 29 per cent

II. Coal, other mining and quarrying, gas, electricity and water, railways, road passenger transport, shipping, harbours, docks and canals, air transport, postal telephone and radio communications, roads and public lighting:
£6,827 million . . . . . 26 per cent

III. Distribution and other services, and bricks, pottery, glass, etc., mineral oil refining, other chemicals and allied trades, iron and steel, non-ferrous metals, shipbuilding, mechanical engineering, electrical engineering, motor vehicles and cycles, aircraft, other vehicles, metal goods, n.e.s., precision instruments, jewellery, etc., rayon, nylon, etc., and silk, other textiles, leather, fur and clothing, food, drink and tobacco, manufactures of wood and cork, paper and board, paper products, printing, etc., rubber, other manufacturing:
£10,200 million . . . . . 38 per cent

The remaining £2,064 million, 8 per cent of the total, is accounted for by agriculture, forestry and fishing (£1,163 million), building and contracting (£429 million) and legal fees, stamp duties, etc. (£472 million).

It can be calculated from the table that housing and the social services have taken a smaller share of total investment in the years 1948–58 than in 1938—29 per cent against 42 per cent. Total expenditure has also been lower in real terms, largely because annual real expenditure on housing has been on average £92 million less in the last eleven years than in 1938. In only two years, 1953 and 1954, did it exceed the level of 1938. Expenditure on "other public services" has been consistently lower in real terms than in 1938, the 1948–58 average of £79 million being 39 per cent lower than in 1938. The average annual real capital expenditure on the social services was about one million less in 1948–58 than in 1938, but this average is particularly misleading.

Although real investment in the social services was only £59 million in 1948 (54 per cent of the 1938 figure), it was steadily rising during the eleven-year period. By 1954 it had regained the 1938 level in real terms, and in 1958 it reached £153 million, an increase of 40 per cent over 1938.

Investment in transport and public utilities since 1948 has been taking a slightly larger share of total investment than in 1938, 26 per cent between 1948 and 1958 against 24 per cent of the total in 1938. But the real value of capital expenditure in this sector has been, on average, 31 per cent higher than in 1938, and expenditure in 1958 reached £803 million at 1954 prices, an increase of nearly 69 per cent over 1938. Investment in mining and quarrying and in gas, electricity and water has been steadily rising over the whole period. In transport and communications, although real investment in 1948 was £13 million more than in 1938, it was falling between 1949 and 1953, and in 1954 was only just above the 1938 level in real terms. But since 1955 investment in transport and communications has been rising rapidly, from £274 million in 1955 to £384 million in 1958, an increase of 40 per cent in four years.

Manufacturing and distribution and other services have been taking a larger share of total investment than in 1938, 40 per cent of the total on average between 1948 and 1958, and 42 per cent of the total in 1958 compared with 30 per cent in 1938. In real terms investment in this sector has almost doubled since 1938, rising from £603 million in 1938 to £1,252 million in 1958, and over the eleven years 1948–58 as a whole it has been on average 60 per cent more than in 1938. Investment in distribution and other services averaged £324 million per annum at 1954 prices between 1948 and 1958. Between 1948 and 1953 it was fluctuating between £206 million and £272 million but from 1953 to 1958 it rose steadily and rapidly from £272 million to £473 million. Investment in manufacturing averaged £603 million a year at 1954 prices between 1948 and 1958. Investment in manufacturing also fluctuated between 1948 and 1953, but then rose rapidly from £550 million to £731 million.

Investment in building and contracting has risen in real terms from £28 million in 1948 to £48 million in 1958, with particularly large rises between 1950 and 1951, and between 1954 and 1955.

TABLE 12

GROSS FIXED CAPITAL FORMATION IN MANUFACTURING, 1948–1958

(£ million)

	1948	1949	1950	1951	1952	1953	1954	1955	1956	1957	1958	Total 1948–58
1. Food, drink and tobacco	42	45	53	58	57	56	60	73	84	91	102	721
2. Mineral oil refining	6	18	32	34	40	33	16	13	22	42	36	292
3. Other chemicals and allied industries	34	43	57	75	81	92	96	103	140	153	154	1,028
4. Iron and steel	32	42	49	54	55	52	69	69	83	107	116	728
5. Other metals	8	10	9	10	10	10	11	13	20	22	14	137
6. Engineering and electrical goods	57	58	62	71	88	88	97	121	141	143		
7. Shipbuilding and marine engineering				6	7	8	9	9	10	16		
8. Motor vehicles and cycles				26	30	26	26	47	57	57		
9. Aircraft	21	21	33	25	37	38	22	18	23	22	255	2,021
10. Other vehicles				3	3	3	3	3	3	4		
11. Metal goods not elsewhere specified	15	16	18	17	19	20	22	29	35	33		
12. Textiles	38	51	53	54	46	43	55	64	58	62	78	711
13. Leather, leather goods, fur and clothing	14	13	11	9	8	10	10	11	12	11		
14. Bricks, pottery, glass, etc.	19	18	20	19	18	22	24	25	30	31		
15. Timber, furniture, etc.	6	8	11	10	8	8	10	12	10	10		
16. Paper, printing and publishing	23	22	24	30	29	27	36	47	64	73	140	995
17. Rubber	13	12	12	7	7	5	8	12	15	14		
18. Other manufacturing				6	6	6	7	9	10	12		
TOTAL	328	377	444	514	549	547	581	678	817	903	895	6,633
AT 1954 PRICES	430	486	559	591	566	550	581	644	731	767	731	6,636

Source: National Income and Expenditure 1959 (HMSO), Table 53, and for 1954 prices, Table 52.

THE SOCIAL SECTOR

Housing

The provision of housing is by far the largest part of social investment. Between 1948 and 1958 it took £507 million out of the total average of £696 million for all social investment. Housing alone accounted for no less than 21 per cent of national fixed investment between 1948 and 1958. But the proportion of national investment going to housing was at its peak in 1953, when it accounted for 26 per cent of all fixed investment. By 1958 the proportion had fallen to 17 per cent and this reflected a real fall in the volume of fixed investment in housing from 1954 onwards.

The Labour Government restrained house-building, which was strictly controlled from Whitehall, to under 200,000 dwellings per annum in England and Wales in 1949, 1950 and 1951, in order not to impose an additional strain on the balance of payments. The Conservative Government entered office in 1951 bearing a pledge to build 300,000 houses a year. When interest rates were raised in March 1952 in accordance with the new economic policies, housing was deliberately excluded from the effects of dearer credit by an increase in the subsidy which compensated for the additional interest charges. Municipal house-building was encouraged, and the restrictions on private house-building were relaxed and finally removed. In 1954 354,000 houses were built. Then from 1955 a new housing policy was initiated. The general needs subsidy for municipal housing was first cut and then abolished. Private housing was also hit by dearer money and credit restrictions, and did not expand as quickly as local authority building contracted. The total number of houses completed in the United Kingdom fell from 354,000 in 1954 to 308,000 in 1956 and 1957, and 279,000 in 1958. The number completed by local authorities fell from 239,000 in 1954 to 143,000 in 1958. Within the falling total private housing was expanding, but only slowly, from 92,000 completions in 1954 and 116,000 in 1955 to 130,000 in 1958.

Has investment in housing since the war been excessive? There are a variety of difficulties in arriving at a judgement on this point. Housing demand—at subsidised or controlled rents—is not the same as housing need: nor is housing need accurately measured by a census, which counts as families people living in the same house whether they wish to do so or not. Undoubtedly there was a severe housing shortage at the end of the war, one of between 1 and 1·5 million houses. In addition the number of households has since increased by over 150,000 per annum. Whether or not there is still a shortage is a controversial matter in the absence of adequate information. The 1951 Census found that, on average, there were 1·08 rooms per person in households sharing dwellings and an average of 1·67 rooms per person in those households which had separate dwellings to themselves. This represents a higher standard of housing than has ever before been enjoyed in this country. On the other hand, the Census also revealed that there were about 1·1 million actual and potential households without dwellings to themselves.

Some argue that the continuing "shortage" is the result of under-occupation at one end of the scale together with over-occupation at the other. The decontrol of rents initiated in the 1957 Rent Act has done something to resolve this question, within the range of property which was decontrolled.

Taking a general view, if there are after twelve years just about sufficient houses, the investment effort that has been required may be considered not unreasonable. But what of the future? Can expenditure on housing now be cut and attention diverted to more directly productive investment? In the last few years the numbers of houses built have fallen. There is, however, a vast problem of replacing about 4 million houses that are now over eighty years old, and half of the local authority houses built each year are needed for the slum clearance programme. No relief from a falling number of households can be expected in the next decade or two. It seems that on general grounds a further cut in housing investment cannot be recommended, unless a clear sacrifice of personal and social amenities in this respect is intended to make way for urgent investments elsewhere.

The proportion of total investment devoted to housing in the United Kingdom is by no means excessive in comparison with that in other European countries. In 1957 housing was taking a smaller proportion in the United Kingdom than in Italy, Belgium and Sweden and probably smaller than in France and Germany, although recent figures for these countries are not available. The table below compares gross investment in dwellings as a percentage of total gross investment in 1950, 1954 and 1958.

TABLE 13

GROSS INVESTMENT IN DWELLINGS AS A PERCENTAGE OF TOTAL GROSS FIXED CAPITAL FORMATION IN 1950, 1954 AND 1958

	1950	1954	1958
United Kingdom	17·6	24·0	16·9
Western Germany	21·7	28·4	22·6*
France	15·3	24·6	24·6*
Italy	16·4	23·3	27·4*
Belgium	23·2	24·6	25·3*
Denmark	16·7	17·3	15·3
Sweden	24·5	23·8	25·5
Norway	18·2	16·7	13·0

Sources: 1950 and 1954 figures calculated from ECE *Economic Survey of Europe in 1955*, Table 29. 1958 figures calculated from OEEC *General Statistics*, 1959, No. 4. July.

* These figures refer to 1957 and are taken from OEEC *General Statistics*, 1959, No. 2, March.

In 1954, when the share of housing in the United Kingdom was the highest of the three years cited, it was still lower than in Western Germany, and was about the same as in France, Italy, Belgium and Sweden. Only Denmark and Norway were devoting a significantly smaller share of investment to housing. Compared with 1950, the share of housing in the United Kingdom rose more by 1954 than in most of the countries. But it had fallen back in 1957 to a share not much greater than in 1950, while in most of the other countries the share of housing continued to rise. Of the countries cited, the share taken by housing fell over the whole period only in Norway.

Investment in housing varies, for special reasons of housing need or political considerations, from country to country. Thus in Western Germany, the need for housing to replace wartime devastation and to house the refugee population has determined the relatively high rate of investment in this sector. On the other hand, the effect of rent control in France has probably been to depress the level of investment in new housing by making old houses artificially cheap.

Education

Capital expenditure on education in the post-war period has been considerably greater than before the war. From about £17 million in 1938–39 it rose to £51 million in 1950, and to £122 million in 1958 at current prices.[1] This means that in real terms, investment in 1958 was probably about two-and-a-half times as great as in 1938–39. Investment in education is now taking a larger share of total gross fixed capital formation at home—3·5 per cent in 1958 compared with 2·6 per cent in 1938–39—and also represents a slightly larger proportion of total expenditure on education—14·3 per cent in 1958 compared with 13·4 per cent in 1938–39.

Because of the post-war increase in the birthrate, a considerable increase in total expenditure on education, and particularly on school buildings, would have been needed merely to maintain pre-war standards of education. Between 1950 and 1958 the total number of pupils in state maintained or state assisted schools rose from 5,651,000 to 6,839,000, an increase of 20 per cent. By 1968 the Ministry of Education expects the number to have risen to over 7 million. However, the level of investment in education has been high enough to secure an increase in real standards of accommodation in spite of the larger number of pupils. Expenditure in money terms was two-and-a-half times greater in 1958 than in 1950. Moreover, investment in new schools has been particularly efficient, and the average cost of providing school places has actually been falling in the post-war period. In 1949, it cost an average of £200 for each primary school place, and £320 for each secondary school place.[2] In 1958, the average net cost on tender was £146 and £252 respectively,[3] an exceptional fall in the face of rising costs throughout the period. The Ministry of Education stated that:

> A calculation made during 1958 showed that, for the same reasons, the 1,700,000 new places started since 1949 at approved costs totalling £439,000,000 exceeded by some 600,000 the number of places which could have been started for the same sum had the costs of new schools been allowed to rise from the average costs per place ruling in 1949 at the same rate as the increases in costs of labour and materials.[4]

[1] 1938–39 estimate from *The Cost of Social Services 1938–52*, PLANNING No. 354 (P E P), 15 June 1953. Post-war figures from *National Income and Expenditure 1959* (HMSO), Table 41.

[2] *Education in 1956*, Report of the Minister of Education (HMSO), Cmnd. 223. p. 54.

[3] *Education in 1958*, Report of the Minister of Education (HMSO), Cmnd. 777, p. 94.

[4] Ibid., p. 95.

Since the war, over 4,000 new schools have been completed, and considerable progress has been made along the lines of the Education Act of 1944 to provide proper secondary education for all children. In 1947 only 75 per cent of children of secondary school age attending publicly maintained schools were in secondary schools, but by 1956 this figure had risen to 90 per cent; whereas in 1938 only one child in ten could expect to go to a secondary grammar school, today one in five may do so.[5] The number of pupils still being taught in the senior classes of all-age schools has been progressively reduced, though in January 1958 there were still 139,000 pupils in such classes, and 6·7 per cent of children aged thirteen in state maintained and assisted schools were attending all-age schools. A drive to reorganise all-age rural schools was launched in December 1954 and it was estimated that 400 extra secondary schools would be required to do this, one-third of which had been brought into use by the end of December 1958.

Many problems still remain. About 35 per cent of all classes are still above the regulation maximum of forty for junior classes and thirty for senior classes, which means that about 42 per cent of all pupils are being taught in oversized classes. The explanation is partly the shortage of teachers, but also, particularly in the older schools, the shortage of classrooms. In many schools, classes are still being held in improvised and unsatisfactory rooms.

The scope of secondary education still needs widening. The alternatives of grammar, technical or secondary modern school education are not yet available in all parts of the country. In fact 40 per cent of local education authorities do not provide technical schools.[6] There is a serious gap in the education facilities for the 15- to 18-year-old age group. The Crowther Committee, investigating the facilities for this group, noted that

> . . . the country is a long way from tapping all the available supply of talent by present methods. Half the National Service recruits to the Army who were rated in the two highest ability groups had left school at 15.[7]

The Committee went on to recommend that:

[5] *Education in Britain* (Central Office of Information), March 1958, pp. 2 and 3.

[6] *Fifteen to Eighteen*—a Report of the Central Advisory Council for Education (England), [the Crowther Report] (HMSO), 1959, p. 22.

[7] Ibid, p. 131.

> Both the unfulfilled provisions of the Education Act of 1944 affecting older children—the raising of the school-leaving age to 16 and the creation of county colleges for compulsory part-time day education to 18—should be reaffirmed as objectives of national policy.[8]

The Committee finally concluded, "the education that is provided for the great mass of children is inadequate both in its quality and in its duration."[9]

A five-year building programme for secondary schools starting in 1960 was announced in December 1958, involving expenditure of £300 million. This is to be devoted mainly to developing a wider range of opportunities in secondary education and completing the reorganisation of all-age rural and urban schools and of other overcrowded or inadequate schools, but deficiencies in the provision of primary schools will also be made good under this programme.

Any improvement in the standard of education depends, however, on expanding the supply of teachers. The introduction of a three-year training course for teachers in 1960 also necessitates an expansion of facilities in training colleges. The Government proposes to create 12,000 additional places in training colleges by the autumn of 1962, at a cost of £15 million. This plan, although involving an increase of 50 per cent in the number of general training college places, provides for 4,000 fewer additional places than recommended by the National Advisory Council on the Training and Supply of Teachers in July 1958. Although the plan for expanding teachers' training colleges arises out of the decision to extend the teachers' training course to three years, and was precipitated by the falling off in the annual net increase in the number of teachers (this averaged about 6,700 between 1953 and 1955, and 7,000 in 1956 but only 4,400 in 1957), it is doubtful whether these factors, together with the increasing size of the secondary school population, have been adequately provided for in the present expansion.

The importance of technical and technological education to the supply of skilled manpower and, even more essential, to the supply of good managers has long been recognised but here is a field where expansion and re-organisation have only recently been given their due priority. In 1956 the Government announced a

[8] Ibid., p. 452.
[9] Ibid, p. 472.

five-year building programme for technical education costing £70 million in England and Wales, an average of £14 million per annum. About one-seventh of this sum was to be devoted to the colleges of advanced technology, eight of which were designated in 1956 as colleges which would concentrate on work at an advanced level. The number of students taking advanced courses expanded according to plan, from 9,500 in 1955 to over 11,000 in 1958. The number of sandwich courses increased from 2,327 students in 1955–56 to 6,492 in 1957–58, but between 15,000 and 20,000 students need to enroll for these courses before the annual output of advanced students reaches 6,000. The institution of the Diploma of Technology at a standard broadly equivalent to a university honours degree and of the post-graduate award of Membership of the College of Technologists will provide a long overdue stimulus for advanced work in this field. However, the development of work of university level in the colleges also requires the provision of facilities for residence and informal student activities akin to those available in the universities.[10]

So investment in education has been considerable but by no means adequate in relation to needs that are continually expanding particularly in the technological field. In view of the vital role which education plays, not only at the level of schools but also in technical colleges and universities, in overcoming the shortage of trained manpower referred to in Chapter 2, investment in education must be given priority for economic as well as for other reasons. The final conclusion of the Crowther Report[11] puts the case in its correct perspective.

> We plead, then, for a forward plan for education. Just as with similar plans for transport or for power, there need be nothing immutable; ... but if the objectives are to be attained, there will have to be a programme, with dates fixed in the future for the execution of its various component parts.... And though the children... flash through the schools in a few brief years, we know within close limits, how many of them there will be, at least in the secondary schools, for a long way ahead. The problem is to make sure that an instrument requiring many years to prepare will be ready for opportunities that must be seized at once or they are gone for ever. Only by the most careful planning can we make sure that most of them are taken.

[10] See Ministry of Education Report for 1958, p. 55.
[11] Op. cit., p. 473.

Health

Investment in the health services is probably only very slightly higher in real terms than in 1938–39 before the existence of the National Health Service, although in money terms it has risen from £7 million in 1938–39[12] to £16 million in 1950 and to £28 million in 1958.[13] It is taking a much smaller share of the total national gross fixed capital formation, 0·8 per cent in 1958 compared with 1·7 per cent in 1938–39. The importance of investment expenditure in the total of expenditure on health has fallen sharply in the post-war period: in 1938–39 between 8 and 9 per cent was for capital projects, but in the years 1950–58 only about 3 per cent. This suggests a very serious neglect of the future needs of the health services. The building of hospitals in particular appears to have suffered serious neglect, and only two new hospitals have been built since the war. Expenditure from Exchequer funds for improved services and increased ward accommodation in the first seven years of the National Health Service, averaged only just under £9 million a year. In 1956 an expanded programme for hospital building and capital improvements was begun, and this will raise the rate of expenditure from public funds to over £20 million a year, and some funds will also be available for hospital extensions and improvements from voluntary sources.[14]

The level of capital expenditure on hospitals has been so inadequate that throughout the period 1949–57 there were never fewer than 400,000 on hospital waiting lists, and in 1950–53 there were 500,000—greater than the total of 400,000 beds in use.[15] Despite this appalling shortage, the number of available staffed hospital beds rose only 6 per cent between 1949 and 1958. Investment in the health service is a most urgent call on resources.

TRANSPORT

Investment in roads

In the period 1924–39 investment in roads and public lighting

[12] *The Cost of Social Services 1938–52*, PLANNING No. 354 (P E P), 15 June 1953, p. 12.

[13] *National Income and Expenditure 1959* (HMSO), Table 41.

[14] *Health Services in Britain* (Central Office of Information), December 1958, pp. 17–18.

[15] *Report of the Ministry of Health for the year ended 31 December 1958* (HMSO), Cmnd. 806, p. 8.

averaged about £30 million per annum at 1948 prices. In 1948–53 it averaged only £7 million per annum.[16] Further, Redfern's calculations suggested that after allowing for depreciation, real net fixed capital formation in roads in the post-war period to 1953 was negative, ranging from −£7 million in 1949 to −£11 million in 1953 at 1948 prices. These calculations indicate that road investment in the post-war period to 1953 was not even keeping pace with the deterioration of existing roads, let alone catering for the rapid increase in the number of vehicles. The chief reason for the neglect of road investment seems to be that Governments have considered road development to be low on the list of national priorities and long-term investment has been sacrificed to more immediate demands on the national product.

In 1909 Lloyd George imposed taxation on motor vehicles and fuel and established a Road Fund, the revenue from which was to be devoted exclusively to building roads. The Fund was, however, "raided" during the first world war as a temporary measure, and from 1926 onwards became a regular source of revenue to the Exchequer. In 1937 the Road Fund was completely amalgamated with the general body of taxation; it ceased to receive revenue from licence duties but was financed by grants from the Exchequer provided in the budget each year. In April 1956 the convention of a Road Fund was abolished and road investment is now financed by direct grants through the Civil Estimates, and grants to local authorities to cover 75 per cent of the cost of works undertaken by them.

In 1946 a ten-year plan for road development was announced with some £80 million to be spent in the first two years, but during the economic crisis of 1947 the plan was abandoned. In December 1953 the Government announced a three-year plan for major improvements and new construction involving the authorisation of schemes costing £50 million in the period 1954–55 to 1956–57. In 1955 an expanded programme of authorisations for the period 1955–56 to 1958–59 was announced involving an ultimate Exchequer expenditure of £147 million. This figure excluded the cost of certain major projects of national importance, such as the London–Yorkshire motorway, which were estimated to cost a further £65 million. A further expansion became

[16] P. Redfern, *Journal of the Royal Statistical Society*, Series A (General), Vol. 118, Part 2, 1955, p. 160.

possible before the 1955 programme had run its full course, and in July 1957 the Minister of Transport and Civil Aviation stated that during the four-year period 1958–59 to 1961–62 schemes would be authorised for England and Wales which would ultimately involve the central government in expenditure of £240 million. For the same period the road programme of major improvements and new construction for Scotland was estimated at £40 million.

In England and Wales alone nearly £100 million was spent on roads in 1957–58 by the Government and local authorities together, and £26 million of this represents investment in new construction and major improvement works. In 1958–59 this latter figure rose to some £52 million and in 1959–60 it is estimated that it will be between £60 million and £63 million.

The fact that this programme was specifically excluded from the investment cuts in 1957 suggests that the Government was at last prepared to give road development some priority.

This priority is long overdue, for the present expenditure is amply justified, and investment on a much greater scale should be seriously considered. The density of traffic has been increasing at a very high rate, and density in Great Britain is much higher than in Europe or America. Between 1954 and 1956 alone the number of motor vehicles per road mile in Great Britain rose from 22·7 to 27·4.[17] A sample investigation of road traffic has shown traffic to be in excess of design capacity on 62 per cent of Trunk roads, 23 per cent of Class I roads, and 6 per cent of Class II roads.[18] The number of vehicles has more than doubled, from 3 million in 1946 to just under 7·5 million in 1957, and in the next ten years a further increase of at least 75 per cent is expected.

The costs of congestion

The expenses of delays arising from traffic congestion impose a considerable burden of cost on industry which might be reduced by the provision of better roads. For instance, W. H. Glanville and R. J. Smeed have also calculated that an increase of 1 mile per hour in the average speed of traffic—20 miles per hour

[17] British Road Federation, *Basic Road Statistics, 1958*, p. 12.

[18] W. H. Glanville and R. J. Smeed, "The Basic Requirements for the Roads of Great Britain", paper read to the Conference of The Institution of Civil Engineers, 13 November 1957, para. 141.

in urban areas and 32 miles per hour in rural areas in 1956—would result in savings in vehicle operating and labour costs of just under £30 million per annum in urban and £7 million per annum in rural areas. If savings of non-working time were included and valued at the same rate as working time, the total saving would be as much as £100 million per annum. An estimate of the total cost of road congestion on the basis of a "reasonable" speed for traffic—25 miles per hour in urban and 40 miles per hour in rural areas—shows the total economic cost to industry and commerce of road delays to be £155 million per annum. The inclusion of non-working time brings the total to more than £450 million. Further, the number of vehicles using the roads is increasing at the rate of 7·4 per cent per annum, but the time cost through congestion increases at roughly twice the rate for a given percentage increase in traffic, so that the rate of increase in the cost of delays is 14 per cent per annum. If traffic is doubled in ten years, the total time cost of delay will rise to over £600 million, or over £1,800 million including non-working time.[19]

The increase in traffic has been accompanied by an increase, though not a proportional one, in the number of road accidents. The number of accidents increased by about 68 per cent between 1946 and 1956.[20] The cost of road accidents to the community, as estimated by the Royal Society for the Prevention of Accidents, increased from £136 million in 1950 to £175 million in 1957. The Road Research Laboratory estimated the purely economic cost, including damage to property, medical treatment and loss of output, at £110 million for 1956.[21] There is no doubt that road investment directed specifically to the elimination of "black spots" will help to reduce road accidents.

Is enough being invested?

Traffic problems arising from the density of motor vehicles and consequent congestion are much more serious in this country than in Europe. Great Britain has the highest traffic density in Europe, but in spite of the fact that there are more vehicles per road mile in Great Britain, the amount spent on construction and maintenance over the past five years has been smaller than in any of the

[19] Ibid., paras. 52–56.

[20] British Road Federation, *Basic Road Statistics, 1958*, p. 15. 1946: 162,546 persons killed or injured; 1957: 273,858 persons killed or injured.

[21] W. H. Glanville and R. J. Smeed, op. cit., para. 60.

other European countries. Between 1950 and 1955 Britain spent less than £30 per annum per vehicle compared with between £70 and £90 per annum spent by most other European countries. As a percentage of the national product, British investment in roads is again well behind that of the other European countries.

TABLE 14

	Number of vehicles per road mile, 1954	*Investment in roads as a percentage of Gross National Product, 1953–55**
Great Britain	20·8	(United Kingdom) 0·09
Holland	15·9	1·00
Belgium	14·1	0·60
Germany	9·8	0·75
France	5·8	0·69

Source: British Road Federation, *Basic Road Statistics 1958*, p. 12; and ECE, *Economic Survey of Europe in 1956*, Chapter 5, Table 8.

* Holland 1954 to 1955, France 1952 to 1954.

In this situation it seems fair to ask whether enough is being invested in roads, even with the new programme, and whether planning should not be on a more long-term basis than at present. In 1957 R. Nicholas and J. H. W. Wilkes[22] produced detailed estimates of the cost of necessary road development over the next twenty years, and suggested that expenditure of £3,500 million would be necessary. This would mean an average expenditure of £175 million per annum, which is more than two-and-a-half times the present planned level. These calculations were based on the cost of motorway schemes already undertaken or under consideration, and on the cost of bringing the rest of the road system into line with the traffic capacity figures recommended by the Ministry of Transport.

Long-term planning by local authorities seems to be inhibited by annual budgets and by the unwillingness of the Government to spend large sums on roads. Thus, when in 1954 the County Councils' Association asked the counties to provide estimates of their expenditure on new construction and major improvements to classified roads based on a twenty-year plan, the highly un-

[22] "An Assessment of the Cost of an Adequate Highway System", Institution of Civil Engineers Conference 1957, Paper No. 10, p. 9.

realistic figure of £339 million emerged as total local authority capital expenditure over this whole period.[23] These estimates were tailored to fit the grants for such projects expected to be forthcoming from the Government. In the County of London alone, a conservative estimate of the cost of accommodating traffic, based on a 50 per cent increase in traffic, was £300 million; the proposals the County submitted for inclusion in the twenty-year Development Plan were, however, for only £90 million. Taking the estimate by Nicholas and Wilkes of £3,500 million over twenty years, and excluding the provisions for motorways (£280 million) and trunk roads (£900 million), for which local authorities are not responsible, the inference is that local authorities should spend £2,320 million in order to meet traffic needs over the next twenty years, compared with the proposals of the counties for £339 million. There is apparently a case for a more serious official assessment of the country's overall traffic needs over a longer period as a basis for an investment programme.

Such a long-term programme would also enable the best use to be made of the experience of the contractors who have undertaken the building of Britain's first motorways. It would be a great help if the teams of workers, supervisors and technicians brought together for this work were retained at the end of the current programme. Further, the experience of building motorways has shown modern road building to be a much more capital intensive process than was thought, and contractors have already invested in heavy equipment which could be utilised for further road construction. It seems that both the contractors and the manufacturers of the equipment could work more efficiently and at lower costs if road development were more fully planned well in advance.

The yield on road investment

One of the factors which probably accounts for the relative neglect of roads in the past is the dispersed nature of the yield, and the fact that it does not accrue directly to the authority responsible for the expenditure. None the less some estimate of yield is possible, and shows road investment to be an attractive economic proposition. Taking calculations of annual savings in vehicle hours, fuel and other operating costs, accidents, etc., as

[23] This figure would not include expenditure on trunk roads.

the economic return on road development schemes, it can be estimated that the rate of return on road investment may vary between 1,000 per cent and 3 per cent according to circumstances. This kind of calculation would provide a rough and ready criterion for the allocation of priorities in road investment. For example, on this basis the rate of return on the Slough By-pass would be 10 per cent and on the Brentwood By-pass 35 per cent. If the national estimates of wastage from road congestion referred to earlier are taken as the economic cost of an unimproved road system (taking the figure of £600 million for annual wastage in ten years' time) and if it is assumed that this would be eliminated by the twenty-year plan of Nicholas and Wilkes, the yield on their estimated capital expenditure of £3,500 million would be 17 per cent per annum. It has been estimated in Japan that the return on capital invested for the first year after the completion of a five-year road programme will be about 25 per cent.[24]

Thus, on the basis of present and expected trends in road transport, considerable investment in roads would seem to be economically justified. If the consequent widely dispersed benefits are measured it seems that the real yield from such investment compares very favourably with yields from ordinary industrial investment. But the yield is only realised if road investment is successful in reducing traffic density, and relieving congestion and the high accident rate. If the attempt to cater properly for increased traffic on the roads itself serves to stimulate further increases in traffic, the net result of all extra investment in reducing congestion will be negligible. Increased investment in roads is necessary to improve transport facilities in Great Britain, but it must be accompanied by measures which ensure that the best use is made of all the country's transport facilities.

The economics of the distribution of heavy traffic between road and rail deserves a more thorough investigation. It seems likely that the building of motorways will further encourage manufacturers to send regular large consignments of goods for long distances by road, and this is the type of traffic most economically dealt with by railways. Given that a railway system is to be maintained, it would seem advantageous that it should be used

[24] C. T. Brunner, "Assessment of the Economic Loss to the Country due to Inadequate Highways", Institution of Civil Engineers Conference 1957, Paper 4, paras. 62 and 63.

as near to full capacity as possible. Since the marginal cost of rail transport is usually much less than that of road transport, railway investment designed to meet manufacturers' requirements more fully and to reduce handling costs may be as effective in reducing road congestion as the construction of motorways.

Investment in railways

From £48 million per annum at 1948 prices in 1935–38, railway investment fell to £35 million per annum in 1948–53.[25] Between 1948 and 1952 investment at current prices remained stationary at just over £40 million. There was a steady rise between 1952 and 1956 from £40 million to £90 million as a result of the first stages of the railway modernisation programme, and then a more rapid rise took it to £126 million in 1957 and £140 million in 1958. However, even in recent years the rate of investment in road goods vehicles has been far in excess of that in railway rolling-stock. The table below compares the total investment in road

TABLE 15

	Gross Fixed Capital Formation in road goods vehicles, passenger cars and buses and coaches*	*Gross Fixed Capital Formation in railway rolling-stock*	*Gross Fixed Capital Formation in railway rolling-stock as a percentage of that in road vehicles*
	£m	£m	%
1938	50	14	28
1948	144	28	19
1949	170	29	17
1950	164	31	19
1951	175	33	19
1952	188	27	14
1953	196	36	18
1954	216	48	22
1955	266	55	21
1956	270	65	24
1957	260	89	34
1958	301	86	29
TOTAL 1948–58	2,350	527	22

Source: National Income and Expenditure 1959 (HMSO), Table 49.

* Excluding cars owned by private individuals.

[25] P. Redfern, op. cit., p. 160.

goods vehicles, buses and coaches and passenger cars with the total investment in railway rolling-stock between 1938 and 1958.

In investment in railways, as in roads, the United Kingdom lags behind other European countries. In the period 1953 to 1955 the United Kingdom spent 0·4 per cent of the gross national product on railway investment, compared with 1·1 per cent by France in the period 1952 to 1954, 0·7 per cent by Western Germany in 1953 to 1955, and 0·9 per cent by Belgium in 1953 to 1955.[26] However, the serious neglect of investment in the railways is now being remedied: the programme published in 1955 provided for capital expenditure of £1,500 million over the fifteen years to 1970.[27]

In the first four years of the programme to the end of 1958, a total of £421 million has been invested in British railways. Of this, the largest item, investment in freight vehicles, took £159 million and investment in locomotives took only £45 million.[28] In the next five years between 1959 and 1963 total investment is expected to be just under £1,000 million and it is estimated that the annual level of investment will rise from £178 million in 1959 to £210 million in 1962 and 1963.[29]

The advantages of modernisation

The main emphasis in modernisation over the next five years will be on rationalising the railway system. The re-appraisal of the programme published in July 1959 stated that:

> The essential requirement of the next five years is that a more compact railway system and a more economic scale of operations shall be achieved more quickly. Despite the far-reaching nature of the Modernisation Plan it was never intended that the whole of the existing railway network should be retained and modernised . . . the contraction of the railway system as a part of modernisation is thus far from being a negative process, because it aims at the revival of British Railways as a whole.[30]

[26] ECE, *Economic Survey of Europe in 1956*, Chapter 5, Table 7.

[27] The proposal published in 1955 provided for expenditure of £1,200 million, but it was later on announced that the cost had increased to £1,500 million.

[28] British Transport Commission, *Re-appraisal of the Plan for the Modernisation and Re-equipment of British Railways* (HMSO), July 1959, p. 4.

[29] Ibid., p. 14.

[30] Ibid., p. 7.

The British Transport Commission are therefore trying to achieve a more compact network which will concentrate on the services for which the railways are better suited than the roads and provide these more cheaply.

The modernisation of the railway system will not only make it possible to work more economically, but will also lead to improvements in the quality, speed and reliability of the services. These improvements are as important to the ability of the railways to compete with road transport as the level of their charges, because the dominating factor in the rapid increase in the number of road goods vehicles is the use of "C" licence vehicles by firms for the distribution of their own products. "C" licence vehicles were responsible for 95 per cent of the increase in the total number of road goods vehicles between June 1938 and December 1957.[31] Sometimes manufacturers choose to provide their own transport because the immediate economic costs are lower, but more usually they are prompted by considerations of punctuality, flexibility, expert handling of goods, reduction in the amount of packing required and in loss and damage, the time and handling saved as a result of door-to-door service, the use of drivers as representatives and salesmen and for servicing goods, and the prestige and advertising value of a fleet of vehicles. Some of these advantages, like prestige, advertising, and the skilled servicing of equipment, cannot be matched by any improvements in the quality of the railway services, but the railways will be able to improve their performance considerably in respect of other requirements when modernisation has been completed. For instance, the amount of handling and consequent risks of damage and loss can be reduced by palletisation and road-rail containers; time saved by door-to-door service can be balanced by speedier transit between rail terminals when the vacuum brake has been fitted to all freight trains; and the need for greater punctuality and flexibility can also be met by bringing marshalling yards up to date, and by generally improving the efficiency of the railway service. These improvements, together with correct pricing policies, should help to slow down the rate of increase in road goods transport and so allow road investment effectively to reduce traffic congestion.

The Commission expect that when their programme is com-

[31] Calculated from British Road Federation, *Basic Road Statistics 1959*, p. 20.

plete the gross return on railway modernisation will be about £85 million per annum.[32] The interest on the capital borrowed for the programme was originally estimated at £40 million per annum, but in view of the increase in its cost it will be about £50 million, assuming the same rate of interest. Thus, if these expectations are justified, the initial cost of the modernisation programme will be met by the improved revenues. The improvement in the standard of railway services, combined with new pricing arrangements, should enable the railways to attract more traffic and so, in the long run, contribute to improving the financial position. If estimates of the savings which will arise from modernisation and of the improvements which will take place in railway freight and passenger traffics are correct, then once the programme is completed the railways will no longer lose money.

FUEL AND POWER

Coal

The British economy still depends primarily on the coal industry for its energy, despite the fact that oil and nuclear power will provide increasing proportions of total energy supplies in the 1960's, and despite the situation of inadequate demand which arose in 1958. In 1938 some 93 per cent of Britain's total energy supplies came from coal, and this proportion had only been reduced to 80 per cent by 1958.

During the period between the wars the coal industry suffered from a chronic deficiency of demand, and there was little investment. Redfern's estimates, at 1948 prices, show average annual investments of £5–6 million for the periods 1924–29, 1930–34, and 1935–38. For the period 1948 to 1953 the comparable figure was £19 million per annum.[33] Between 1948 and 1951 investment in coal fluctuated between £20 and £30 million at current prices, but since 1951 has increased rapidly year by year to reach £95 million in 1958.[34] This big increase in investment has been the result of the industry's *Plan for Coal* of 1950. The original estimate was for a capital expenditure of £635 million over fifteen years, but the plan was revised in 1955 (*Investing in Coal*) and the total investment put at £1,350 million. This doubling of

[32] Cmnd. 585 (HMSO), November 1958.
[33] P. Redfern, op. cit., p. 160.
[34] *National Income and Expenditure 1959* (HMSO), Table 53.

the original figure was accounted for partly by the rise in prices from 1949, but largely by the fact that the plans for new pits and the development of older pits as contained in the original programme were later seen to be insufficient to offset the constant loss of productive capacity. The net increase in output to be achieved by 1965 was only 18 million tons above the 1955 level of 222 million tons per annum. But without any investment output would have fallen to 180 million tons by 1965, in the face of a constantly increasing difficulty in getting coal from the older pits.

In October 1959 the Coal Board published a revised plan for coal which reduced the estimate of total planned capital expenditure for the period 1960 to 1965 from £712 million to £511 million. This was made necessary by the reduction in the demand for coal which became apparent from the end of 1957. The most important cause of this decline was the increased use of oil at the expense of coal and it was further aggravated by the industrial recession of 1958–59. The Coal Board stated:

> In Britain, it is no longer necessary to plan to meet a continuous increase in demand . . . [the National Coal Board] are planning to meet a demand which is about equal to present production. This output will be got at higher efficiency.[35]

It is now estimated that total demand in 1965 will be between 200 and 215 million tons a year and not 240 million tons a year as was estimated in the original *Plan for Coal*. Investment in the next six years will therefore be reduced by about £200 million at current prices, but it will still be necessary to invest £511 million over this period in order to maintain the same level of output as in 1959.

The distinction between gross and net investment has little meaning in the coal industry since replacement of exhausted seams often requires new major colliery development schemes, but it is certain that a large part of the investment of the 1950's may be regarded as having been necessary to meet depreciation, that is, to maintain the existing level of output. The Coal Board estimated in their report for 1957 that £289 million of colliery expenditure in the years 1947 to 1957 was replacement expenditure and could therefore be regarded as part of the cost of current output. This means that only the remaining £218 million of

[35] National Coal Board, *Revised Plan for Coal*, October 1959, p. 5.

colliery investment in the period 1947 to 1957, or 43 per cent, which was devoted to major schemes, could be regarded as creating fresh productive capacity. But this fresh capacity still had to meet the decline of capacity, estimated at 4 million tons a year, natural to an extractive industry. Some of the investment has increased output per man shift but since investment has in fact failed, since 1950, to increase output significantly, most of the investment in the coal industry since then must be regarded as simply replacement.

In assessing the investment and pricing policies of the coal industry it is necessary to take account of the two radically different market situations that may exist in the 1960's. The present surplus and excessive stocks of coal may be a temporary phase, related to the industrial recession, or it may prove to be the beginning of a new era for the industry, which will make all the arguments of the early and mid-1950's irrelevant. The fortunes of the coal industry depend above all on the general level of industrial prosperity, but they may come to depend much more on the competition from alternative sources of energy, especially oil and in the longer term nuclear energy. But here again much depends on the policy which is pursued with regard to oil imports, which may be freely permitted, or may be limited by the balance of payments, by strategic considerations and by the need to make political concessions to the coal-producing regions. Within this background of uncertainty it is possible only to point out alternatives, and to sum up the arguments as they appear at the end of the 1950's.

The argument for investment in coal is not that it will yield more coal but that it is necessary to prevent a fall in output. This is true looking ahead for several decades, and would constitute an unanswerable case if the country were still deeply concerned about its future fuel and power supplies. Now that these appear more assured, it may be better policy to get as much coal as is needed currently by concentrating on the more efficient working of existing capacity, and to spend less on opening up future capacity. If it is certain that in 1970 and 1980 the country will still require over 200 million tons of coal each year, then the investment is justified. If on the other hand it becomes apparent that the demand for coal will decline significantly, a cut in new investment is one of the ways of bringing about an orderly contraction of the industry.[36] Output would fall, but only slowly at first, and the size of the industry could be reduced in line with the rate at which other fuels were eroding its markets.

Electricity

The most dynamic factor in investment in the provision of energy has been the development of electricity. Investment in the generation and transmission and distribution of electricity has far outweighed all other investments in the fuel and power industries or, indeed, in any sector of manufacturing industry. Already in the 1930's a large increase in investment in electricity was under way. From an average of £69 million per annum in the years 1924 to 1929, expenditure rose to £90 million per annum in 1930–34, and to £97 million per annum in 1935–38 (all at 1948 prices). In the period 1948–53 investment in electricity averaged £120 million per annum at 1948 prices.[37] In the post-war years investment in electricity has risen, at current prices, from £99 million in 1948 to £295 million in 1958, with particularly rapid increases in 1953–54, 1954–55, and 1957–58.

The demand for electricity has been rising at a rate which implies that it will roughly double every ten years: hence the extremely high rate of investment. The Report of the Central Electricity Authority for the year ended 31 March 1958[38] showed that output capacity rose by 115 per cent between the year ended 31 March 1948 and the year ended 31 December 1957, and a further increase of 44 per cent in output capacity was planned for the six years 1958 to 1963.

In addition to the high rate of increase in demand over the coming years, capital requirements will be increased by the fact that much of the new capacity will be contributed by nuclear power plants. Of the net addition to capacity in 1958–63 of 9,800,000 kilowatts, some 1,575,000 would come from nuclear plant. It was expected that by 1965 nuclear stations would be providing nearly one-quarter of the total number of units consumed, and that half the annual increase in capacity that year would be nuclear.[39]

[36] Unless pits can be newly developed at lower costs.

[37] P. Redfern, op. cit., p. 160.

[38] Pp. 22–24.

[39] The programme was slowed down in June 1960. See Ministry of Power, *The Nuclear Power Programme*, Cmnd. 1083 (HMSO), 1960.

The effect of nuclear development on investment in the years ahead should be noted. At present prices nuclear stations cost three times as much as conventional stations per kilowatt of installed capacity, or three-and-a-half times as much if the initial charge of nuclear fuel is included. If 6 million kilowatts are provided by nuclear plant by 1965, and 9 million kilowatts by conventional capacity, as estimated in the 1956–57 Report of the CEA, using current costs as the basis of calculation,[40] this would mean spending £450 million on conventional plant of 9 million kilowatts capacity, and £900 million on nuclear plant of 6 million kilowatts capacity. So the total cost would be £1,350 million compared with only £750 million if the extra capacity were to be provided in the conventional form. In other words, £60 million per annum must be added to the capital expenditure on electricity due to the advent of nuclear power. Such a large addition to capital costs adds emphasis to the charges that electricity may have claimed too large a share of capital resources since the war.[41]

Has too much been invested in supplying electricity since the war, in relation to all the other calls on capital resources? Down to 1953 there were continual shortages of supply resulting in power cuts and all the dislocation and loss they involved; and it is clear that, if output is to expand in the future, electricity supply must keep pace with the growing demand. But it is often suggested that if the pricing policies of the electricity authorities were other than they are, wasteful use could be avoided, and in particular the peak load reduced.

CONCLUSION

The strongest argument for more investment is not simply that the rate of investment in the United Kingdom has been lower than that in some other countries, but rather that there exist areas of the economy where more investment can fill urgent needs and can yield a social if not always a financial return. This chapter has described briefly where the investment has gone, and has examined

[40] Roughly £50 per kilowatt installed for conventional plant, and £150 per kilowatt installed for nuclear plant, excluding the initial fuel charge.

[41] In mitigation it should be pointed out that with further technological advances the cost per kilowatt of nuclear capacity may be significantly reduced in the future. Operating costs of course will be lower for nuclear than for conventional power stations, and total costs may be expected to be almost competitive.

the more important industries in the public sector in an attempt to assess the value of the investment that has taken place in them.

Clearly, urgent needs have existed for social investment in housing, education, and health services since the war. A great deal has been done in house-building and education, but in the health services a clear priority for the 1960's should be to replace antiquated hospitals and to increase the number of hospital beds. The education programme also needs to go forward, for the "bulge" will soon be reaching the higher level of colleges and universities, while some schools are still overcrowded or inadequate, even though a reduction in the number of school children will eventually afford some relief. For a wealthy country such as Britain, slums and areas of very old and decaying houses are a disgrace, and a continuing high rate of house-building will be needed for many years.

This social investment is sometimes criticised on the ground that it is unproductive, and diverts scarce capital resources away from industry where they could earn a much higher financial yield. It is difficult, and sometimes impossible, to calculate the yield on social investments, but there is reason to believe that, for education at least, it is very high. Provision for housing and for health services may also yield a good economic return, apart from its apparent social value. But the true comparison here is not between investment in social services and investment in "productive" industry, but between investment in social services and the more marginal forms of consumption. The country that can afford to bring television within reach of all its citizens within a decade can also see that every family has a decent home.

Social investment is a particularly worthy cause at a time when there are unused resources available. Its acceleration can help to reduce any unemployment that may result from a falling off in other forms of construction. But even in times when the economy is running at full pressure, it has the strongest of cases for a share in the available capital.

The need for social investment cannot be entirely divorced from the prices that are charged or from the methods of financing social services, but prices do not play a predominant role in the determination of this investment and the consequences of getting them wrong or not charging any price at all are not too serious. In contrast to this relative unimportance of prices in the social sector, the price that is charged for a product of a nationalised industry is extremely important in determining the correct level of investment in that industry. In particular, it is essential that where there is more than one way of supplying a particular product or service, the *relative* prices of these different forms of energy or alternative forms of transport should accurately reflect differences in the costs of supplying them. Here what is involved is not so much consumers' choice but the allocation of scarce resources so as to achieve a given objective in the cheapest possible way. The result of faulty pricing policies is waste.

It is therefore impossible to arrive at conclusions about the level of investment in the nationalised industries independently of the consideration of their pricing policies.

CHAPTER 4

PRICING POLICIES IN NATIONALISED INDUSTRIES

PRICING policies play a significant part in determining the amount and the distribution of investment. They influence the demand for a product or service and in consequence the need for investment to expand production. In addition they affect the profitability of the enterprise and therefore the funds available for financing investment. This happens throughout the economy in the private as well as in the public sector. However, in the private sector the corrective of competition and the profit motive will often prevent gross distortion of prices.

In the nationalised industries many decisions about production and investment are taken centrally on the basis of forecasts of the need for particular goods or services, and are not left to the workings of a free market system. For example, as was shown in Chapter 3, investment in the coal industry is not decided by the profitability of the industry, but by a long-range forecast of future demands for coal. Investment in electricity generation and distribution is not determined by the size of profits but on the basis of the general forecast that demand will roughly double over ten years. When production and investment are determined in this manner, prices have to be managed as well and it is important that they should be the servants and not the masters of the policies of these industries. If prices are set too low they encourage wasteful use of the products of these industries and distort the allocation of finances for investment by making the need for the products of the industry appear to be greater than it really is. Prices must reflect costs of production if they are to do their proper job of ensuring the correct allocation of resources and particularly of investment resources between the various industries.

Much difficulty is encountered in determining what are the costs of production in these industries and it is not pretended that pricing policies can be any other than extremely difficult to formulate. But in addition to natural difficulties arising out of the technological and market circumstances of each industry, the task of those concerned with drawing up the prices has been made very much more difficult by a number of interferences with the job they ought to be doing. Some industries have suffered from traditional and often unrealistic methods of fixing or regulating prices dating from the years before they were publicly owned and in some cases even back to the nineteenth century. In the case of the railways, practices were imposed by legislation which, though appropriate for the circumstances of the time when it was first passed, was quite out of date by the 1930's. Even then it had already become a source of great difficulty in adjusting prices to reflect relative costs and so to secure a rational use of resources.

Much has been done to bring up to date pricing policies that had become unrealistic and where necessary to amend legislation affecting prices. But at the same time new burdens have been imposed on the nationalised industries which have prevented them from pricing their products and services correctly. In particular the Government has frequently intervened in the determination of prices in pursuit of economic policies designed to prevent inflation. This has been done even though the theoretical basis of such action is uncertain and in spite of the fact that these interventions have had a harmful effect on the industries concerned. While the desire to prevent a cycle of price increases from being passed on from the nationalised industries to other parts of the economy has been the main motive of Government intervention, another motive has been the prevention of increases in the prices of goods or services to which workers were thought to be particularly sensitive. Sometimes this may have appeared sound policy on social grounds, but at other times it has appeared far too much like electoral manoeuvring.

This chapter considers in some detail the relationship between investment and pricing policies in three major industries: the railways, electricity and the coal industry.

THE RAILWAYS

The financial position of the railways has suffered as a result of outdated regulations. The level of railway charges has been subject to regulation for almost as long as the railways have been in existence, the first general regulation being introduced in 1840. The early restrictions on charges had their origins in a fear that the railway companies would abuse their monopoly position.

However, the policy of regulation has persisted beyond the era when the railways had a monopoly in inland transport right up to the present day. The failure to adapt pricing policies to the emergence of alternative forms of transport has led in turn to other disadvantages in competing for traffic. This, too, has had an adverse effect on the railways' financial position.

In recent years, the Government has aggravated the situation by intervening to prevent or modify increases in railway charges as part of its policies to combat inflationary increases in prices. For instance, in March 1956, the Ministry of Transport refused to sanction a 10 per cent increase in freight charges and permitted an increase of only 5 per cent. In addition the Transport Tribunal, which has authority over changes in railway rates, has taken into consideration the social implications of such changes and this is reflected in the survival of cheap early morning fares[1] and specially low rates for season tickets.

A general result of this discrimination has been that passengers on the railways have been shielded from the full effects of the increases in charges that have been necessary to keep up with the general inflation of costs since the war. During the period 1950–58 gross receipts from passenger traffic rose by 29 per cent in money terms, and there was also an increase of 9 per cent in the number of passenger miles. In the same period gross receipts from a *declining* volume of freight traffic rose by 41 per cent. Although the volume of freight traffic is now less than in 1948, this smaller volume has been accounting for a larger proportion of total receipts: 69 per cent of the total in 1958, compared with only 63 per cent in 1948.[2] It is, to say the least, doubtful whether the consumer should have been protected in this way from inflation at the expense of industry.

This regulation of railway fares and charges has meant that a lengthy procedure has had to be followed before any increases could take place. This involved delays which were in themselves costly and served to make railway charges lag behind general price movements. The British Transport Commission have estimated that the total loss of receipts between 1948 and 1955 due

[1] Although the margin between ordinary fares and early morning rates has been greatly reduced.

[2] British Transport Commission, *Annual Report and Accounts 1948* (HMSO), p. 218A; *1950*, p. 216A; and *1958*, Vol. II, p. 16A, and p. 260.

solely to delays in sanctioning increased charges was over £50 million. Further, as they stated in their report for 1955: "The Commission have throughout been prevented from keeping any margin in newly adjusted charges to provide against further price movements against them in the period lying ahead." Losses arising in this way were estimated at a further £50 million, making a total loss of £100 million between 1948 and 1955 due solely to the effects of inflation.[3] The machinery for raising charges is inevitably cumbersome when an industry is required to modify commercial practice in accordance with social and national economic considerations and both these factors have combined to keep increases in railway charges behind general price movements. In real terms railway charges are below the pre-war level. In 1955 average charges for the bulk loads of coal and minerals were only slightly below the 1938 level but charges for both merchandise and passenger fares were about 75–80 per cent of the 1938 level.[4]

However, a significant all-round rise in the general level of railway charges is no longer regarded as a practicable means of increasing the net revenue of the Commission, for charges experts consider that under the present fiercely competitive conditions in inland transport more revenue would be lost as a result of traffic transferred to the roads than would be gained from the increased receipts from the traffic which continued to use the railways. But selective increases—for peak commuter traffic, for example—could yield more revenue and reduce the peak load at the same time. Changes along these lines have been embodied in the fare increases which came into operation in November 1959.

The net revenue can also be increased in the future by attracting to the railways traffic of the kind that adds more to revenue than to costs. In addition to the limitation on the general level of prices, however, railway traffics and revenues have suffered from further restrictions which prevented them from using price discrimination to attract profitable traffic. Government regulation in this field again dates from the era of railway monopoly, and was designed to prevent undue discrimination among users. The

[3] British Transport Commission, *Annual Report for the year ended 31 December 1955* (HMSO), para. 35.

[4] British Transport Commission, *Annual Report for the year ended 31 December 1958* (HMSO), pp. 50–2.

railways had a legal obligation dating from 1845 to provide "equality of treatment in similar circumstances", and from 1854 to refrain from "undue preference to any company or person". The survival of these restrictions into a period of fierce competition between road and rail undertakings constituted a handicap to the railways in attracting traffic from road hauliers. Railway rate makers became afraid to offer a reduced rate to traders when particularly remunerative traffics were at stake for fear that the "undue preference" clause would be invoked by others, so that the favourable rate would have to be extended. Until July 1957 the railways had also been required by law to make their freight charges public, although road hauliers did not have any such legal obligation. As a result, road hauliers competing with the railways were able, when they so desired, to tailor their rates to published rail charges and at short notice could quote "snap rates" below the rail charges for particular traffics without any obligation to publish these for the information of other customers who might be paying higher rates.

Although this legislation was designed to prevent unfair discrimination by a monopoly undertaking, some kind of "discrimination" in charges is inevitable in an industry which has the cost structure of the railways. A large proportion of the industry's costs cannot be attributed to specific traffics, since they are incurred in the provision of a railway service over a large area, and are not much affected by the extent to which the service is used. For instance, the costs of track provision and maintenance, signalling and administration, are common to large groups of traffics, while other capital equipment whose original cost is so heavy, such as locomotives and wagons, has a very low rate of depreciation which makes it impracticable to try to allocate depreciation costs to particular traffics. Costing techniques are being evolved which will give a more accurate indication of the long-term direct costs of carrying particular consignments of goods, but no analyses of costs can solve the problem of allocating the common costs of the railways' operations. The method of covering these must always be somewhat arbitrary.

Ad valorem pricing

The railway companies in their early years evolved a system of charging by which traffics contributed to common costs according to their value. It was felt that the more valuable a commodity, the greater the transport costs it could bear without its sales being adversely affected. This system of *ad valorem* pricing was a policy of charging "what the traffic will bear". Freight was classified according to its value (although factors like bulk in relation to weight, risk of damage, and cost of handling also had a slight influence on the grading), and a standard rate per mile was fixed for each class of traffic. As a virtual monopoly the railways were able to practise this kind of discrimination without losing traffic.

Since the mid-1920's they have been operating in an increasingly competitive atmosphere, and yet it was not until July 1957 that they were able to abandon *ad valorem* pricing for freight traffic. Over the last thirty years the system has not only been a handicap to economic operation, but has also resulted in a distribution of transport between road and rail which is extremely wasteful of the country's transport resources. This has arisen because the cost structure of road haulage undertakings, and of manufacturers who operate a "C" licence fleet, is quite different from that of the railways.

At the outset road transport undertakings require relatively little capital investment, although they work on a much higher rate of depreciation. The contribution towards road building and maintenance takes the form of vehicle and fuel taxation and is therefore to some extent variable with the amount of traffic which is handled, while overheads like the costs of administration, garage facilities, and so on, are a relatively small proportion of total costs. As a result, costs are determined by factors like ease of loading, bulk in relation to weight, distance, and so on. Manufacturers can assess their transport needs on this basis when deciding whether to use their own "C" licence vehicles, and road hauliers can use the same criteria when fixing their charges. The charges fixed by road hauliers have therefore been more closely related to the actual costs of carrying particular loads.[5]

For example, while the railways were charging more for bags of cement than for bags of sand of exactly the same weight and size, road transport undertakings have been able to carry these at

[5] Although there may have been an element of "reflected value" in the charges of hauliers competing with the railways, since the ceiling below which their charges would still attract railway users would be higher for the more valuable merchandise.

identical prices. This meant that high-class merchandise was often sent by road, not because road undertakings incurred lower costs than the railways in carrying it, but because *ad valorem* rail charges discriminated against these goods. Similarly, merchandise of low value was often sent by rail, even for very short hauls, not because carrying costs by rail were less than by road, but because the railway charge was lower. Road haulage was thus able to compete successfully for the "higher class" traffic, but, while the railways tended to lose these "prosperous" traffics, many of which were of good loading characteristics, they retained the "poor relations" which had been virtually subsidised by them.[6]

The structure of railway rates obscured the differences in terms of real costs between rail and road haulage, so that it was impossible for the price mechanism to distribute traffic between road and rail according to which could carry it most economically. The distortion which occurs is summed up by Professor Gilbert Walker as follows:

> Road transport takes that traffic for which costs by road are low in relation to the railway rate; the large consignments and the full loads to big centres whence a load back can always be obtained. The railways are left with the traffic for which the railway rate is low compared with the cost by road, small consignments, traffic to the minor centres from which a return load cannot always be got, and freight to remote areas generally.[7]

Another defect of charging arrangements before 1957 was that although the standard rate per mile fell as the length of haul increased, the charges bore little relationship to the differences in the cost of carrying particular goods, and none at all to the way in which operating costs varied over different routes according to the density of traffic. Road hauliers took these factors into account when fixing their charges, and "C" licence operators when deciding whether it would be economical to use their own vehicles for particular work. The railways could not raise their charges for infrequent loads over little-used routes above the standard rate and as a result they continued to carry these at a loss.

[6] It must not be supposed, of course, that all low-valued traffic was unprofitable. Mineral traffic in full loads was undamageable and might have been priced just as low on a cost as on a value basis.

[7] Gilbert Walker, *Road and Rail* (George Allen and Unwin), 2nd Edition, 1947, p. 114.

They were only allowed to depart from the standard charges in a downward direction. In cases where competitive conditions were keen and costs low, they could charge below standard "exceptional rates" for particular traffics,[8] but they could do nothing to reduce their losses on the traffics which they found most expensive to carry. Their obligations as statutory carriers meant that they had to maintain many services which were not economical and that they could not refuse to carry irregular loads.

The "C" licence operator often used the railways as a standby service for the small or irregular consignments which it did not pay him to send in his own vehicles. The control of maximum charges on the railways meant that they could not price this kind of traffic out of the market but had to subsidise it from the charges on more profitable merchandise. This was a vicious circle which made road competition for these profitable traffics stronger than ever.

Another factor which has probably increased the amount of regular heavy goods traffic sent by road is the system of motor vehicle taxation. There is evidence that, at present, it bears more lightly on the heavy road vehicles, which in fact are those which do most damage to the roads. It is these vehicles in particular which are carrying the traffics which could most readily be transferred to the railways. If the system of distributing the tax burden on road vehicles were revised so as to reflect the proportionate costs, in terms of road maintenance, attributable to different types of vehicles, it is possible that more of this regular heavy goods traffic might be sent by rail.

This history of pricing policies inappropriate to a competitive situation has meant that the railways have been unable to make the profits needed to finance capital investment, and since nationalisation the Government has not accorded them a high priority for capital out of public funds. The industry has not yet been able to take full advantage of all the new types of equipment and techniques which have been evolved, and which are being successfully utilised in other countries. Nor has it in the recent past had the capital to adapt its services to the changing needs of modern industry, in respect of handling devices, punctuality, and

[8] Though even in these cases the railways had still to observe the undue preference and equality of treatment regulations, and to publish details of these exceptional rates.

speed of service. This has been a serious handicap in meeting competition from road transport, particularly from "C" licence vehicles, since manufacturers have not suffered to the same extent from a shortage of capital.

Changes in the distribution of traffic between road and rail may therefore have been influenced to some extent by the past inability of the railways to invest sufficient capital to keep the industry in line with modern developments. Although since 1955 investment has been rising with the impact of the modernisation programme, the present state of the railways reflects their past history of starvation of capital. Thus, the result of this history of inadequate investment in both roads and railways, and incorrect pricing policies, has been an uneconomic use of existing transport resources, both road and rail.

In the last decade, however, a series of fresh approaches has been made to the problem of securing a rational allocation of transport.

Post-war policies

The first post-war approach was to attempt a planned rather than a competitive solution. In 1947, both the railways and long-distance road haulage undertakings were nationalised under the the control of the British Transport Commission, which was to implement a policy of co-ordination and integration of inland transport. However, little was done in this direction in the relatively short time before this policy was reversed by the denationalisation of road transport in 1953.

It was decided to restore competition between the railways and road hauliers, and the Commission were instructed to sell most of the road haulage concerns they had acquired since 1947. At the same time, they were to be given more freedom to compete with road transport. The regulations regarding undue preference and equality of treatment were repealed and the Commission were required to draw up a new freight charges scheme appropriate to competitive conditions. This scheme, which came into operation in July 1957, has abandoned both the practice of pricing according to value and that of charging a standard rate per mile. Only maximum rates have been fixed and these are graded according to consignment weight and loading characteristics. Within the maxima, however, rate makers are free to negotiate charges with individual traders and to vary their charges to different traders according to commercial considerations. For instance, they are able to allow a preferential rate to the trader who sends all his traffic by rail. They are no longer restricted by the need to publish their charges, since under the new scheme the Commission are required to make public only the maximum charges for freight and livestock, and the chargeable distances between stations or destinations. The Commission will be able to use their freight charges to attract the type of traffic most suited to rail transport, consignments in large quantities and wagon loads, regular and good loading traffic, and to divert to the roads those which are uneconomic if carried by rail, such as the shorter distances and irregular traffics.

Nevertheless, because maximum charges have been laid down by the Transport Tribunal, the freedom of the railways to price uneconomic traffic out of the market is still limited, and as common carriers they cannot refuse such traffic. Nor can they refuse to cater for the marginal requirements of "C" licence operators, many of whom use the railways as a standby service in special circumstances, while sending the bulk of their traffic in their own "C" licence vehicles, though they do now have the power to charge them rates well in excess of those they are paying. Thus, even under the new charges scheme some high-cost traffics will still be subsidised by others which the railways carry more cheaply, and this will affect the efficiency with which the price mechanism can distribute traffic between road and rail.

Conclusion

Because of the different cost structures of road and rail transport it would be naive to rely entirely on the price mechanism to bring about the best distribution of transport. The railways have to cover the costs common to their operations as a whole, and there is no "correct" method of allocating these between traffics. The present method, adapted to competitive conditions, demands the greatest contributions towards common costs from the traffics for which there is least actual or potential competition from road transport, and this in fact means that a large sector of railway users is being deprived of the lower cost service which the railways are capable of providing. To the distortion in charges which arises inevitably from the importance of common costs to railway operations, must be added the costs of covering unprofitable services or levels of charges which must also be recouped from more profitable operations. This latter distortion is one that can and should be removed. The railways should either be given freedom to function as a commercial undertaking with no obligation to modify their policies in the public interest, or, if they are to continue to fulfil any "social service" type of obligations, then this must be explicitly recognised in the financial arrangements that are adopted, and payment must be made by the State to cover the costs.[9]

If the former alternative is adopted, then the British Transport Commission must be completely free to apply commercial principles to all their operations. This would imply that they could close any lines and restrict or withdraw any services which were unprofitable; that they could raise thair charges to penal rates to drive unprofitable traffic off the railways; and that they could raise charges selectively in order to maximise revenue. Such a policy would probably result in a considerably smaller and more efficient system. Unfortunately there is no guarantee that the smaller system would run at a profit. The comprehensiveness of the public transport system helps to determine the public attitude towards the alternative attractions of private transport. Each contraction of the railway system might therefore accentuate the trend towards private transport and so reduce the field over which the railways could operate profitably. The case for the railways continuing to fulfil public service obligations may rest on rather stronger grounds than the social value of the particular routes or services which are at the moment being run at a loss.

However, whether or not fully commercial policies are adopted, it is essential that efforts should be made to adjust charges so that they reflect differences in marginal cost. Prices could not actually be *based* on marginal cost for two reasons. First, the marginal cost of railway operations is relatively low, since fixed costs are so heavy, so that marginal cost pricing would lead to heavy losses. Secondly, it is very difficult to determine the full marginal costs of particular railway operations. However, in the cases where costing analyses can show relative differences in marginal cost for

[9] Alternative methods of dealing with this problem are more fully discussed in *Paying for the Railways*, PLANNING No. 429 (P E P), 19 December 1958.

different goods or services, charges should reflect this relationship.[10]

ELECTRICITY

The cost of a unit of electricity depends partly on the cost of fuel, which comprises about 60 per cent of total costs of electricity from coal-fired stations, and partly on the cost of installing generating capacity. Since electricity cannot be stored, the cost also varies with the extent to which generating capacity is being used at any given time. Consumption of electricity is unevenly distributed over the twenty-four hours of each day, and over different seasons of the year. The heaviest seasonal demands on the supply system occur in December and January, and the peak daily demands usually occur between 8.0 and 10.30 a.m. and between 4.15 and 5.45 p.m. when the industrial and commercial load coincides with the domestic load. The demand at such periods of maximum consumption determines the amount of generating capacity required by the industry, but the average cost of each unit of electricity is determined by the extent to which the generating capacity is fully used over a period.

The ideal electricity tariff should do two things. First, it should minimise average cost and, second, it should help to minimise capital expenditure. Both these objects would be attained if the current total demand were evenly spread over the day and over the year. Considering only the more practicable objective of spreading demand evenly over the day, while assuming that capacity must be available to meet maximum seasonal demand, it should be noted that on the day of maximum demand in the year 1957–58, 16 December 1957, the *average* demand over the whole day was only around 13 million kilowatts, compared with a "marginal" maximum demand of over 19 million kilowatts.[11]

[10] The clearest case of long-run marginal cost pricing is found in the steel industry. The Iron and Steel Board appear to have changed the method of price control in recent years. It used to be on the basis of average cost, with some exclusion of extreme results. The 1958 Report of the Board shows that the main principle now is the cost, both operating and capital, at a modern, efficient plant. To quote: "The general basis is that in an expanding industry prices should reflect the costs of production and reasonable capital charges at new plant, incorporating the most modern techniques favourably situated for raw materials and markets, and operating at a high degree of efficiency." (*Annual Report of the Iron and Steel Board for 1958*, p. 32, para. 154.)

[11] Central Electricity Authority, *Reports and Accounts 1st April–31st December 1957 with additional data and accounts covering the twelve months ended 31st March 1958* (HMSO), p. 238.

If only 1 million kilowatts of this marginal demand could have been removed by reducing the peak demand to 18 million kilowatts, some 5 per cent of generating capacity would not have been required. At £50 per kilowatt installed capacity, some £50 million of investment could have been saved for every further 1 million kilowatts taken off the peak load. The average cost per unit would also have been reduced by avoiding the need to operate high-cost stations for short periods to meet the peak demand, thus raising the load factor, the average utilisation, of the remaining capacity.

Domestic and industrial charges

In 1957–58 domestic consumers took just over 30 per cent of total output, industry nearly 51 per cent, and commerce about 12·5 per cent.[12] The domestic consumer is paying, on average, more for each unit than the industrial user but less than the commercial user.

England and Wales

1957–58 average domestic price per unit —1·673d.
1957–58 average industrial price per unit —1·313d.
1957–58 average commercial price per unit—2·086d.[13]

It is hard to understand why the commercial price should be so much higher than the other charges, since it can hardly cost more to supply commerce with electricity than to supply households. Domestic consumers are paying more than industry, but even so are they paying enough to cover the extra costs of supplying them? In 1937–38 the average industrial price per unit was only about 40 per cent of the average domestic price per unit. Since then the average domestic price has risen very slowly (only by about 8 per cent) while the average industrial price has doubled.[14]

Industrial tariffs are now just under 80 per cent of domestic tariffs, but in other countries the differential between domestic and industrial tariffs is much greater. In Western Germany, for instance, industrial tariffs are only about 33 per cent of domestic tariffs. In both Europe and America pricing policies and other measures, such as domestic load limitation in France, have been

[12] Ibid., p. 52.
[13] Ibid., pp. 230–1.
[14] Ibid.

used to prevent the development of a domestic space-heating load. Only 15 per cent of the electricity sold in the United States is for domestic consumers,[15] compared with 30 per cent in England and Wales, and the American electricity undertakings have been able to achieve a higher annual load factor, 60 per cent as against 47 per cent in England and Wales.[16]

Electricity tariffs

The present structure of electricity tariffs, both domestic and industrial, appears to be directed at improving the load factor, but in fact it gives the consumer little incentive to use electricity in the most economical way; that is, to spread his load more evenly over the day so as to increase the load factor, and to keep his peak-hour consumption as low as possible so as to minimise the generating capacity which must be maintained solely to satisfy peak-hour demands. Consumers are usually charged according to a two-part tariff which consists of a standing charge and a relatively low charge per unit of electricity consumed. The standing charge for industrial and commercial consumers is based on their maximum demand, sometimes accurately measured by meters, but this is not necessarily the same as the system peak demand. Some area boards offer special night rates for electricity consumed within restricted off-peak hours. For domestic consumers the standing charge is based on the number of rooms, a rough and ready guide to potential electricity consumption and therefore to the capacity costs attributable to a consumer. This standing charge sometimes takes the form of a block tariff with a much higher unit charge for the first block of units consumed, and a low charge for succeeding units. Either way, the marginal cost of electricity to the consumer—the cost of increasing his own consumption—is relatively small and in fact encourages him to use more electricity, perhaps in place of alternative fuels, in order to spread his own "fixed" costs. While revenue from tariffs may cover the costs of supply, this structure gives the consumer a wrong picture of how his consumption affects total costs. His conception will be "the more I consume, the lower the cost", although it may in fact cost

[15] Cheap oil also contributes to this small proportion of consumer demand for electricity.

[16] I. M. D. Little, *The Price of Fuel* (Clarendon Press), 1953, p. 94, and Central Electricity Authority, op. cit., p. 55.

more to supply a few extra units than to provide his normal supply, if some of his extra consumption is taken at peak periods.

Time-of-day tariff

The basic defect of the present two-part tariff is that the fixed charge (or charge for the first block of units) does not in fact represent the contribution of the individual consumer to the capacity costs of the industry. These are determined, not by size of house, number of appliances or total consumption, but by the rate of consumption over the whole system *at peak hours*. The only kind of tariff which could allocate capacity costs between consumers on a correct basis would be one which charged them according to the demands they made on the supply system at peak periods, that is, some kind of "time-of-day" tariff. Electricity would not be priced, as now, as though it were a uniform commodity, for "midnight electricity" and "8.0 a.m. or 5.0 p.m. electricity" are not the same things. There is plenty of "midnight electricity" available, and not much demand for it, while "8.0 a.m. electricity" is in great demand and extra generating capacity, less efficient than that used to supply the base load, must be used to supply it. Even then demand has sometimes been in excess of supply so that load spreading or load shedding has been necessary.

Charging according to the time of day would involve installing meters which record the amounts of electricity used between different hours. Would their introduction reduce peak-hour demand enough to cover the costs of installation? In industry "consumption per meter" is large enough to suggest that, even if only small marginal adjustments were made, the effect on total consumption at peak hours would justify installing the meters.

For domestic users the question is rather more open, since it is not known if peak demand for electricity would be affected very much by a higher charge. The very nature of the peak, however, suggests that the demand for electricity at these times is dictated by necessity rather than choice—cooking and space-heating at breakfast time and in the evening when workers are coming home—so that, at the most, only small adjustments could be expected. The reduction in peak demand for each household might not, in the short run, cover the costs of installing time-of-day meters.

In the long run, however, such tariffs could influence buying and production decisions and have a far more significant effect on the level of peak demands. Householders who could not reduce their demand for heating and cooking at peak hours might choose to use gas rather than electricity when buying new appliances or replacing their existing ones. Further, manufacturers would have an incentive to increase or develop the production of thermal storage heaters, floorwarming and so on. Even in the short run, however, there is probably scope for small adjustments to peak period domestic consumption which could be made if there was the inducement of a time-of-day tariff. Just over 1·5 million or about one-eighth of the total number of domestic consumers account for about half the total domestic electricity consumption. It would probably pay to install time-of-day meters selectively in households like these which are themselves large consumers of electricity.

Has the industry given this question sufficient consideration? The Authority told the Herbert Committee that they did not consider a differential charge for peak and off-peak consumption was justified because the discrepancy between the running costs of "base-load stations" and the less efficient plant used to satisfy peak demands was not great enough. In 1957–58 the fuel cost of the least efficient plant, supplying 7 per cent of the total maximum output capacity, was over 1·3d. a unit, while 80 per cent of output capacity is produced at a running cost ranging between 0·3d. and 0·8d. per unit.[17] However, these figures take account only of the extra fuel costs of supplying peak demands and not of the capital costs of providing generating capacity for use at peak hours only. Moreover, they do not take account of the overall improvement in the load factor which might result if demand at present concentrated on the peak hours were more evenly distributed over the day.

At times when the resources available for investment were limited, and when the expansion programmes in other industries were being curtailed, the electricity industry was investing at the rate of over £200 million a year. Between 1957 and 1965 about £1,350 million will be spent on generating plant alone. The Central Electricity Generating Board is concentrating on improving the load factor through the increased use of electricity stimulated by low running charges, and the promotion of sales

[17] Central Electricity Authority, op. cit., Appendix 19, Table B, p. 264.

of all kinds of electrical appliances in the hope that the more widespread the demand, the more evenly it will be distributed over the day. But this policy may be defeating its own ends if more of the new demand falls in peak than off-peak periods. As the Herbert Committee commented: "More needs to be known about the load characteristics of appliances and the nature of demands made by various classes and types of consumers."[18]

From the point of view of both improving the load factor and reducing the required level of investment in generating capacity, the time-of-day tariff seems the best solution. Some other possibilities should however be briefly considered.

Other methods

With a load-limiting device as used in France, the maximum load consumers may take at any one time is automatically limited below the level at which space-heating would be practicable. Consumers who wish to use more power than the permitted level must meet the cost of metering for payment according to a time-of-day tariff. This system would, however, prove unfair to consumers who have already invested in electrical space-heating appliances, and would also reduce demand unnecessarily at off-peak periods.

The cost of individual electricity consumption could be increased by either charging more for the cheaper units in a two-part tariff, or charging on a flat-rate basis, or by raising the general level of all electricity charges in winter. These would all encourage consumers to reduce their demand for electricity but might have an adverse effect on the load factor. They would discourage consumption not only at peak hours, but also at off-peak periods, and since the peak demands seem to be the most urgent, they might even increase the discrepancy between the levels of peak and off-peak demands.

Conclusion

All these measures could be expected to have some effect in reducing the total consumption of electricity, and if all that were needed was a reduction in the amount of investment required in the electricity industry, these last two measures might be helpful.

[18] *Report of the Committee of Inquiry into the Electricity Supply Industry* (HMSO), January 1956, para. 403.

However, if the industry is also concerned to reduce the real costs of supplying electricity, then the effect of these measures on the load factor makes them inferior to the time-of-day tariff, although they would be easier to operate. The industry has been faced with a constantly rising demand for its product, which has been growing at the rate of just under 7 per cent per annum. With able advocates at its head, it has been able to secure a large proportion of the total investment resources available, so that by 1958 it was taking about 8 per cent of the total gross national investment, and 23 per cent of the gross fixed investment of public utilities and manufacturing industry together. As a result of its preoccupation with growth, the industry has probably not been paying enough attention to the question of satisfying this rising demand with the minimum of investment. Since other sectors have suffered from inadequate investment in the post-war period, it would seem to be in the national interest that the Ministry of Power should instruct the electricity authorities at least to experiment with such devices as the time-of-day tariff, to try to divert some capital from electricity to other industries that need it more urgently.

Charges based on the varying costs of electricity supplies at different times of day would have a tendency to increase the proportion of total costs which is paid by the domestic consumer. They would reduce the peak problem, and therefore lower the cost per unit, and yield a higher return on capital. The massive investments in electricity have been carried out on a basis of yields far lower than those that are obtainable on the average industrial investment. There may be some reasons why this yield should be slightly below that for industrial investments, but there is no economic justification for the great disparity which has existed in the post-war period.

COAL

Down to 1957, when the prospect of a surplus of coal first became clear, arguments about the pricing and investment policies of the coal industry took place in the context of the apparent inability to raise output, and the rising demand for energy which could only be met by importing oil or coal. More recently the situation has changed radically. The promise of nuclear power has removed the long-term fear of a shortage of fuel for the generation of electricity in the later decades of this century and the industrial recession of 1958–59 has created a problem of a surplus of coal output over current consumption so that stocks have been accumulating at an embarrassing rate. It is by no means certain, however, that a shortage of energy could not recur in the 1960's, and this gives relevance to arguments about coal pricing policies that might otherwise appear outdated. But, although these controversies may have been passed by events, they are still interesting as examples of the connection between pricing policies and investment since the war. There have been five main arguments to suggest that the real value of coal to the community may be, or may have been in the past, higher than its average cost of extraction, on which coal prices have in fact been based.

First, it has been argued that the real value of coal was almost infinite since the country had limited, though considerable, reserves of coal, the only indigenous fuel, with which to supply the basic power requirements of industry. From this point of view saving coal became an end in itself. This position is no longer tenable. Although the full potentialities of nuclear power will not begin to be realised for some years, there is now clearly a feasible alternative to coal for the production of electricity, the form of energy for which the demand is expanding most rapidly. Moreover, this alternative is one which does not increase dependence on imports.

Secondly, it was suggested that the price of coal ought to be high enough to equate supply and demand without the need for rationing. Demand for coal at current prices was in excess of supply by between 15 and 20 million tons according to the estimates of the Ridley Committee in 1952. United Kingdom consumers would have been willing to take about 5 million tons more coal than they were being allocated, and between 10 and 15 million tons more could have been sold on the export market. A rise in price of about £3 a ton followed by a gradual fall as coal output expanded would probably have made it possible then to de-ration coal, but the regressive effect on the distribution of income, together with the speculation in coal stocks which would have followed this recourse to a free market solution of the coal shortage, outweighed its advantages. At the present time the Coal Board is faced with the problem of a surplus of coal. Their stocks of undistributed coal were nearly 35 million tons in the latter half of 1959. Some of the fall in demand was the result of temporary factors, such as the slackening of industrial production aggravated by a mild winter in 1958, but some was the result of the more efficient utilisation of coal and permanent changes in the pattern of fuel consumption, especially the changeover to oil. Domestic coal has now been de-rationed, and recruitment for the pits has been temporarily suspended in some areas, which suggests that excess demand for coal may be a thing of the past.

A third argument was that if at any time coal output and stocks were insufficient to meet the needs of industry, as in 1947, the real value of coal was equal to the total value of the output lost. So long as there is any danger of a repetition of the 1947 crisis, the value of coal is considerably greater than the cost of producing it. Similarly the real cost of domestic consumption of fuel, in particular wasteful or excessive consumption, which endangers supplies to industry, is equal to the social cost of unemployment. How great is the danger of another fuel crisis? The 1947 crisis occurred before the coal industry had fully recovered from the effects of failure to invest in coal mining in the previous decades. At the present time, with a better-equipped mining industry, and with oil—and soon nuclear power—catering for the increase in industrial and domestic fuel consumption, the risk must be much less, even if the industry contracts in order to reduce the current level of coal stocks.

Fourthly, the value of coal to the economy was said to be at least that price for which it could be sold abroad. The export price of coal until the change in market conditions was on average £1–£1 5s. 0d. more than the price at which it was being sold on the home market. While the country is suffering from balance-of-payments crises the value to the economy of coal exports is even greater than their export price. Further, the heavy home demand for particular grades of coal has necessitated imports, mainly of large coal, totalling about 25 million tons between 1947 and 1958. The value of comparable grades of home-produced coal to the economy must again be at least as much as the cost of importing it. In 1956 coal was being imported at a cost of over £3 a ton more than the internal price. Moreover, its value to the economy was probably even greater than this since half the coal imported between 1947 and 1956 came from the United States and was paid for in dollars. This higher-cost coal was sold at the lower, internal price, on the grounds that such imports were only a temporary measure, and in order to avoid the need to allocate home-produced coal if imported coal were to be sold at a price high enough to cover its actual cost. This practice obscures the real cost relationship between imported coal and oil. However, the situation has now changed, whether temporarily or permanently, and imports of coal have been stopped. It is impossible to increase exports of British coal to Europe, since excessive stocks are also a serious problem there. Unless the situation in world markets changes, it cannot now be argued that domestic consumption of coal should be regarded as an alternative to increased exports.

Prices and future costs

The last argument for increasing the price of coal was based on the fact that coal output can often only be expanded under conditions of increasing costs per unit, since the more accessible and productive seams are exhausted first. The argument is that the price of coal should not be based on the average cost of producing the whole of the current output, but should reflect the scarcity of the coal which can be mined at current costs and the higher costs of production of the coal needed to replace or to increase current supplies. This gap between the average and the long-run marginal cost of coal is difficult to estimate. Large estimates are needed to replace capacity, and these investments are not financed out of current prices, but largely by loans which impose a future charge on the revenues of the industry. In the financial year 1958–59, it was estimated that total investment in the industry would be £162 million. This included £108 million for capital investment, of which only £35 million could be provided by the Coal Board from their own resources.[19] It has already been suggested above in Chapter 3, page 79, that it may be appropriate in the present circumstances to concentrate on getting the coal that is needed by more intensive use of existing capacity, and not to continue to invest a lot of money in developing new capacity, except where this could produce at lower cost than current capacity. This would probably mean that the capacity of the industry would eventually decline, and this might match the rate at which other fuels were capturing traditional markets for coal even with the present pricing policy.

[19] National Coal Board, *Annual Report and Accounts for the year ended 3 January 1959* (HMSO), Vol. I, p. 7.

The long-run marginal cost of coal is a better guide to the price that should be charged than is the short-run marginal cost of coal from the most inefficient existing pits and seams. Although there may in some circumstances be a theoretical case for raising the price as high as the short-run marginal cost, so that demand is sufficiently reduced to enable this high-cost capacity to be withdrawn, these pits should be closed in any case if the Coal Board can replace them with new lower cost capacity. So far, investment in the coal industry has been devoted primarily to raising or at least maintaining the existing capacity. Now that the fuel situation is more competitive, it is important to consider the efficiency of investment. If new capacity could produce at a profit at the existing level of prices, then, although the demand for coal may be stationary, or may even decline, there would still be a good case for more investment for the replacement of the older pits that are making losses greater than their capital charges. In a private enterprise industry a price based on the costs of the more efficient firms would automatically tend to drive out the high-cost producers. In a nationalised industry the same replacement of inefficient capacity should be carried out by a management that is concerned to produce at the lowest possible average cost.

The price of coal should be that price which will cover average costs, including a reasonable provision for future capital needs, and investment should only proceed if it opens up capacity which can produce coal at a lower cost including capital charges than the average. Capacity producing at higher than average cost, even ignoring capital charges,[20] can then be closed, and the average cost of coal, and therefore its price, can be steadily reduced. Unfortunately, there appear to be few investment opportunities in this increasing cost industry that meet these requirements. If, with prices based on its existing cost of production, the coal industry continues to lose markets, then high cost pits should be closed until the average cost is brought down to a level which permits the output of coal to be sold at a competitive price. If at this lower price some new investment should still be profitable, then the industry need not decline.

This of course is only the crude economic argument. The social

[20] Such capital charges as remain on old pits will have to be paid in any case, whether the old pit continues in production or is replaced by a new one, so they are not relevant to the decision whether or not to replace capacity.

arguments against accelerating the closure of pits and redundancy of miners are strong, more so than in many other industries since the pits are mostly located in scattered mining villages which offer little alternative employment. The miner's skills are in any case very specialised and applicable only to his own industry. There are also international political and strategic issues involved in allowing oil to fill some of the traditional markets for coal. It would be foolish to argue that policy can be determined solely on arguments about prices and costs. The decision has clearly to be related to a policy for the future supply of fuel and power in this country. If a social cost for maintaining mining communities has to be incurred this should be a national obligation and not a charge on the users of coal since to impose such a charge only increases the uncompetitiveness of the coal industry. But the Government must beware of being drawn into a position where, by subsidising low prices and continuing to lend money for further capital development, it would be maintaining the size of an industry that possibly ought to contract.

During the last war, a series of flat rate increases in coal prices narrowed the differentials between different grades, making the better grades relatively cheaper than they had been and the lower grades relatively dearer. Thus, in the early post-war period industries relying largely on low-grade coals were paying more than their share of the increased costs of coal, and users of large coal (which forms a large proportion of domestic consumption) were paying less than their share. In particular, electricity undertakings, which use a great deal of poor quality coal, were affected in this way.

The National Coal Board have since been applying their price increases in a more discriminatory manner, and recent adjustments reflect more closely the demand for different grades of coal.

Industrial users have (rightly) fared better than domestic consumers in obtaining supplies of coal in times of scarcity. They have usually been allocated their full requirements, although post-war rationing of domestic consumers meant that householders' demands were not always fully satisfied. But industry has not always been supplied with the grades desired, and has often had to make do with fuels not suited to existing appliances, with a consequent loss of thermal efficiency. The gas, electricity and railway undertakings have complained of inefficiency caused in this way.

Thus it seems that in the past there may have been some discrimination against industrial users of coal, but that this has now been corrected. Higher prices have not been needed to restrain domestic consumption in order to ensure adequate supplies for industry because the rationing system gave industry a priority.

The present excessive stocks are mainly of small coal, especially suitable for power stations, while large coal is still quite scarce. The future trend will be towards a greater output of small than of large coal. Recent price increases have, therefore, tended to affect large coal more than small coal, but they have probably not yet increased the differential sufficiently to reflect the relative strengths of demand.

CONCLUSION

The discussion of pricing policies on the railways, in electricity supply and in the coal industry has shown that while these industries have been nationalised and could be expected therefore to form a rationally planned part of the economy, the influence of the past, and in particular of outmoded pricing policies, has prevented the emergence of the best distribution of investment.

In the transport sector the chief problem is that of co-ordinating road and rail transport. The railways have been burdened with pricing policies and common carrier obligations which were not designed for a time when there are alternative forms of transport. It is essential to decide what kind of railway system is required, and then to design a pricing policy that will enable this to work efficiently. The roads have been systematically starved of investment over many years, but again, more investment, though urgently needed, is not in itself a sufficient answer to the problems. Measures are required to ensure that improvements are not immediately negated by the number of vehicles expanding to fill and overfill the whole capacity of the new roads. This implies again a co-ordinated transport policy to see that traffic that is better carried by rail—for example, long-distance and regular heavy freights, and urban commuter traffic—is in fact carried by rail, and not diverted on to the roads by faulty pricing policies, badly distributed taxes or the imposition of unrealistic obligations.

Investment in the electricity industry has been criticised as excessive. Down to 1953 there were power cuts which detracted from industrial efficiency, and, given the existing pricing policies, it was obviously essential to expand generating capacity. Until the problem of differential pricing for peak loads is tackled, however, there will always be reason to argue that a lot of generating capacity is being inadequately used. The encouragement of overnight storage heating and similar techniques is a step in the right direction but their advantages have not so far been by any means fully exploited. The coming of nuclear power stations has increased the capital cost of electricity generation and therefore made this problem even more urgent. This addition to capital costs was justified on the grounds of a general fuel shortage but may not be so acceptable now that there is plenty of fuel. Of course the excessive stocks of coal may be only temporary, but one feature which is likely to continue in the future is the plentiful supply of small coal which is ideal for power stations, and this may be considered to alter the valuation of investment in atomic power stations *vis-à-vis* conventional coal-fired stations.

In the coal industry, the high level of investment has been criticised on the ground that it does not give an adequate return in terms of more coal, but in defence of this policy it is said that most of the investment is necessary to prevent a fall in coal output. Various critics have in the past suggested that for one reason or another the price of coal is too low and a higher price would certainly help to cut losses, to pay better wages, to reduce the size of the industry and to promote efficient coal utilisation with the added social benefits of clean air. Most of the arguments about the coal industry have been related to the period up to 1957 in which a general shortage and rationing prevailed, and the position has changed very considerably during—though not simply as a consequence of—the recession of 1957–58. Certainly the coal industry would find it even harder to justify a price increase now than it appears to have done in past years of shortage. In addition, there are social and political and long-term strategic arguments against allowing oil to fill, as it is increasingly doing, some of the traditional markets for coal. However, the immediate economic incentive should certainly be allowed some influence, and the Government must not allow itself to be put in the position of subsidising any form of energy supply that is not efficient.

More important perhaps than these conclusions about each individual industry are some considerations that are common to the pricing policies of all of them.

First, they have tended to weight prices adversely against industry and in favour of the domestic consumer. The examination of the differentials between domestic and industrial tariffs in the fuel and transport industries shows that prices have been rather more favourably biased in favour of domestic consumers in this country than in other European countries. It is not always easy to say whether this means that the domestic consumer has been subsidised by industry in this country, or whether the reverse was taking place in the European countries. The evidence in the case of the railways, however, clearly shows that industry has borne an increasingly larger share of total costs while rail carryings were falling and passenger fares were being shielded from the effects of inflation. From the point of view of keeping industry's costs down, and from that of the long-term interests of railway freight traffic and revenue, the political pressures which have held down passenger fares at the expense of freight charges should be removed.

Other countries have deliberately arranged their charges for electricity to discourage its use for domestic space-heating, and so reduce the amount of investment in generating capacity needed. It is not clear, however, if the higher European charges for domestic electricity which have had this effect reflect higher relative costs of supply, but it would be desirable to reduce the domestic space-heating load in this country. Time-of-day tariffs which would ensure payment according to the pressure on capacity at peak hours would be a more accurate way of allocating costs than merely raising domestic electricity charges as a whole. The use of gas for intermittent domestic space-heating is more economic than electricity since the peak problem is not so acute for the gas industry.

In the case of coal, it is suggested that in the past large coal for domestic use had probably been underpriced in relation to small coal, and the tendency for discriminatory price increases to replace flat-rate increases is welcome. In view of the current stocks of small coal, there is undoubtedly scope for further widening the differential between large and small coal prices, and it is hoped that the Coal Board will continue to adjust its prices in this way.

The unfavourable treatment of domestic prices in the United Kingdom has been part of a policy of keeping the cost of living, and therefore labour costs, down. This, however, may be an entirely wrong policy if it means keeping industrial costs up. A correct pricing policy, if it resulted finally in higher labour costs but lower general industrial costs (and therefore the same final price level) would increase the pressure to economise in labour and would lead therefore to higher productivity. The contrast between the Continental and the United Kingdom pricing of domestic and industrial supplies from the publicly owned industries is instanced by Sir Robert Shone and H. R. Fisher in a paper to the Royal Statistical Society[21] as one of the factors responsible for the slow growth of productivity in the United Kingdom.

The table below is taken from this paper and gives some examples of comparative prices in the United Kingdom and in the countries of the European Coal and Steel Community at the end of 1957. For the three industries considered, domestic prices are higher in the ECSC countries while industrial prices are lower.

TABLE 16

DOMESTIC AND INDUSTRIAL PRICES IN THE UNITED KINGDOM AND THE ECSC COUNTRIES

	United Kingdom			*ECSC*		
	Domestic	*Industrial*	*Ratio D/I*	*Domestic*	*Industrial*	*Ratio D/I*
(*a*) Gas	19·9	11·4	1·75	27·8	8·9	3·13
(*b*) Electricity	1·6	1·3	1·23	3·6	1·2	3·00
(*c*) Transport	2·0	2·7	0·74	2·5	2·3	1·09

(*a*) Prices per therm charged by the East Midlands Gas Board in the United Kingdom: in the Ruhr for the ECSC.
(*b*) Pence per kilowatt-hour: ECSC, Germany.
(*c*) Pence per passenger-mile and pence per ton-mile for an average of iron ore, steel scrap, and steel charges.

A second general point is that the prices charged in these industries have been inadequate to provide funds for expansion, and recourse has been had therefore to the Treasury to provide the capital needed for increasing, or even for maintaining, output. There is good reason to believe that this procedure is more

[21] Sir Robert Shone and H. R. Fisher, "Industrial Production and Steel Consumption", *Journal of the Royal Statistical Society*, Series A (General), Vol. 121, Part 3, 1958, p. 293.

inflationary than if a substantial proportion of the capital were made available by raising prices of peak loads particularly. Prices in these industries may justifiably be raised for two reasons: first, in order to raise more revenue so as to provide internal finance for a greater proportion of investment, and secondly, in order to cut out traffics and sales that are not desired because they are not profitable. In either case the effect would be to raise the yield on investments. These industries have long continued to operate on the basis of a yield of around 5 per cent—sufficient to cover the low rate of interest on gilt-edged borrowing—while private industry expects, and gets, a yield between 15 and 20 per cent, out of which it is able to finance much of its own future development. Even after allowing for the possibly greater risk involved in some private investments there seems no clear justification for this vast difference in the assessment of the profitability of public enterprises.

Finally, there is clearly an urgent need for co-ordination of investment and pricing policies throughout the public sector if these basic industries are to develop correctly, and fulfil their role in the economy efficiently. It is not proposed to elaborate this conclusion here since a similar conclusion arises out of later chapters discussing other features of the economy. The need for a greater degree of co-ordination of economic objectives and particularly a more thorough co-ordination of investment is therefore examined in Chapter 10.

CHAPTER 5

THE IMPACT OF TAXATION

THE last chapter has considered the influence on investment, enterprise and production of certain important pricing decisions in nationalised industries. A survey of the effects of taxation, the most prevalent form of intervention in the free production and sale of goods and services, has been held over for separate treatment. Through the tax system some 30 per cent of the national income is every year diverted from the hands of persons and companies into those of the State, and whatever combination is employed of the many methods available for effecting this diversion, there are bound to be significant effects on investment and production.

The sums which the Government removes from individuals and firms in order to finance its expenditures may be considered from at least three points of view. First, one form of tax may be more effective than another in raising the total revenue that is required. Secondly, there is the problem of the justice of the tax system as between one individual and another, and especially the question of the redistribution of income, of progressive versus regressive taxes. Thirdly, there is the problem of the impact of taxation in general, and of the particular forms of tax, on industrial efficiency and growth. The present chapter is concerned only with the last set of problems, except of course for the necessity to temper rhe conclusions reached with due consideration of the needs of the tevenue and of social justice.

Even within the bounds set by this delimitation of interest, the issues concerning taxation and industry are multiple and complex. They are complex not only in a theoretical economic sense—the effect of a given tax is not easy to deduce—but because of the difficulty of obtaining and assessing the relevant facts, and because many of the questions are political rather than economic. The various pressure groups use economic arguments to support their case, but the very existence of this or that body seeking to influence policy in some (to them) desirable direction means that decisions cannot be taken only after a rational appraisal of the economic facts of each case, but must also be influenced by what can be made acceptable.

There is a tendency in discussions of the effects of taxation on industry to start from the assumption that only unfavourable effects are in question. But while taxes as a whole may be on balance harmful (though even this cannot be accepted without examination) it is clear that particular methods of arranging taxes and allowances may be either harmful or favourable to industry. Many of the results of particular taxes are recognised and the methods of levying them are deliberately arranged so as to have a positive and helpful influence on industry and commerce. This chapter starts without bias: it will consider positive as well as negative aspects of taxation.

One matter that is not discussed here is the way in which the money raised by the Government is then spent. Chapter 6 discusses the two major items of Government expenditure, defence and the social services.

The first part of this chapter deals with the general criticisms of the level of taxation in this country, and with the effect of personal taxes, income tax and surtax, on individual effort and enterprise. The larger second part is devoted to the taxes and allowances affecting business. First the profits tax is discussed, and then the particular aspects of company taxation which have a special importance: the provision for overseas trading profits, and the depreciation allowances together with their variants, the initial and investment allowances. Death duties are, strictly speaking, a personal tax, but they have a special impact on small family firms. Finally, purchase tax, which has a sharp but deliberate effect on production, is reviewed.

THE GENERAL LEVEL OF TAXATION

Much of the argument about the level of taxation is informed rather by emotional prejudice than by reasonable analysis. On the one side, there are those whose instinctive reaction is to oppose any tax because they are fundamentally opposed to the increase of the role of Government in the economy. On the other, are those who prefer to see public in place of private spending. Given a need for revenue arising out of certain defence and social policies, a case can always be made out for any particular tax and the issue crystallises into whether the general level of tax which is the

TABLE 17

ANALYSIS OF EXCHEQUER ORDINARY REVENUE 1938–39 TO 1957–58

	Actual			*Per cent of Ordinary Revenue*			*Per cent of National Income in*		
							1938	1950	1957
	Financial years			*Financial years*			*Financial years*		
	1938–9	1950–1	1957–8	1938–9	1950–1	1957–8	1938–9	1950–1	1957–8
Inland Revenue		£ million							
Income Tax (including Companies)	336	1,404	2,208	36·2	35·3	41·3	7·0	13·2	12·5
Surtax	63	121	157	6·8	3·0	2·9	1·3	1·1	0·9
Death Duties	77	185	171	8·3	4·7	3·2	1·6	1·7	1·0
Stamp Duties	21	55	64	2·3	1·4	1·2	0·4	0·5	0·4
Profits Taxes	22	273*	255*	2·4	6·9	4·8	0·5	2·6	1·4
TOTAL INLAND REVENUE	520	2,038	2,855	56·1	51·2	53·4	10·8	19·1	16·2
Customs and Excise									
Tobacco	85	604	713	9·2	15·2	13·3	1·8	5·7	4·1
Hydro carbon oils	58	144	322	6·3	3·6	6·0	1·2	1·3	1·8
Purchase Tax	—	303	494	—	7·6	9·2	—	2·8	2·8
Other Customs and Excise	198	579	621	21·4	14·6	11·6	4·1	5·4	3·5
TOTAL CUSTOMS AND EXCISE	341	1,630	2,150	36·8	41·0	40·2	7·1	15·3	12·2
Miscellaneous	66	310	338	7·1	7·8	6·3	1·4	2·9	1·9
TOTAL ORDINARY REVENUE	927	3,978	5,343	100·0	100·0	100·0	19·0	37·0	30·0

Source: Annual Abstract of Statistics 1958, Table 298.

* Including special contribution and "other revenue duties".

outcome of the individual decisions is not more than the country can bear. Those who oppose taxes seek to show that they will have serious consequences for the economic well-being, while those who support them argue that these harmful effects are much exaggerated.

In brief, the arguments put forward against the level of taxation that has been maintained in Britain since the war are that it discourages effort and enterprise, encourages extravagant and wasteful expenditure, and strengthens those elements of the economy that acquiesce in the continuation of inflation. It is in the nature of things impossible to quantify these alleged effects of a high level of taxation. Everyone can quote at first or second hand cases where a decision to do a certain job has been reversed on account of the large share that taxation would take of the extra, marginal, earnings that would result from the effort. Extravagant expenditures that would not be made out of net income become more enticing with the thought that the Chancellor of the Exchequer will be paying 7s. 9d. in the pound or even more of those expenditures, but no estimates are available of the effects on industrial efficiency and on the growth of the national product.

The most vigorous academic opposition to high levels of taxation has probably come from Colin Clark, who has argued in three papers since the war that taxation should not take more than 25 per cent of the national income. He first expressed this view in an article "Public Finance and Changes in the Value of Money", then in his pamphlet *Welfare and Taxation* and in 1957 in *The Cost of Living*.[1] In the first he adduced statistical evidence from a number of countries to show that whenever the attempt had been made to divert more than about 25 per cent (the exact proportion varying between one country and another) of the national income into the hands of the Government by means of taxation, it had been frustrated by the inflation that was the inevitable result of this strengthening of those forces in the economy that preferred to see rising prices. In *Welfare and Taxation* he attacked the post-war policies which had taken around 40 per cent of the national income in taxes in order to meet vast expenditures on defence and on the social services. In *The Cost of Living* he set out figures showing the comparative lack of economic

[1] Published respectively by: *Economic Journal*, December 1945; Catholic Social Guild, 1954; Hollis and Carter, 1957.

progress in Britain since the war and attributed this to the effects of excessive Government spending out of taxation. But the bringing together of a lot of statistics is not a sufficient proof of this proposition. The following key paragraph shows that the case is one of assertion rather than proof:

> Chancellors are sometimes persuaded by their economic advisers to increase taxation on the supposed grounds that this is the best way of mopping-up surplus purchasing power. Such action may sometimes indeed be unavoidable. But at best it is a short-sighted approach. After a year or two, taxation carried beyond reasonable economic limits begins to have the opposite effect, and to cause a rise in prices. The reasons can be simply stated. By discouraging effort and enterprise, it keeps down the supply of goods and services available for sale; by encouraging businessmen to spend comparatively extravagantly on anything which can be charged to a business expense account, it increases the amount of purchasing power competing for a limited supply of goods, and finally, it brings about a subtle change in parliamentary and public opinion, which can be relied upon to put up a resistance to inflationary proposals under normal circumstances, but under the circumstances of excessive taxation come to think that inflation might be the lesser evil, believing that it may help to reduce the real burden of Government expenditure.[2]

All this may be true, but what is its quantitative importance? By how much is the supply of goods and services reduced? What total sum is spent wastefully? How important is taxation as a pressure towards inflation compared with changes in the level of import prices, the strength of the unions, or the influence of hire purchase on consumer demand?

In their representations to the Chancellor for the 1958 Budget (*The Budget 1958*) the Federation of British Industries used a similar argument:

> Inflation arises from the attempt to spend more than is produced. A principal cause of this has been excessive public expenditure, which is even now, despite the relative moderation in real terms of recent years, well over 30 per cent of the national income. Public expenditure at this level makes the task of mastering inflation by monetary measures difficult, if not impossible.

[2] *The Cost of Living*, p. 3.

This assertion is backed up chiefly by the argument that the extra cash left in the hands of the public by reducing taxes would be mostly saved, thus helping industry to find the funds for investment.

A British Association study on science and industry investigated the effects of taxation on business but produced no very positive conclusions.[3] It concluded that the most important factor might be that businessmen *believed* that taxation prevented a high rate of investment. But even this may not be a correct interpretation of the complaints about the general burden of taxes (as opposed to specific complaints about the operation of particular taxes). An equally respectable explanation is that businessmen do not believe that taxation has really prevented them investing in greater productivity, but feel obliged in the interests of their shareholders to complain about the amounts that go in tax.

There appears therefore to be no good ground for accepting the allegation that public spending, financed by a high level of taxation, has in itself a built-in tendency to harm production and investment to any significant extent, or to produce inflation. But it is necessary to look in more detail at the effects of particular taxes, since it may well be that the incidence of particular taxes rather than the total volume has a significant impact on economic growth.

TAXES ON PERSONS

Income tax

Income tax is levied on the incomes of both individuals and companies. In the case of persons the tax is graduated according to the size of income and subject to exemption limits and allowances depending on personal circumstances. Personal incomes above £2,000 are subject also to surtax at graduated rates, and unearned incomes are more severely taxed than earned incomes. Companies pay income tax at the standard rate, now 7s. 9d. in the pound, and, where profits are over £2,000 per annum, are liable also to profits tax. Income tax provides about 41 per cent of the Government's revenue from taxation. Exchequer receipts from income tax in the year 1957–58 were £2,208 million. Taxation on companies accounts for a larger proportion of the total than taxes levied on

[3] C. F. Carter and B. R. Williams, *Industry and Technical Progress* (Oxford University Press), 1957.

individuals under PAYE. Tax assessments for the year 1956–57 on profits of business and professions (Schedule D) amounted to £1,175 million, of which £954 million were accounted for by companies alone. Tax deducted under Schedule E for PAYE amounted to £861 million in the same year. The rates at which income tax is levied on individuals are graduated, and a progressively larger proportion of earnings is taken in tax as earnings increase. It is frequently argued that this constitutes a disincentive to extra effort to increase earning capacity. The effect on incentives at the margin is particularly important in this context. A worker paying tax on £60 of his earnings is now paying at the rate of 1s. 9d. in the pound. If extra effort could earn him another £50 the rate of tax on these additional earnings will jump from 1s. 9d. to 4s. 3d.—more than twice as much. If he is already paying tax on £210 and has the opportunity of earning a further £100, his rate will jump from 4s. 3d. to 6s. 3d. Once he is paying tax at the standard rate, £30 of every £100 earned will go in tax.

How far are decisions to work in an effort to increase earnings affected by these considerations? There is very little evidence on this question, but the following facts are relevant to the discussion.

First: as long as earnings are below what is necessary to provide for a generally accepted minimum standard of living, there is a very powerful incentive to increase earnings in spite of a large proportion of the increase being paid in tax. That is to say that up to a certain minimum level, increased earnings are not seen as a substitute for anything else, for example, leisure.

Second: a large proportion of wage earners paid on flat hourly rates are not affected by any kind of payments by results scheme and are therefore not in a position to influence their marginal earnings by extra effort anyway. The quality or speed of their work influences not whether they earn an extra pound or not, but, less forcefully perhaps, whether they retain their job.

Third: such factual evidence as there is on this subject does not suggest that income tax affects attitudes to earnings. A social survey undertaken for the Royal Commission on Taxation showed that its influence on incentives was negligible. The most striking finding of the survey was that only between 3 and 5 per cent of the male sample had sufficient knowledge of the tax system to be able to "take that factor accurately into account in deciding their working behaviour". Less than 5 per cent "believed that their personal actions and behaviour had been materially affected by income tax". Of those in the sample who had turned down an offer of overtime during the previous four weeks only 5 per cent gave tax considerations as their reason. The National Coal Board conducted a survey into absenteeism in selected collieries in the East Midlands, and found that only about 0·3 per cent of the shifts lost through absenteeism could be ascribed to tax considerations. The Commission also consulted a number of industrial consultants. "These consultants had encountered no evidence to show that PAYE has any significant effect upon absenteeism or extra effort." The Royal Commission therefore concluded that high taxation would not influence the vigour with which a man pursued his ordinary calling, but that it might make him "disinclined to take on a casual engagement of something out of his usual course".[4]

These conclusions may have to be modified to some extent to take account of the fact that income tax is not the only charge that is graduated according to income. For example, differential rents schemes sometimes result in a heavy extra charge if earnings rise above a certain level. The middle classes are faced with extra payments for educating their children at universities if their income rises above a certain level. While no single one of the several charges that may be graduated according to income may constitute a disincentive to effort, the cumulative effect of them all could be serious.

Surtax

In addition to paying income tax at the standard rate of 7s. 9d. in the pound, surtax at graduated rates ranging from 2s. to 10s. is charged on incomes above £2,000. Taxable income is reduced by the excess of certain personal allowances over the single personal allowance of £140. Thus, a married couple without children are liable to surtax when their joint income reaches £2,100. If they have one child, the additional £100 allowance for the child means that they pay surtax on all income above £2,200. There is, therefore, a jump in the marginal rate of taxation when income reaches the surtax limit. When the joint income of a childless married couple reaches £2,100, each addi-

[4] *Second Report of the Royal Commission on the Taxation of Profits and Income*, Cmd. 9105 (HMSO), April 1954, para. 149.

tional £1 of earnings is taxed at 9s. 9d. in the pound. If they have an income of £4,100, each additional £1 of earnings is taxed at 12s. 3d. in the pound. Further, it is only since the 1957 Budget that some of the allowances for income tax purposes have been deducted from income for surtax purposes also. The position of surtax payers was considerably improved by this concession and, in the same budget, by the extension of the uppermost limit of the two-ninths earned income allowance from £2,025 to £4,005, and the operation of an earned income allowance of one-ninth for incomes of £4,005–£9,945 per annum. Prior to these changes, there had been a very sharp rise in the effective rate of tax, once incomes reached the £2,000 per annum range. This has now been modified, but the steep rise in the marginal rate of taxation remains.

The existence of a disincentive to taking on extra work is most apparent in the case of married women.[5] Below the surtax range, and contrary to a popular misconception, the earnings of married women receive slightly better treatment than those of single persons, and more favourable treatment than if the total joint income of the married couple were earned solely by the husband. This arises from the recognition of the fact that a cost to the household is incurred when a wife works which is not incurred if the family income is earned solely by the husband. The wife's earnings are therefore credited with a personal allowance of seven-ninths of her income up to £140 (the personal allowance for a single person) in addition to the net marriage allowance of £100 per annum which her husband can claim against his earnings, plus the normal earned income allowances and reduced rate benefits which she claims irrespective of her husband's earnings. However, once above the surtax limit, the joint incomes are aggregated for surtax purposes and surtax is chargeable on the total joint income. If the husband is already paying surtax, the wife's earnings, even if very small, can considerably increase the tax liability of the family.

Since business and professional people are especially able to increase their earnings by their own efforts, either because the whole of their income is derived from fees, or because, although

[5] It is, of course, recognised that many married women will work for reasons other than financial reward, and where this is so the provisions of the tax system are unlikely to influence their decision.

paid a basic salary, they can find opportunities for extra work, the heavy marginal incidence of taxation at £2,000 a year is particularly unfortunate. Moreover, not only taxation has its keenest marginal effect at this level of income. Extra payments for educating their children are involved for these same income groups. In so far as these are voluntary, for example, sending the children to private schools instead of to State schools, there may be a case for ignoring such expenses. But when a child of wealthy parents obtains a place at a university, the parents do not get a grant for his maintenance, as do poorer parents. This may be a part of redistributive justice, but it does accentuate the disincentive effects of taxation on this same income group. How far effort is in fact reduced as a result of these burdens is uncertain. Many of these people do their jobs because they are interested in them and get satisfaction from them. Although they complain, there is little evidence that in fact they work less hard as a result of marginal taxation and other burdens which take a large proportion of their extra income. But those who are in business at least have a way out, which has resulted in serious wastes and distortions in the economy, in addition to its harmful moral effects. They contrive to be paid as far as possible in the form of expenses rather than in taxable income. Thus, many restaurants are kept going because they provide lunches, often lavish, for businessmen to entertain clients and contacts. If they were not taxed so heavily the businessmen might prefer to receive the money they spend in this way in the form of income, which they could spend in a more satisfying way.

The proposal for an expenditure tax

The most serious suggestion for an alternative tax system which has been put forward in recent years is that of an expenditure tax.[6] This would replace income tax by a progressive tax levied on expenditure over a given period. The main advantage over the present system would be that incentives to earn and to save would be increased since savings would not be taxed while they remained in the bank. In so far as income tax may involve any general disincentive to increasing earnings this would be reduced by a tax which exempted savings. This exemption would imply not only a deferment of taxes on that part of income that is saved so

[6] Especially by N. Kaldor in *An Expenditure Tax* (Allen and Unwin), 1955.

that almost twice as much could be saved without the individual cutting his standard of living, but also that the interest earned on these savings, if it were not spent, would not attract tax. This would be a powerful combination of incentives to save, for most of the benefit to savers would accrue only so long as they refrained from withdrawing their savings and accrued interest. Even on withdrawal, there would be an addition to consumable income represented by the net interest received on money held by the individual and not by the Exchequer during the period of deferment. Moreover, if savings were only withdrawn, for example, in old age when current income would be small, the individual would pay less tax on his savings if they were then spent gradually than he would have done if he had spent them during his peak earning period. So the incentive to save for old age or hard times would be quite considerable. The other advantage of the system is that it would "catch" concealed income which escapes the present income tax net in the form of capital gains, while not taxing those capital gains which are reinvested. The system would therefore have a built-in bias towards savings and against expenditure. In a rapidly expanding economy this would assist the financing of investment. It would also provide the Government with a far more effective weapon for curtailing consumption than the present income tax, which is often paid in effect at the expense of savings.

There are two disadvantages to the operation of an expenditure tax. Its administration might involve rather more interference in the life of the individual than the present system, since the revenue authorities would need to check detailed accounts of a taxpayer's expenditure, gifts and so on. This consideration affects its acceptability as a tax. More directly relevant to the present discussion, however, is the question whether the system's chief advantage, the built-in bias towards savings, is of permanent value, being justified mainly by an appeal to its advantages in an inflationary period. But if the demand for capital remains high, the proposal could merit fuller consideration than it has so far received.

TAXES AFFECTING COMPANIES

Profits tax

All companies are taxed at the standard rate for income tax, and in addition where their profits exceed £2,000 per annum they are liable to profits tax. This tax does not play a very significant role as a source of revenue, since it yields only about £250 million per annum, or just under 5 per cent of the total of all taxes paid to the central government. The incidence of the tax on particular firms or activities has, however, been important, especially since, up to the 1958 Budget, it was imposed at rates which discriminated sharply between distributed and undistributed profits. From 1947 distributed profits had been taxed at a much higher rate than undistributed profits. The rates in 1947 were 25 per cent and 10 per cent respectively. In 1949 they were changed to 30 per cent and 10 per cent and in 1951 to 50 per cent and 10 per cent. From 1952 to 1955 they were 22½ per cent and 2½ per cent. In 1955 they changed to 27½ per cent and 2½ per cent, and from 1956 to 1958 they were 30 per cent and 3 per cent. The differential has thus been steadily rising from 2½ : 1 in 1947 to 10 : 1 in 1956. In the 1958 Finance Act the differential was abolished, and a single flat rate of tax of 10 per cent was imposed on all profits whether distributed or not. This was raised to 12½ per cent in the 1960 Budget.

The change to a flat rate removed one of the chief disadvantages of the profits tax, namely, that it affected firms differently according to the diversities of financial structure, and in such a way as to penalise what were probably the most progressive firms. While ordinary and preference dividends were treated as distributed profits and charged for income tax at the standard rate and for profits tax at 30 per cent (between 1956 and 1958), interest on debentures or loan stocks was a charge against revenue which did not count as profits and therefore was not subject to profits tax, though of course it was subject to income tax in the hands of the recipient. Thus, a firm that raised its capital by loans paid much less tax than one which relied on equities. Similarly, dividend policies were affected by the incentive against the distribution of profits. When raising capital for future ventures, the tax encouraged reliance on loan capital and was a disincentive to the financing of risky investments.[7] A particular disadvantage of the discriminatory system was that the special relief of 27 per cent on undistributed profits applied only so long as these were not distributed. If at any time a firm distributed profits that had only

[7] See *Final Report of the Royal Commission on the Taxation of Profits and Income*, Cmd. 9474 (HMSO), June 1955, Chapter 20.

been taxed at 3 per cent, the remaining 27 per cent tax had to be paid. If liquidation, reconstruction, or reorganisation was forced on a firm, and the distribution exceeded the paid-up capital and cash premiums on its shares, profits tax was levied on the whole of the excess, to the extent that it had been relieved of tax at the full rate during the life of the company since January 1947.

The decision in the 1958 Budget to charge a flat-rate profits tax in future has thus removed these inequities and distortions arising from the differential rates. There is little danger of losing an incentive to investment through the change since a tax relief that encouraged retention of profits did not necessarily encourage their productive use. The Royal Commission on Taxation had concluded that:

> The mere retention of profits cannot be rated as an economic advantage: on the contrary it would better serve the public interest that a company should be encouraged to distribute those profits which it cannot put to fruitful use, in order that there may be a chance that they may be invested effectively elsewhere. Nor is it advantageous for the economy that the level of dividends should be kept down . . . the market value of shares in industrial and commercial enterprises is artificially depressed and an obstacle placed in the way of raising new capital.[8]

If incentives to investment are needed, investment allowances[9] would seem a better method than one which provided only an ambiguous and somewhat inequitable incentive for the retention of profits. The new flat-rate profits tax means in effect that companies earning profits of more than £2,000 per annum are being charged income tax at 2s. in the pound above the standard rate, that is, at 9s. 9d. instead of 7s. 9d. in the pound. An individual is allowed two-ninths of his income free of tax if it is earned. This brings his rate (on that part of his income on which tax is payed at the standard rate) down to about 6s. in the pound compared with the 9s. 9d. paid on profits, though part of the two-ninths earned income allowance is an allowance towards the expenses of the individual in equipping himself for and travelling to work. The rate of tax on earnings created by investment is thus over half as high again as the rate on earnings of individuals from employ-

[8] Ibid., para. 536.

[9] See p. 129.

ment. This difference in the tax rates on the two main sources of wealth is considered later.

Overseas trading profits

The profits tax has been modified in respect of the overseas earnings of British companies trading abroad in order to prevent their being at too great a disadvantage in comparison with their local competitors. First, a system of double taxation relief operates, by which taxes paid to the country where the profits are earned are credited against taxation due at the rates applying in the United Kingdom, so that tax is paid in this country only to the extent that the tax already paid in the country where the earnings originate falls short of the amount which would be due at United Kingdom rates.

However, until April 1957 all companies whose management and control were exercised from the United Kingdom were liable for the full rate of United Kingdom income and profits tax. This meant that where local taxes were not so severe as in the United Kingdom, companies trading abroad were put at a disadvantage *vis-à-vis* their local competitors, or other foreign competitors whose governments gave tax exemption or preferential treatment to overseas earnings. Such competitors included the United States, Canada, Belgium, Holland and Switzerland. Further, the system of double taxation relief did not take account of other concealed forms of taxation which might be imposed by the country in which the profits were earned. Thus a government royalty on production, or an export tax, would not qualify for discount against United Kingdom taxation. This meant that a company trading abroad might have to face an even greater liability to taxation than if it were trading in the United Kingdom, and so constituted a disincentive to foreign trading. Finally, where local governments might wish to encourage foreign investment by means of tax concessions, they had no incentive to do so for British firms, since the only beneficiary of such a concession would be the British Government.

British companies had two alternatives open to them for avoiding United Kingdom taxation on overseas earnings, though after 1951 these could only be adopted subject to Treasury control. First, they could emigrate their management and control overseas, and second, they could operate their overseas activities via subsidiary overseas companies with independent local management.

In the Finance Act of April 1957 overseas earnings were accorded a privileged position in the tax structure. A company or a subsidiary which was controlled and managed in this country but whose actual trading operations were wholly conducted abroad could be classified as an Overseas Trade Corporation and thereby be exempted from income and profits taxation in the United Kingdom. Earnings made overseas are now subject to United Kingdom taxes only when they are distributed to shareholders in this country. They are then liable to the normal rates of income tax, and in addition to profits tax if they are distributed to companies. This measure was estimated to cost the Exchequer only about £35 million per annum.

It has, however, improved the competitive position of British companies abroad only at the expense of creating new inequities in the tax structure. If the burden of taxation is justified as a contribution to the needs of the State, companies earning profits abroad are as able to make their full contribution as those which earn their profits in this country. Further, on the question of the danger of putting British firms at a disadvantage *vis-à-vis* their foreign competitors, which has been met by this new exemption, the Royal Commission pointed out in 1955[10] that it is "not confined to those firms which possess overseas establishments. It is common to all businesses which produce for export, and it may even affect industries which produce for the home market, if they have to face overseas competition upon that market."

It seems that equity and expediency cannot both be satisfied at one and the same time. If equal liability were insisted on at a time when overseas earnings were vital to the economy, the balance of payments would suffer. On the other hand, it may not always be in the interests of the economy that overseas earnings should be made more attractive than earnings at home. The 1920 Royal Commission on Taxation was worried about this problem and asked: "Should we be justified in recommending differential taxation which will become more and more favourable to the British resident as he employs more and more of his capital abroad?"[11] The 1955 Royal Commission pointed out that for the

[10] *Final Report*, para. 650.
[11] Cmd. 615, para. 33, quoted ibid., para. 647.

period 1951–53 the level of net overseas investment was about £180 million per annum.[12] Would some of this money have been better devoted to reducing the short-term debt or building up the reserves?[13]

The question of the taxation of overseas earnings must be decided in relation to the relative importance of overseas earnings and the desirability in particular periods of exporting capital. It might, therefore, be better if any exemption from taxation which might be justified at a particular time were not embodied too firmly in the tax structure but made as a special, and easily withdrawn, concession.

Depreciation allowances

Depreciation allowances in this country are based on the original or historical cost of assets. In a period of inflation this means that the total sum provided out of untaxed income to finance the replacement of assets will be insufficient, and further provision will have to be made out of taxed income to cover the difference between historical and replacement cost. It has been strongly argued that the allowances set against profits for the depreciation of "wasting assets" should take into account changes in money values by periodically revaluing assets, or by basing them directly on the replacement cost. Schemes which include allowances for price changes are operated in many other countries, including France, Italy, Belgium, Germany, and the Netherlands, so that British firms are put at a disadvantage in finding the funds to replace capital assets.

The replacement cost basis for depreciation allowances has the advantage of giving a truer picture of *real* profit. Allowances based on historical cost tend to give an inflated picture of the level of profits which in turn may encourage wage claims and so aggravate inflationary pressures.

There are, however, some drawbacks to the adoption of allowances based on replacement cost. First, this change would involve more complicated machinery for administration and assessment. Valuations would be somewhat arbitrary and not as certain nor as uncontroversial as those based on the actual cost of buying assets.

[12] *Final Report*, para. 653.
[13] See Chapter 7, pp. 174-81.

Secondly, if replacement cost were substituted for the present historical cost as the basis for allowances, but the rates of tax were adjusted so that profits tax continued to yield the same revenue, there would be a shifting of the tax burden among firms. The firms that would gain most would be those whose existing stock of capital equipment is greatest, and the new or rapidly expanding firm would not be assisted by this change. So it would not necessarily help the most dynamic sectors of industry.

Thirdly, if depreciation allowances are to be adjusted upwards when replacement cost is above historical cost, they would have to be adjusted downwards in a deflationary period when replacement cost is below historical cost.

There is no evidence to suggest that the burden of taxation on industry, income tax plus profits tax, combined with historical cost depreciation, has led to any erosion of capital. On the contrary, estimates show that net company savings available for expansion in the years 1951 to 1953 were almost twice as great in real terms as those of 1938.[14] It is interesting also to compare investment in this country with that in the United States and on the Continent, where more generous allowances are made for depreciation. In the steel industry, for example, roughly the same amount is being invested per ton of output in this country, the United States, and Western Europe. More profits are being ploughed back into the industry in Britain to offset the lower depreciation reserves. Of course it may still be thought unfair that British industry should be expected to bear this burden of making good out of taxed income capital sums that its competitors overseas can lay aside out of gross income before tax.

British firms have, however, been assisted in financing both replacement and new investment by means of initial and investment allowances which the Government has made from time to time in order to influence the level of investment. Initial allowances provide for a larger proportion of the total depreciation allowance to be claimed in the first year of the life of a new asset, so that although the total sum allowed over the life of an asset is not increased, there is some assistance to firms in finding liquid funds for financing investment. This is particularly helpful in cases where the new assets cost more than those they are replacing so that the accumulated depreciation reserves may be inadequate.

[14] N. Kaldor, op. cit., p. 155.

Investment allowances are claimable in the year of purchase in addition to the normal depreciation allowance, so that over the life of the asset a sum in addition to the original purchase price is allowed against profits. Both types of allowance have been in operation at different times in the post-war period and they have been used as instruments of Government economic policy, being introduced or suspended according to the needs of the economic situation.

The investment and initial allowances of the post-war period have been of considerable value to expanding firms, and, over the period as a whole, allowances against profits have probably been roughly equivalent to those which would have operated if depreciation allowances had been calculated on the basis of replacement cost. Thus, there is no reason to suppose that the historical cost method of depreciation allowances has in this period put British firms at a disadvantage in relation to competitors in countries operating replacement cost depreciation allowances, except where these competitors have also received in addition special depreciation provisions similar to the British initial allowances.

The best policy would appear to be to allow firms to write off assets as quickly as they wished for tax purposes. However, one condition would need to be attached to this concession. It is, that they must also write off the assets in their books at the same time. Some firms have in the past not written off assets as quickly in their books as they were allowed to do for tax purposes, thus in part defeating the objects of the concession.

Death duties

The duty applicable to deaths occurring at the present time is estate duty. This is levied at progressive rates on property valued above £3,000 which changes hands at death or within the previous five years. The yield from estate duties, like the profits tax, plays a relatively minor role as a source of Government revenue; it was £171 million in 1957–58, about 3 per cent of total revenue from central government taxation. None the less, the duty constitutes a heavy burden at the higher levels, which may be having serious effects on the growth of the family business.

The duty rises from 1 per cent for estates valued at £3,000–£4,000 to 10 per cent for estates of £15,000–£17,500. Estates of

£100,000–£150,000 incur duties at 50 per cent, those of £750,000–£1 million at 75 per cent and those over £1 million at 80 per cent. These duties must be met in cash. Under Section 55 of the Finance Act, 1940, where a director of a private family company has control of the company, his estate is valued according to the proportion of his holding multiplied by the present value of the assets of the firm. Consequently, if family control is to be maintained without the need for selling the business to meet estate duties on death, money must be constantly withdrawn and held idle to meet this contingency. Further, the system of valuation up to 1954 was based on the current real value of the assets and might have led to insolvency if the estate had to be sold to meet death duties, since the market value in a forced sale of the assets could be below this assessment. From 1954 onwards, however, if the estate was sold within three years the sale value would be accepted.

The value of the tax as an equitable contribution by property to the revenue is diminished by the numerous devices by which it can be avoided. Specialist consultants publish information on ways of minimising the effects of death duties via gifts under the Married Women's Property Act, gifts *inter-vivos*, etc. However, the fact that the tax can be partly avoided does not minimise its serious effects on the growth of small businesses. The position was summed up by Carter and Williams[15] as follows:

> These devices, and especially the withdrawal of funds to be held idle to meet estate duty, are inimical to the development of the business (including the improvement of its technical equipment) and may prevent far-sighted planning of that development by concentrating attention on short-term gains. The danger is particularly acute in some declining industries, in need of technical improvement, which are dominated by small family firms. . . . We conclude that there is a likelihood that the weight of estate duties is a hindrance to the adoption in certain firms of improvements in product or process, in which those firms might have been pioneers.

The yield from death duties is relatively small, and their harmful impact on industry as a whole is perhaps slight, but in their attempts to avoid the very heavy rates at the upper limits of the scale, owners of some small firms are induced to take measures prejudicial to the growth and efficiency of their undertakings. In

[15] Op. cit., p. 153.

addition, the system provides such owners with very little incentive to develop the long-term interests of their firms.

If it is considered necessary that this amount of revenue be raised by a tax on property at death, it would be more rational to levy the tax at rates less severe than those operated at present, and at the same time effectively to close the loopholes to evasion so that revenue would not be affected. This would reduce the incentive to dispose of the business in order to avoid the tax, and at the same time make it possible for the small family business to play a more dynamic role in the economy. The suggestion that the duty should be a legacy duty, levied on the inheritors, rather than a duty levied on the estate of the deceased, would encourage the splitting-up of estates among a larger number of inheritors. This may achieve a more democratic distribution of property, but it is doubtful whether its economic effects would be preferable to those of the present duty. Family firms might be disrupted just as much by coping with the problem of too many owners as they are at present in trying to avoid selling out to pay the death duty.

Purchase tax

In the financial year 1957–58, £494 million or 9 per cent of total central government revenue was raised in the form of purchase tax. This tax was first introduced in 1940 with the chief intention of increasing the revenue for war purposes. It was intended to cover the whole range of consumer products that were not already subject to excise duties, and was levied at the rate of $33\frac{1}{3}$ per cent, with a reduced rate of $16\frac{2}{3}$ per cent for certain "essential" products such as clothing, household utensils, and medicines. From as early as 1942, however, the nature of the tax was changed so as to transform it into primarily an instrument of economic control, and only secondarily a source of revenue. The tax came to be used as a means of restraining consumer demand for articles in short supply, and in general for restraining inflationary pressures. Although since the war the revenue deriving from this tax has steadily increased from the £100 million per annum of the war years, to almost £500 million, the changes in the tax have been based always on broad economic rather than on narrower revenue considerations. It is probably true to say that the purchase tax has had more direct effect on industry than any of the taxes whose effects have been outlined above, so it is important to state at the outset that these effects have not been a chance and unforeseen outcome of the needs of the Government for more revenue, but have been deliberate results of steps taken specifically to produce those effects.

It would be tiresome to outline all the changes in the rates of purchase tax since 1945, but a few examples of the type and scale of change and their effect on industry will serve to illustrate the foremost objection to the tax, namely, that the rates have changed far too frequently and often unpredictably. In 1945, for example, various domestic appliances, heating and kitchen equipment were exempted from purchase tax. Plans were made by several firms to expand their output of these goods in expectation of a prospective high demand from consumers who had been unable to obtain these goods during the war. Then in 1947 following the power cuts of the late winter and spring, and the balance-of-payments crisis, the exemption was withdrawn and these goods were taxed at the rate of 66⅔ per cent. The most important group of goods in the present purchase tax classification are "motors and household durables". Motor-cars, wireless and television sets, refrigerators and washing machines, were taxed at 33⅓ per cent from 1945. In 1951 the rate for these goods was raised to 66⅔ per cent and, passing through further changes in 1953 and 1955, they now stand at 50 per cent. Given time, a firm can adapt itself to even these extremely high rates of tax, but frequent changes in the rates are costly in terms of the disorganisation of production they involve. It is difficult to assess the validity of this criticism of the purchase tax, in view of the deliberate nature of the measures. Any proposal for avoiding frequent changes in the rates to meet varying economic conditions would have to be founded on a broad review of the whole system of Government control over economic fluctuations.

The use of variable rates of purchase tax as a weapon of economic control has the effect of distorting the consumers' choice by stimulating the demand for goods that are not taxed in this way. The consumer is not allowed to adjust his purchases in such a way as to reflect the real prices and real costs of production. Against this consideration it must be remembered that any economic controls are open to the same criticism: even the most general, monetary control affects some interests more severely than others.

Other defects of the purchase tax are: that if the rates are reduced, the retailer faces a loss on his stocks because no refund of tax already paid is allowed (though equally he makes a windfall gain if the rates are increased); that uneconomic changes may be made in products and materials in order to take goods out of a classification that is subject to the tax or out of a classification subject to a high rate into one subject to a lower rate; and that a problem is created regarding the treatment of goods which pass directly from manufacturer to retailer, the tax being levied at the wholesale stage.

The high rates on certain products, if maintained over a long period, have a serious effect on the growth and development of industries, which can only be justified if there are good long-term reasons why the growth of these industries should be suppressed. For example, a high purchase tax on cars for the home market may be justified if for many years it is desired to divert a large share of a limited total output to export in order to assist the balance of payments, but not if the reason is that the Government has failed to spend sufficient on the roads, unless the tax on the cars is part of the revenue needed to pay for the roads—and for the hospitals for casualties! But it should also be noted that the purchase tax may help to maintain stability in an industry. If it is increased in boom conditions and reduced in time of recession, it may assist an industry to maintain a more regular and healthy growth of output than would otherwise be possible.

In the Budgets of 1958 and 1959 the system of purchase tax has been simplified and the burden particularly at the higher levels has been reduced. In 1958 the number of rates at which it was levied was reduced from seven to four. The 90 per cent rate was abolished and the number of goods charged at the 60 per cent rate was reduced, household goods and electrical appliances in particular being charged at 30 per cent. In 1959 the three highest rates were reduced by one-sixth.[16]

[16] The most important items currently taxed are as follows:

50 per cent .	Cars, radio and television sets, gramophones and gramophone records and cosmetics.
25 per cent .	Jewellery, fur coats, refrigerators, washing machines, vacuum cleaners, electric irons, luggage, clocks, mirrors, gas and electrical equipment, sewing machines, cameras.
12½ per cent .	Carpets, floor coverings, wallpaper, hardware, china, glass, kitchen utensils.
5 per cent .	Clothing, textiles, furniture.

THE BALANCE OF TAXATION

Something must now be said about the general balance of taxes as they affect economic growth. A major aspect of budgetary policy is the allocation of the national overhead, whether the overhead costs consist of welfare services, defence or anything else. It is suggested that one major reason why the British economy has increased its productivity more slowly than those of other industrial countries is that the allocation of national overhead costs is such that to a manufacturer the cost of labour is kept relatively low and the cost of capital relatively high as compared with the corresponding situation in other countries. If this situation were altered, it would become more attractive to replace labour by capital, and investment would be carried further with greater gains in productivity. Also, in applying any given amount of investment there would be increased pressure to utilise the investment to its full potentialities by the maximum economy in the now more costly labour element.

One example of the allocation of national overheads in a sense unfavourable to productivity growth is seen in the United Kingdom in the method of financing the welfare services. Family allowances, pensions, health services, and so on are financed on the Continent mainly by a charge on labour employed paid by the employer. These items of cost therefore appear as a labour cost. The situation is the same in the United States, where the main burden of these charges falls on the employers as a labour cost, associated with the so-called fringe benefits. In the United Kingdom, only a minor part of these items appears as a labour cost, and the major part comes out of general taxation.[17]

The British system of taxation therefore represents a low level of taxation on labour, but a high level on capital employed. The tax on income created by investment is considerably higher than the standard rate of tax on income created by work. This follows from the higher rate of tax on unearned or investment income and from the profits tax.

The extra tax on income created by capital application is partly offset by the initial and investment allowances. In the main, however, these allowances have been a method of compensating for the unrealistically low historical cost depreciation allowed by

[17] See Sir Robert Shone and H. R. Fisher, op. cit.

the revenue. In so far as they might be greater than real replacement cost depreciation they are a mitigation of the extra tax on investment. Even if this factor is allowed for, there is still left a substantial discriminatory tax on capital as against labour income. If some given net return is necessary and accepted as reasonable to induce savings and reward investment, then the augmentation of this by a discriminatory supplementary tax increases the cost of employing capital and is a disincentive to the replacement of labour by capital.

A somewhat different illustration of the choice between taxing the use of labour or the use of capital is seen in the case of rates. Municipal rates are mainly used for services related to individuals. Nevertheless, there has recently been a big increase in the amounts charged on industrial premises in relation to the value of the property. It might have been preferable for the same amounts to be paid by industry on a basis primarily related to employment rather than according to the less relevant value of property.

CONCLUSION

It is necessary to be cautious in arriving at conclusions about the effects of taxation on industrial efficiency and growth. There is insufficient evidence to support the more sweeping assertions that are made about the harmfulness of taxes. The arguments on the subject of the effects of the general level of taxation are inadequately supported, despite the strong views that are held on this question. If it be assumed that the onus of proof lies on those who call for reforms, particularly for a reduction in the total of taxation, then it must be concluded that their case fails for lack of sufficient evidence of the evils they allege. That wastes and distortions of the economy do arise out of heavy taxes is apparent. An example is the growth of the use of the business expense allowance. But this would appear to constitute rather a case for a tightening of the regulations regarding expenses than for an abolition of the taxes that leave room for these abuses, for only a major reduction of income and surtax would sufficiently lessen the desirability of being paid expenses rather than personal income. Admittedly, however tight the restrictions on expenses might be, there would still be abuses. These have to be accepted in view of the offsetting advantages of taxes: that the Government can provide things which the private citizen, and the firm, cannot provide for themselves.

Moreover, when taxes are used as the instruments of Government policies, and not merely as a source of revenue, they cannot be judged in themselves as good or bad taxes. All that can be done is to judge the effectiveness of the policies of which these tax arrangements are the instrument, or the failings that have made these policies necessary. This is the case with regard both to depreciation allowances and to purchase tax. If the Government varies depreciation allowances in order to control investment this cannot be a failing of the tax system as such. Similarly, if purchase tax is used, not primarily to raise revenue, but deliberately to suppress the production of certain items, this again cannot be held to be an example of a bad tax, but only of a bad policy on the part of the Government in its regulation of the economy. Much of the criticism of the tax system is therefore really misdirected. The purchase tax has had severe effects on some industries, and the depreciation allowances given at times when initial and investment allowances have been suspended have probably been inadequate to allow for replacement costs. But both should be regarded not as taxes but as deliberate measures of economic control.

However, despite these doubts, this chapter has revealed some areas where it would be worthwhile to examine very carefully the effects on growth of the methods of taxation. In particular, although it is difficult to be certain of the actual impact of any given tax, since taxes may be passed on from those on whom they are levied to other sections of the community, it is important that taxes should not have the effect of distorting the correct relationship of capital and labour costs. Social charges are properly a cost of labour, yet social services have been financed primarily out of general taxation rather than by taxes which reveal the real social cost of labour. This has the effect of weighting the economy in favour of the use of labour and against the use of more capital, and this is an influence tending to prevent industry from making use of all the worthwhile opportunities for saving labour that exist.

CHAPTER 6

DEFENCE AND THE SOCIAL SERVICES

THE previous chapter has briefly raised the general question, whether or not the total burden of taxation (as well as the particular ways in which it is levied) has been detrimental to effort and enterprise and investment, and may therefore have contributed to the low rate of growth of productivity since the war. On such a wide issue it was not possible to be very conclusive. However, Government expenditure goes very largely to two main items, defence and the social services, which in 1958 absorbed between them some 25 per cent of the gross national product,[1] and the direct effect of these two types of expenditure on the economy can be more readily assessed than can the indirect influence of the level of taxation required to finance them. Certainly neither can be ignored in considering factors affecting the growth and flexibility of the economy. Both defence spending and the provision of social services have come under fire, from different quarters, as being excessive and contributing in no small measure to Britain's economic weakness. The aim of this chapter then is to examine the *economic* effects of these Government expenditures.

Most of the discussion of expenditure on defence and on the social services has been essentially political rather than economic, the critic of defence expenditure being opposed to the policy of rearmament and the critic of social expenditure being opposed to the principles of the Welfare State. However, another type of discussion has also been taking place and criticism has been put forward on a different level. The political objectives of either defence or social policy are not challenged, but instead critics have asked whether these have been pursued in the most efficient and economical way. These critics have made it respectable to count the cost of defence and the social services in terms of the effects on economic growth and the balance of payments. The stigma of opposing Britain's military objectives cannot be laid upon a critic who wishes to state that strategically the country is more vulnerable if it runs down its economic machine than if it spends less

[1] Including transfer payments in social service expenditure. If these are excluded the percentage is 18.

on building up its war machine. Equally, the keenest supporter of social welfare schemes could oppose expenditure on the social services on the ground that it would significantly increase total consumption, thereby seriously restricting investment and depriving the community of social benefits and a higher standard of living at a later date.

Further, it is becoming increasingly important to determine whether there is any foundation for the fear that the defence burden has had a debilitating effect on the economy which is preventing fuller use of the economic weapon. The question is not, however, simply a matter of whether the actual sum spent each year on arms would have better furthered Britain's political objectives if it had been used to provide economic aid for underdeveloped areas, which may be vulnerable to Communist infiltration as a result of backwardness and poverty. It is rather whether the defence effort has been in itself so great that it has hindered the expansion of the economy at a rate which would have made it possible to spend more on economic aid—and possibly more also on armaments at a later stage. This aspect of the argument first became prominent when Mr. Aneurin Bevan, Mr. Harold Wilson and Mr. John Freeman resigned from the Labour Government in 1951. More recently critics like Andrew Shonfield have made similar objections to the scale of defence expenditure.

DEFENCE

Since 1953 defence spending on current account has been running at around £1,500 million per annum, which is in money terms about double the level of 1948. In real terms defence spending has increased by about 17 per cent between 1948 and 1958, whereas consumers' expenditure has risen in real terms by 22 per cent over the same period. But gross fixed capital formation has risen at a faster rate, being in 1958 some 59 per cent greater in real terms than in 1948.[2] It seems that by 1948 the process of reducing military expenditure from its wartime levels had been completed, and the share of resources taken by defence had become adjusted to what might have been a "normal" peacetime expenditure in a troubled world. The share of the national product taken by defence in 1948 and 1949 was only very slightly higher

[2] *National Income and Expenditure 1959* (HMSO), Table 13.

than in 1938. However, the outbreak of the Korean war led to a considerable acceleration in the defence programme. In 1951 it was decided to embark on a programme costing £3,600 million in three years, and then within a few months this was increased to £4,700 million, although it was later found to be physically impossible to spend as much as this on defence.

Although the share of the gross national product taken by defence expenditure was 7·7 per cent in 1958 compared with 6·6 per cent in 1938, the share taken by defence and consumption expenditure together has actually fallen from 83 per cent in 1938 to 71 per cent in 1958. This is due to the fact that, apart from slight fluctuations during the early post-war period when consumers' habits were being readjusted to peacetime conditions, the share of the national income taken by consumption has been steadily falling, from 76 per cent in 1938 to 63 per cent in 1958. Part of this fall in the share of consumption is attributable to the less favourable trading position after the war, and the figure for consumption does not include expenditure on the social services. It may be noted, however, that the share taken by consumption dropped from 67 to 65 per cent between 1951 and 1952 when the share of defence expenditure rose from 8·5 to 10·4 per cent, so that almost the whole of the increased share of defence spending was covered by a fall in the share of consumption expenditure. Part at least of the fall in the share of consumption between 1951 and 1952 must be directly attributed to sacrifices made in order to finance the defence effort. But, while it could be argued that the same sacrifices might have been made in order to finance an increase in investment, it is doubtful whether any such policy would have been practicable. Just as in wartime the population can be persuaded to restrain its demands for material goods in the interests of the war effort, so the shock of the Korean war created a similar if milder atmosphere of danger. It would be wrong to suggest that a policy of restraining consumption in order to finance a programme of economic expansion is not feasible but a frightened population will contemplate more drastic measures than one which is rationally balancing present against future satisfactions. The fact that at any period it may seem that consumption paid or helped to pay for part of the defence effort does not necessarily mean that without that defence expenditure consumption would have paid for something else.

TABLE 18

DEFENCE EXPENDITURE, CONSUMPTION, AND CAPITAL FORMATION, 1938–58

	Gross National Product at Factor Cost £ million	Current Defence Expenditure £ million	Gross Fixed Capital Formation at Home at Market Prices £ million	Consumers' Expenditure at Factor Cost £ million	Current Defence Expenditure as a percentage of GNP Per cent	Gross Fixed Capital Formation at Market Prices as a percentage of GNP Per cent	Consumers' Expenditure at Factor Cost as a percentage of GNP Per cent	Consumers' Expenditure plus Defence Expenditure as a percentage of GNP Per cent
1938 . .	5,175	343	656	3,950	6·6	12·7	76	83
1948 . .	10,446	740	1,452	7,219	7·1	13·9	69	76
1949 . .	11,129	770	1,603	7,588	6·9	14·4	68	75
1950 . .	11,687	820	1,726	7,986	7·0	14·8	68	75
1951 . .	12,839	1,090	1,913	8,590	8·5	14·9	67	75
1952 . .	13,987	1,450	2,131	9,069	10·4	15·2	65	75
1953 . .	14,922	1,540	2,384	9,585	10·3	16·0	64	75
1954 . .	15,945	1,554	2,578	10,323	9·7	16·2	65	74
1955 . .	16,892	1,524	2,841	10,967	9·0	16·8	65	74
1956 . .	18,267	1,625	3,137	11,504	8·9	17·2	63	72
1957 . .	19,370	1,550	3,400	12,107	8·0	17·6	63	71
1958 . .	20,130	1,551	3,516	12,737	7·7	17·5	63	71

Source: *National Income and Expenditure 1959*, Tables 1, 11 and 35, and for 1938 figures *National Income and Expenditure 1958*, Tables 1 and 11, and *National Income and Expenditure 1955*, Table 24.

Table 18 compares defence expenditure, consumption and gross fixed capital formation in the eleven years from 1948 to 1958, and in 1938. It can be seen from the table that the share of the national income available for purposes other than consumption and defence was 29 per cent in 1958 against only 17 per cent in 1938. The stepping up of the rearmament programme in the years 1950–52 did not result in an increase in the total share of resources devoted to consumption and defence. This remained around 75 per cent of the national income for the years 1950–54. However, the tendency for this share to decline, which did not become apparent until after 1954, might possibly have shown itself earlier in the absence of an accelerated rearmament programme. The tendency for the share of resources taken by consumption to decline as the real value of the national income increases, has meant that the defence burden could be absorbed without any reduction, and even with a small increase, in the share available for investment. This does not mean of course that the defence burden has had no impact on this share. The difficulty is to distinguish between the extent to which the share of consumption has fallen as a result of restraints imposed in order to finance the defence programme, and the extent to which it would have fallen anyway. If all or most of this decline would have taken place in any case, then the fact that it has more than compensated for the increase in defence expenditure is of no significance in measuring the economic costs of defence.

The strain on physical resources

The above attempt to estimate the financial costs of the defence effort needs to be supplemented by an estimate of the cost in terms of physical resources. The strain on physical resources was most acute during the period when the accelerated three-year rearmament programme of £4,700 million was inaugurated in 1951. The 1951 *Economic Survey* estimated that:

> Of the three-year total, some £2,800 million is attributable to production of arms, equipment and clothing, to works and buildings and to research and development. . . . Production of engineering and metal goods directly for defence is expected to increase from about £170 million in 1950–51 to about £360 million in 1951–52, with a total of £1,650 million for the three years 1951–54.[3]

[3] Cmd. 8195 (HMSO), paras. 12–13.

It was later found impossible to carry out this three-year programme in full, and in the first year expenditure fell £120 million short of what had been planned. The demands made on the engineering industries, and on supplies of steel, reduced not only the supplies available for consumption goods on the home market but also those available for export. Further, the *Economic Survey* warned that:

> The increased claims of defence are not distributed evenly over the economy, but are concentrated upon particular sectors—most of all upon the metal using industries. The great bulk of the output of these industries goes to home investment and exports and only a very small part consists of consumption goods. This makes it much more difficult to shift the main burden of rearmament on to consumption.[4]

As the defence effort continued to increase the pressure on the capital goods sector of the engineering industry, it began to have further repercussions on exports. The 1953 *Economic Survey* posed this problem:

> The main objective of the internal economic and financial policies of the government in 1952 was to assist in creating the general conditions in which an improvement in the balance of payments could be brought about. This was not an easy problem. Although home demand for many consumer goods was low, and more such goods could have been made available for export if they could have been sold abroad, other countries' demand for consumer goods had also slackened off. Export prospects appeared in general to be best for capital goods; but defence expenditure and investment at home were making heavy demands on the output of the industries producing such goods, while steel was still scarce, and these demands could not be quickly curtailed.[5]

In 1950 the metal-using industries were responsible for about two-fifths of all United Kingdom exports[6] and also for the great bulk of the plant and machinery used for home investment. However, the rearmament programme was in fact given priority over exports and home investment in certain sectors of industry. The *Economic Survey* of 1951 stated that:

> One of the most difficult problems arising from rearmament will be the supply of machine tools. The re-tooling of existing plant and the

[4] Ibid., para. 22.
[5] Cmd. 8800, para. 53.
[6] Cmd. 8195, para. 64.

creation of new capacity will together involve an expenditure of over £100 million on machine tools during the next two years. . . . Production will be expanded where practicable, and supplies for home civilian uses and export will be reduced to make way for defence orders. Even so, it is clear that many of the machine tools needed will have to be imported.[7]

Table 19 below shows the percentages of total supplies, including imports, of metals, engineering products and vehicles which were used for defence, export, and gross fixed capital formation at home, between the years 1950 and 1957. The value of the total supplies of these industries, taken at 1948 factory prices (or c.i.f. values for imports) rose from £2,995 million in 1950 to £3,910 million in 1957, an increase of 30 per cent. The value of those supplies taken for defence calculated on the same basis rose from £200 million in 1950 to £470 million in 1953, an increase of 135 per cent. By 1957 these defence expenditures had fallen to £405 million, but this was still more than 100 per cent above the 1950 level.

TABLE 19

THE USE OF METALS, ENGINEERING PRODUCTS AND VEHICLES, 1950–57

	Percentage of total supplies							
	1950	1951	1952	1953	1954	1955	1956	1957
Defence . . .	7	9	13	14	13	12	11	10
Exports . . .	33	31	30	29	28	28	31	32
Gross fixed capital formation at home	30	29	27	27	27	28	30	31

Source: Calculated from *National Income and Expenditure 1958*, Table 17.

Between 1950 and 1952 imports of metal goods increased from £65 million to £110 million in terms of 1951 prices.[8] Commenting on this rise, the 1953 *Economic Survey* stated that most of the increase was accounted for by the import of machine tools from the United States and Europe for equipping armaments factories.[9]

Considerable demands on restricted supplies of steel were also being made at this time. The steel requirements in 1952–53 for the defence programme were estimated at 1 million tons out of a total

[7] Ibid., para. 68.
[8] *Economic Survey 1953*, Cmd. 8800, Table 24.
[9] Ibid., para. 79.

of about 12½ million tons available for consumption in the United Kingdom,[10] but by 1954 this had fallen to half a million tons while total home consumption was roughly the same.[11] While, therefore, steel consumption for defence purposes fluctuated between 4 per cent and 8 per cent of total supplies, it is hard to measure how significant this consumption was in a period in which supplies of steel were scarce. If it is fair to take amounts of steel imported as a measure of the scarcity, then the defence consumption was important. Imports of finished and semi-finished steel in 1950 and 1951 were about half a million ingot tons; in 1952 they were one and three-quarter million tons.[12] It would be wrong to relate the fluctuations in steel imports only to changes in the defence programme, though this is very tempting for the years 1951–52, because changes in the accumulation of stocks and availability of foreign supplies particularly affected these figures in the early 1950's. But it does seem that the steel consumption of the defence industries has been important when related to the general levels of steel imports. Half a million tons of imported steel at current prices was costing the balance of payments about £30 million.

Since 1948 the numbers of men and women in the armed forces have fluctuated between seven and eight hundred thousand, equivalent to between 3 and 4 per cent of the working population. In addition, some sectors of the engineering industry, notably aircraft, had to expand their labour forces with the increases in defence production. The *Economic Survey* estimated that in 1950 just under half a million workers were engaged on the production of munitions and equipment for the armed forces, and that when the rearmament programme reached its peak in 1953–54 this number would need to be doubled. Some of this increase, however, was to be achieved by switching existing factories over to defence production so that the actual movements of labour necessitated by the defence effort would be considerably less than the half a million or so extra workers expected to be engaged on defence production. Together with the men in the armed forces, the possible peak figure of manpower absorbed by defence was

[10] *Statement on Defence, 1952*, Cmd. 8475 (HMSO), para. 44.

[11] *Development in the Iron and Steel Industry*, Special Report (HMSO), 1957, p. 21.

[12] Ibid., p. 98, Table 44. Figures are in terms of ingot equivalent.

nearly two million, equivalent to about 9 per cent of the working population in 1953. This increase caused some concern in 1951 when the unemployment figures were the lowest since the end of the war, but the labour supply began to ease slightly with a recession in consumer demand in the early part of 1952. The resulting shortages of labour appeared in specific sectors, for instance there was a severe shortage of certain classes of skilled workers in the engineering industry, particularly draughtsmen, toolmakers and jig makers. In February 1952 the Notification of Vacancies Order was introduced to channel labour into work with a defence priority. As a result the shortage of certain categories of skilled labour, including scientists and research workers, had its chief impact on those sectors of industry not concerned with defence contracts, where there was already a scarcity of labour. The situation in these sectors was therefore aggravated.

The impact on the balance of payments

The strain imposed on the balance of payments by the defence effort is the result rather of the way in which defence has added to the general pressure on economic resources than of direct payments in foreign exchange necessitated by defence policies. Although the latter have not been insignificant, the United Kingdom has had some assistance towards meeting them, and towards reducing the amounts of foreign exchange needed to finance the defence programme. Direct grants to supplement Government defence expenditure have been received from the United States and Canada under various aid agreements, and between 1951 and 1958 these totalled £372 million. They have been falling considerably in recent years, however, from £102 million in 1953 to £21 million in 1957 and only £3 million in 1958.[13] More important in recent years has been the aid received from American offshore procurement. This aid takes the form of placing orders for military equipment in this country, paying for it in dollars, and then donating the finished product to the Government for the defence effort. In 1957 the dollar equivalent of £40 million was spent in the United Kingdom in this manner and £18 million in 1958. From 1953 to 1958 the total offshore procurement expenditure was £193 million. In addition, the

[13] These figures are net of repayments to the United States Government in sterling counterpart, and are taken from the Balance of Payments White Papers.

stationing of American and Canadian forces in this country has resulted in dollar expenditures in the United Kingdom. In 1957 these amounted to the sterling equivalent of £90 million, and in 1958, £70 million. Although these are only a by-product of the British defence effort, they are the outcome of NATO agreements, as is much of the defence expenditure. When considering the balance of payments, these earnings should also be offset against the expenditure in foreign exchange on British troops stationed abroad. Thus in 1958 Britain received some £91 million of foreign exchange, mostly in dollars, on account of defence programmes, and in 1957 as much as £151 million was received from these sources.

In 1958 British military expenditure abroad was £181 million. The total was falling steadily in the first half of the post-war period, from £374 million in 1946 down to £100 million in 1950, but after 1950 it began to rise. In addition, colonial grants have been rising during these years, from £10 million in 1946 to £18 million in 1950 and to £38 million in 1957 and £36 million in 1958. However, foreign exchange is also received as a result of British participation in the common defence policies of NATO and other Western alliances, and estimated above at a total of £151 million in 1957. In terms of foreign exchange, the net effect of direct defence spending abroad in 1957 was only a matter of some £10 million a year. In 1958, however, defence expenditure abroad increased while there was a fall in receipts from defence aid, offshore procurement and the expenditure of American forces in this country, and in that year the net burden in terms of foreign exchange was £90 million.

Defence expenditure also affects the economy as a whole, and the consequent repercussions on the balance of payments may be much more serious. The defence effort has undoubtedly affected export producing capacity, and this can be partially measured by figures such as those on page 143 for consumption of metal goods. In 1951 and 1952 an increase in defence expenditure coincided with increases in the prices of world commodities and with raw material shortages, and in these circumstances had a direct and observable effect on both exports and the balance of payments. Between 1950 and 1951 defence expenditure rose by £270 million and between 1951 and 1952 by a further £360 million. The pressure on physical resources has already been noted. There was also a marked reduction in the supply of metal goods, engineering products and vehicles for exports. Real exports of these goods, valued in terms of 1948 factory prices, fell from £990 million in 1950 to £985 million in 1951, £975 million in 1952, and £960 million in 1953, and not until 1954 did they resume their pre-1950 trend of absorbing in real terms steadily increasing amounts of the products of these industries.[14] Total exports of goods and services, measured in 1954 prices, continued to increase between 1950 and 1951 though at a slower rate than previously, but between 1951 and 1952 they fell a little from £3,415 million to £3,390 million, and in 1953 to £3,347 million. Between 1948 and 1950 exports had increased in real terms by 28 per cent; between 1950 and 1952 they increased by only 0·7 per cent.[15] The balance of payments was being adversely affected by the sharp increase in raw material prices which followed the Korean war and by the general world-wide acceleration of defence expenditure and stock piling. This also resulted in shortages of strategic materials such as sulphur, which created further difficulties for the export industries. Responsibility for the 1951–52 crisis must, therefore, be divided between the effects of British attempts to speed up rearmament and the cumulative effect of a world-wide increase in expenditure on armaments.

Apart from this one instance, it is not possible to be quite so specific about the influence of defence expenditure on the balance of payments. To the extent to which resources have been devoted to defence production export producing capacity has been reduced, assuming that markets could have been found for the extra goods that would have been available for export in the absence of defence expenditure. This assumption is reasonable for most of the post-war period, though perhaps not correct in more recent years. The defence effort has also added to the inflationary pressures which have contributed to balance of payments difficulties by reducing the manpower available for private industry and so exerting an upward pressure on wage rates. Thus, the defence effort is one of the factors the removal of which might, at the least, have reduced the severity of balance of payments crises in the post-war period. It certainly played a major part in the crisis of 1951–52.

[14] *National Income and Expenditure 1958*, Table 17.
[15] Ibid., *1959*, Table 13.

Defence and investment

As in the case of the balance of payments, discussion of this question must be divided into two parts. First, specific occasions or instances can be discerned where defence expenditure has had a clear effect on the level of investment, and, secondly, the indirect repercussions on investment of the other economic consequences of defence expenditure must be assessed. The specific case where the defence effort reduced the level of investment is again in the years 1951 and 1952 when the accelerated rearmament programme was in operation. In these years gross fixed capital formation at home, at constant prices, remained virtually static, while between 1949 and 1950 it had risen by 5 per cent and between 1952 and 1953 was to rise by 11 per cent.[16] In the metals, engineering and vehicles industry, the value, in real terms, of the supplies used for gross fixed capital formation fell in the year between 1951 and 1952 by 6 per cent and in 1953 were only marginally higher than the 1950 level. Measured in terms of 1948 factory and import prices, gross fixed capital formation at home took the following amounts of the products of these industries.[17]

£ million

1948	1949	1950	1951	1952	1953	1954	1955	1956	1957
785	835	890	920	865	900	980	1,090	1,130	1,210

In 1951 the Government took various measures to restrict investment in order to free resources for the rearmament programme. The suspension after one year's notice of the initial allowances, 40 per cent for new plant and machinery and 10 per cent for industrial buildings, was announced in April 1951 and took effect in April 1952. In his Budget speech on 10 April 1951 the Chancellor of the Exchequer, Mr. Gaitskell, said:

> . . . in our present circumstances to stimulate capital expenditure in this way would, I am satisfied, positively endanger the defence and export programmes too much. When the period of re-armament is over and we can increase home investment again, it will no doubt be desirable to reintroduce allowances of this kind.

He went on to say:

> I feel justified in allowing only for a very small increase in the total expenditure civil and defence, on investment at home—a small

[16] *National Income and Expenditure 1959*, Table 13.
[17] Ibid., *1958*, Table 17. The figures include imports.

increase of £30 million. Having regard to the rise in prices of investment goods—capital equipment and so on—this implies no increase in total real investment and, indeed, a significant fall in investment for civil purposes.[18]

The suspension of initial allowances lasted for only one year: they were restored in April 1953, though at a lower rate of 20 per cent, for plant and machinery. In April 1954 they were superseded by investment allowances, which were paid in addition to the depreciation allowance and provided a more powerful stimulus to investment than the initial allowance.

The relationship between the balance of payments and investment is dealt with in Chapter 7, pages 161–63. In so far as defence expenditure has aggravated balance of payments difficulties, it also shares responsibility for the consequent cuts in investment.

It is tempting to conclude that the only observable repercussions on the general level of investment took place in 1951 and 1952, for apart from these years the statistics show investment to have been steadily, if slowly, rising in real terms. But in fact all that the statistics show is that apart from the period 1951–52, the share of resources devoted to defence was one which could be combined with some increase in capital expenditure and in exports. The attempt to increase the share of resources devoted to defence from 7 per cent of the gross national product in 1950 to over 10 per cent in 1952 and 1953 brought defence expenditure to a level which could not be combined with this expenditure, and indisputably halted the rate of economic expansion during those years. Of course, this is not to say that the smaller share of the national product spent on defence in the years 1948–50 and 1954–57 did not result in a slower rate of expansion than could otherwise have been achieved. Some part at least of the 7–9 per cent of the national product being spent on defence in these years could have been used to increase the rate of investment. The fact that an extra 3 per cent of the national product devoted to defence could have the serious effects noted provides some indication of the benefits which could have been obtained, and could still be obtained, by a reduction of defence expenditure. This conclusion may not apply, however, in a period of recession, when a cut in defence spending could result in further unemployment of men and materials.

[18] *Hansard*, Cols. 842 and 843, 10 April 1951.

Defence expenditure in other countries

The defence expenditure of the United Kingdom is the highest in Europe, and second only to the American among the countries of the Western alliance. Estimates of the defence expenditure of the NATO countries for 1957 showed United States expenditure as $44,278 million; United Kingdom expenditure as $4,505 million, and French as $4,268 million.[19] The conversion of budget estimates of different countries at current rates of exchange does not, however, give an accurate picture of the economic sacrifices involved for the various countries, since it ignores differences in internal price relationships, in national wealth, and in size of populations. When considering the share of the national product taken by defence, the British contribution appears to be much more nearly comparable with the American. Table 20 shows the proportions of the gross national product spent on defence by nine member countries of NATO in 1957.

TABLE 20

COMPARATIVE DEFENCE EXPENDITURES IN 1957

	Defence Expenditure as a percentage of Gross National Product
United States	11·5*
United Kingdom	8·4
France	8·6
Canada	7·1
Western Germany	4·3
Netherlands	6·5*
Norway	4·0
Italy	4·3
Denmark	3·6*

Source: Report on the State of European Security, Western European Union, Assembly Document 105 of 8 December 1958.

* Estimate

In 1949 and 1950 British defence expenditure actually took a larger share of the national income than did American defence expenditure. But the American effort after the outbreak of the Korean war was much greater than anything that Britain could have contemplated. Between 1950 and 1952 American defence

[19] *Report on the State of European Security*, Western European Union, Assembly Document 105 of 8 December 1958.

expenditure in money terms was more than trebled, and its share of the gross national product rose from 5·5 per cent to 14·4 per cent.[20]

THE SOCIAL SERVICES

Social services have been linked with defence expenditure in this chapter because both are Government expenditure which adds to the total demand on national resources and therefore influences the amounts available for investment. Both are authorised by the Government and paid for, wholly in the case of defence and mainly in the case of the social services, out of general taxation. There are, however, important differences between the two. In the case of defence expenditure, it is safe to assume that if these sums were not spent by the Government, they would not be spent by anyone else either. The resources of manpower and materials consumed by the armed services and their ancillaries and by the industries producing armaments would be available for other purposes, and the Government would have an additional £1,500 million to dispose of either by tax reliefs or by spending in other ways. Similar assumptions cannot be made about the social services. If, for instance, medical treatment were not provided by the National Health Service, individuals would have to make this provision for themselves. Some minor ailments might go unattended, but, basically, individuals would need to make the same type of provision for themselves that is now being made for them by the State. The same applies to housing, where again the standards might not be the same but the greater part of the expenditure would still be made.

A large part of social service expenditure takes the form of grants to persons, which are also part of consumers' expenditure as calculated in the national income accounts. These transfer payments must for many purposes be distinguished from social expenditure on goods and services.

Transfer payments neither increase nor decrease consumption directly, since their effect is merely to redistribute the power to consume among different classes of consumers. That part of Government expenditure on the social services which takes the

[20] Defence expenditure as a percentage of gross national product cost. OEEC *General Statistics*, 1959, No. 1, January, p. 125.

form of the direct provision of goods and services increases the total amount of resources devoted to these goods and services only to the extent to which they are an improvement in quantity or quality over what individuals would be willing and able to provide for themselves, and to the extent that the alleged wasteful and unnecessary uses are made of the services. This difference between what is being provided by the State and what would be provided by individuals cannot be estimated, but it must fall a long way short of the total estimates of Government social service expenditure on goods and services. While the figures for total defence expenditure do in fact measure what would be saved if defence expenditure were reduced or abolished, figures for total social service expenditure do not tell us anything about what resources would be taken up by these services in the absence of Government expenditure on them.

Quite a large proportion of social service expenditure is investment according to the definitions of the official statisticians. In 1958, of the total social service expenditure—including transfer payments—of £3,149 million, £403 million, or 12 per cent, came under the category of gross fixed capital formation, nearly two-thirds of this capital spending being on housing. If transfer payments are excluded the percentage was 20 per cent. But much of the expenditure is also investment in another sense. Whenever the National Health Service has made earlier diagnosis possible and so helped to prevent serious illness, it has reduced the costs of treatment, hospital accommodation, and lost man-hours. If education services are improved, young people are of more value to industry. There are no statistics to prove these points, but, without entering into the merits or demerits of the present social services, it can be stated that it is wrong to regard the whole cost of providing such services as an item which must be deducted from the total available for adding to the productive capacity of the nation. Social service expenditure rightly used can be a way of improving both quantitatively and qualitatively the productive capacity of the nation.

The cost of the social services

In 1958 total expenditure by the central and local government authorities on the social services, including transfer payments, came to £3,419 million.[21] This expenditure represented just over £66 per head of the population and was equal to about 17 per cent of the gross national product at factor cost. This share of the national product was about the same as in 1950. A narrower definition of the social services expenditure, excluding housing and education, gives a total of £2,197 million, which was about 11 per cent of the national product in 1957. In the period 1950–58 total expenditure on the social services only just kept pace with the growth in the national product. Current expenditure on the social services has risen at a faster rate than consumer prices so that there has been a real increase in current spending on the social services. Between 1950 and 1958, for instance, the value of public authorities' expenditure on health and education increased in real terms by 22 per cent.[22] Expenditure on national insurance and pensions and assistance is the largest single item of social service expenditure, taking 40 per cent of the total estimated expenditure in 1958, while education and child care took 25 per cent and the Health Service 22 per cent. The item which has grown fastest in the last seven years is education, which has increased in money terms by 124 per cent between 1950 and 1958, while pensions and national assistance have increased by 104 per cent, and Health Service expenditure has increased by only 54 per cent.

The rapid increase in expenditure on education is partly due to the increase in the size of the school population, but for the social services as a whole there has been a significant increase in current expenditure per head of the population. Total social service expenditure per head of the population has increased in money terms by 73 per cent between 1950 and 1958, while consumers' expenditure per head in money terms has risen by 56 per cent in the same period.

However, in the post-war period the structure of the population has been undergoing important changes. The sections of the population which make the heaviest calls on the social services, the very young and the very old, have been increasing at a much faster rate than the population as a whole. Table 21 shows the proportion of the total population in the United Kingdom

[21] This figure includes housing, education, school meals and welfare foods, health, national insurance and pensions, and is taken from *National Income and Expenditure 1959*, Table 41.

[22] Ibid., Table 13.

which can be classified as "dependent" (those under 15 years of age and those over retirement age, 65 for men and 60 for women) for the years 1939, 1948 and 1958.

TABLE 21

UNITED KINGDOM:

THE DEPENDENT POPULATION, 1939, 1948 AND 1958

	1939	1948	1958
Total population (000)	47,761	50,065	51,870
Total dependent population (000)	15,750	17,566	19,502
Dependent population as a percentage of total population	33	35	38
Percentage increase in dependent population since 1939	—	12	24

Source: Annual Abstract of Statistics, No. 88, 1938–1950 (HMSO), Table 7, and *Monthly Digest of Statistics*, No. 163, June 1959 (HMSO), Table 10. Estimates for 1948 and 1958 include members of the forces serving overseas and merchant seamen at sea.

Taking these figures as a very rough indication of the increase in the numbers making demands on the social services, it would seem that current social service expenditure needed to rise in real terms by a quarter merely to cater for the increase in the number of dependents in the community at the pre-war standard of social service provision. Social service expenditure has risen from £610 million in 1938–39 to £3,419 million in 1958 and in real terms this probably represents an increase of 100 per cent. The true measure of improvements in the quality and scope of the social services in 1958 compared with 1938–39 is, therefore, about 80 per cent.

Social services and consumption

While the State provision of social services may result in only a moderate increase in the resources actually devoted to providing the welfare services themselves, the indirect method of financing them (about 75 per cent of the total is financed out of general taxation), may result in an increase in the total of resources devoted to consumption.

Table 22 shows the relationship between consumers' and social service expenditure and the gross national product in 1938 and in 1950 to 1958. Transfer payments have been subtracted from consumers' expenditure to arrive at a figure for consumers' expenditure *before* the receipt of social service grants. To this "net" consumers' expenditure has been added the total expenditure on the social services to arrive at a combined total of net consumers' and social service expenditure.

Total consumers' expenditure including social service grants took a larger share of the national income before the war than it has in the post-war Welfare State. In 1938 consumers' expenditure at factor cost was equal to 76 per cent of the gross national product at factor cost. In 1950 it was taking 68 per cent of the gross national product and after two sharp reductions in 1950–52 and in 1955–57, was taking by 1958 only 63 per cent of the gross national product. But between 1938 and 1950 total social service expenditure rose from 12 per cent to 17 per cent of the gross national product. Adjusting to allow for the transfer payments, the proportion of the national product taken by the combined net consumers' and social services expenditure fell from 83 per cent in 1938 to 79 per cent in 1950. Since 1950, with total social services expenditure taking a steady 16–17 per cent, and the share of net consumers' expenditure falling from 62 per cent to 56 per cent, the proportion of the national product going to both forms of expenditure has fallen from 79 to 73 per cent. Most of this fall was concentrated in the years of rearmament in 1951 and 1952.

Since 1950, the total share of the resources devoted to consumption and the social services has faithfully followed the fall in the share of consumers' expenditure but does not appear to have assisted it. Does this suggest that the total would have fallen faster in the absence of the same rate of expenditure on the social services or would a reduction in the share of Government spending on social services have been balanced by an increase in private consumption expenditure to compensate for this? The question is a difficult one to answer because it depends on whether the public would have been prepared to accept a cut in the standard of social services. While it might be true that if there had never been social service expenditure on its present scale, total consumption expenditure might be taking a smaller share of the national product because individuals would have to make provision for their own medical treatment, insurance, and so on, and so have less to spend on other less necessary items, it does not follow that this would happen now if large cuts were made in the already established system of social services. The indications are that trade unions and

TABLE 22

SOCIAL EXPENDITURE AND CONSUMPTION, 1938 AND 1950–58

(Current £ million)

	1938	1950	1951	1952	1953	1954	1955	1956	1957	1958
Gross national product at factor cost	5,175	11,687	12,839	13,987	14,922	15,945	16,892	18,267	19,370	20,130
Consumers' expenditure at factor cost	3,950*	7,986	8,590	9,069	9,585	10,323	10,967	11,504	12,107	12,737
Consumers' expenditure as percentage of GNP	*76*	*68*	*67*	*65*	*64*	*65*	*65*	*63*	*63*	*63*
Less grants to persons (transfer payments)	278†	726	759	884	975	986	1,086	1,164	1,217	1,453
Net consumers' expenditure	3,672	7,260	7,831	8,185	8,610	9,337	9,881	10,340	10,890	11,284
Total social services' expenditure	610†	1,934	2,071	2,328	2,514	2,555	2,699	2,924	3,121	3,419
Social Services' expenditure as percentage of GNP	*12*	*17*	*16*	*17*	*17*	*16*	*16*	*16*	*16*	*17*
Total of net consumers' and social services' expenditure	4,282	9,194	9,902	10,513	11,124	11,892	12,580	13,264	14,011	14,703
Social services' expenditure plus net consumers' expenditure as a percentage of GNP	*83*	*79*	*77*	*75*	*75*	*75*	*74*	*73*	*72*	*73*

Source: National Income and Expenditure 1959, Tables 11 and 41.

* *National Income and Expenditure 1955*, Table 24.

† These figures refer to the financial year 1938–39 and are taken from *The Cost of Social Services, 1938–1952* PLANNING No. 354 (P E P), 15 June 1953, p. 12.

other pressure groups have come to regard these almost as an element in the wage packet, and when, for instance, subsidies are reduced, or national insurance contributions increased, they tend to demand that their incomes be increased to compensate for this indirect loss of income. Thus, it seems unlikely that a reduction in social expenditure at the present time would be followed by a fall in the total share of resources devoted to consumption and the social services.

CONCLUSION

The superficial similarity between defence and the social services as expenditures both of which reduce the resources available for investment has been found to be invalid. While defence expenditure can be considered in this way, social service expenditure represents rather a transfer of the initiative in expenditure from individuals to Government authorities. While this transfer may result in an increase in total consumption through extra spending or redistributive methods of financing, this is not measured by estimates of total social service expenditure, and indeed, is very difficult to measure at all.

If total consumption has been boosted by social service expenditure it will have been in one of the following ways:

First, by extra wastages arising in nationally run schemes;
Second, by the provision of better facilities, drugs, etc., than individuals would provide for themselves;
Third, by an inflationary redistribution of income arising from financing social services through a progressive tax system.[23]

The first is a minor administrative question, and the second is one of balancing present cost against future savings in terms of man-hours, further treatment and so on, and against human welfare. The third is an important question but one which also concerns the tax system as a whole. The inflationary effect by redistribution of income via the social services consists only in the extent to which total consumption has thereby been increased, without compensating effects on productive efficiency, and it must be emphasised again that this falls very far short of the figures of total social service expenditure.

[23] Chapter 5 has considered other effects of the method of financing the social services.

The real value of social service expenditure, even accounting for population changes, has increased at a faster rate since 1938 than the real value of consumers' expenditure. But there is no evidence to prove that consumption is taking a larger share of national resources than it would if individuals were still making their own provisions in place of the existing social services. Comparisons between the pre-war and post-war period show that the share of the national product taken by consumption and the social services has fallen to a lower proportion than in 1938. It is not possible to verify whether the share of both forms of spending would have fallen faster in the absence of a high rate of social service expenditure.

Estimates of defence expenditure provide a more reliable indication of what would have been saved if the defence effort had been smaller. The only qualification which must be made in this case is to account for specific sacrifices in consumption which have been made to finance the defence effort and which might not have been made to finance an investment programme. A sacrifice of this kind occurred in the years 1951–52.

In spite of the restraint in consumption, however, the acceleration of defence expenditure made extra claims on scarce physical resources which reduced the supplies available for exports and for investment. If this increase above "normal" post-war defence expenditure had not taken place, the worst of the balance of payments crisis of 1951 and consequent stagnation of investment might have been avoided.

However, in the rest of the post-war period, experience suggests that the level of defence expenditure has been one which can be accommodated and combined with a degree of economic expansion. But Chapter 2 concluded that Britain had achieved a far from satisfactory rate of economic expansion, and without the defence effort more could have been done. If only half the annual average defence expenditure in "normal years" could have been diverted to investment, between 3·5 and 4·5 per cent more of the national income would have been added to the share which gross investment has been taking in the post-war period, and this would have made a considerable impact on the rate of growth, on productivity, and on export performance.

The claims of defence on physical resources were most significant in the years of post-war materials shortages, and have continued to have an influence on the demand for skilled labour, the scarcity of which has persisted. These claims on physical resources and labour have aggravated the inflationary pressures in the economy and contributed to balance of payments difficulties and consequent restrictions on investment.

CHAPTER 7

THE BALANCE OF PAYMENTS

THE outstanding economic problem facing the British Government since the war has been that of the balance of foreign payments, and decisions on internal policy have always been taken with one eye on the external position. Economic crises have usually expressed themselves most critically in a payments difficulty, even though they were primarily domestic in origin. Often it has been the payments position that has forced the Government to take action to improve the internal economic situation. The delicacy of the balance of payments, and the recurrent crises when Britain's ability to pay for essential imports has been called in question, have had a marked effect on investment and on the rate of economic growth. Investment has frequently been cut back in times of payments difficulties, and these cuts or restraints, though not always so effective in reducing the level of investment as had been intended, have certainly hindered the expansion of industrial investment. Production has also been affected by various restrictions designed to bring the country through crises in the balance of payments. The impact of balance of payments problems on investment and on production is documented in the first part of this chapter. The remainder of the chapter is devoted to the discussion of two of the most plausible explanations of the chronic difficulties with the balance of payments. First, there is an examination of the export problem. Has the export of new products expanded sufficiently to replace those export industries that have been in decline? How far have new markets been found to replace those of declining importance? How does the British export performance compare with that of other industrial nations? In particular, is the British share in world trade falling, and does this matter? The second explanation of the failure of receipts from overseas to offset payments made overseas is that the total of payments has been unnecessarily high, rather than that the receipts from exports have been too low. The chief issue here concerns long-term overseas investment. Is overseas investment profitable for this country, and should it be maintained and expanded for selfish or for altruistic reasons? Or should it be restricted so that more money can be made available for investment at home? In any case, should capital be allowed to leave the country while the gold reserves are still slender, and the economy still liable to balance of payments crises?

THE EFFECT ON INVESTMENT

The dependence of the level of home capital investment on the condition of the balance of payments has been clearly revealed in every *Economic Survey* since 1948. As the main hope of achieving a healthier balance of payments has reposed in the expansion of exports, home investment and exports have made competing claims on limited national resources, particularly in the sector of metals and manufactures of metals. There has been a direct connection between the state of the balance of payments and the rate of expansion of the economy. Some extracts from the *Economic Surveys* may serve to document this relationship.

The 1948 *Survey* explained how the original capital development programmes for 1948 had been reviewed in September and October of 1947:

> The need to make cuts in the investment programmes sprang from three things. First, the exhaustion of the dollar credits at an earlier date than had been expected had made it necessary to build up exports more rapidly, even at the expense of postponing re-equipment of the home industries. Second, the condition of achieving the necessary export targets was a release of certain materials, notably steel, which were in such short supply as to set an effective limit to production for export. Third, the over-all resources, including manpower, needed to build up the export and import-saving industries, could be secured only by reductions in investment as well as consumption.[1]

The *Survey* for 1950 explained how the restraints on capital expenditure initiated in 1949 through the Capital Issues Committee and by advice to bankers were intended to give

> . . . preference to increases of capacity designed to overcome shortages of basic materials, to projects which were likely to increase exports to, or save imports from, hard currency countries on a substantial scale, to the promotion of technical developments and

[1] Cmd. 7344 (HMSO), para. 176.

practices, and to proposals which would yield marked and immediate reductions in costs.[2]

The 1952 *Survey* spoke of a direct transfer of resources from home investment to export:

In present conditions of world demand the expansion of the total volume of exports must depend almost entirely on increasing engineering exports. World demand for capital goods remains very high, and there is opportunity for a considerable increase in British exports. . . . In the long run our industries must have the equipment they need for expansion and efficiency. At the present time, however, some of these needs must be sacrificed because of the overriding importance of increasing exports of precisely these goods for which investment demand is heaviest. The Government has therefore taken steps to divert resources on a large scale from supplying engineering goods to the home market to production for export.[3]

Even in the more expansionist climate of 1954 the balance of payments remained the chief anxiety:

The outstanding economic problem facing the United Kingdom is still that of paying its way abroad, and the needs of the balance of payments must continue to govern the pace of internal expansion. Internal stability and external solvency are closely linked, the more so now that many of the physical controls over imports have been removed. The growth of production at home and of trade abroad must proceed in step with each other.[4]

Again the warning appeared in the 1955 *Survey*:[5]

For this country to attempt to pursue the long-term objective of expansion without regard to the needs of the balance of payments would be a self-defeating course.

At home the main objective of economic policy is to ensure that, while the level of purchasing power is not so high as to interfere with the growth of exports or to attract a larger volume of imports than the nation can afford, adequate incentives are provided for long-run expansion.

In the 1956 *Survey* a clear explanation was given of the connection between the rise in industrial investment, the renewed

[2] Cmd. 7915, para. 25.
[3] Cmd. 8509, paras. 30–31.
[4] Cmd. 9108, para. 79.
[5] Cmd. 9412, paras. 104 and 97.

crisis in the balance of payments, and the resulting restrictions on investment:

> The amount of industrial building started had been rising rapidly, and it became clear that a considerable up-surge in the capital expenditure of industry was being superimposed on the buoyant level of consumers' expenditure. An increase in industrial development was desirable: but evidence accumulated that the size of the expansion in progress and in preparation was greater than our resources permitted, and was prejudicing both the stability of the home economy and the required growth in exports. A check to the expansion of investment was necessary, but it was also desirable to curb consumers' expenditure, so as to make room for a healthy growth of investment and a surplus in the balance of payments.[6]

It is not possible to state what has been the exact effect on investment of the periodic cuts and restrictions that have been outlined. It is clear that in particular years investment has actually been reduced below the level that had been planned, but the plans may sometimes have been unrealistic, as in 1955, and it is impossible to know if the effect of the cuts has been only to delay the achievement of a certain level of investment for a few years or whether it has in fact held down the level of investment in every year below what would have been achieved in the absence of the crises. The greatest check to investment took place in 1951 and 1952, gross fixed capital formation remaining virtually stationary when revalued at 1954 prices. Gross fixed capital formation at home in 1950 was £2,130 million, in 1951 £2,134 million, and in 1952 £2,143 million, all at 1954 prices.[7] In 1953 investment rose to £2,373 million. Whether this last figure would have been higher if investment had continued to increase steadily in 1951 and 1952 is hard to say, though on the evidence of previous and later years it seems reasonable to suppose that it would have been.

THE DECLINING BRITISH SHARE IN WORLD TRADE

In the early post-war years attention was focused on the rapid expansion of British exports, but when considerable achievements had removed the immediate danger of national bankruptcy, a more insidious fear took its place: that of a slowly but persistently declining trend in the share of British exports in the world total of

[6] Cmd. 9278, para. 69.
[7] *National Income and Expenditure 1959* (HMSO), Table 13.

exports, particularly of manufactures. Although great success had been achieved in the export markets in the 1940's, in the 1950's a steady decline in Britain's share in world trade began to cause concern. Between 1950 and 1956, while the volume of world trade in manufactures rose at a rate of 8 per cent per annum, the volume of British exports of manufactures rose by only 2 per cent per annum.[8]

In some degree it was possible to shrug off this falling share as a natural consequence of the recovery of German and Japanese industry, but as Britain's share continued to decline, this excuse no longer carried much weight. Even compared with 1937, the comparison was disheartening. The volume of world exports of manufactures had risen by 153 per cent; the volume of British exports of manufactures by only 96 per cent. In 1937 Britain's share in the exports of manufactures of the main exporting countries (the United Kingdom, the United States, Germany, other European countries, Canada, Japan) had been 22 per cent, but by 1957 it had fallen to 18 per cent. The share of Germany in 1937 had been 23 per cent. In 1951 the share of Western Germany (which before the war had accounted for about two-thirds of the total exports of the whole of Germany) was only 10 per cent, but by 1957 it equalled that of the United Kingdom, with 18 per cent.[9]

The structure of exports

A partial explanation of Britain's falling share of world exports of manufactures is to be found in a study of the structure of British exports by area and by commodity compared with the structure of other countries' exports in relation to the expansion of world trade. A report by an Inter-Departmental Working Party, extracts from which were published in the Board of Trade Journal[10] showed how

> . . . a country's share of trade may change simply because the commodities in the manufacture of which it specializes expand faster or less fast than manufactures as a whole, or because the markets to

[8] E. A. G. Robinson, "The problem of Living within our Foreign Earnings Further Considered", *Three Banks Review*, June 1958, p. 5.

[9] "Trends in Exports of United Kingdom Compared with other Countries", *Board of Trade Journal*, 30 March 1957, p. 666, and Treasury *Bulletin for Industry*, May 1958.

[10] *Board of Trade Journal*, 30 March 1957, pp. 665 ff.

which it exports the most expand faster or less fast than world markets taken together.

In the first half of 1956 just over 46 per cent of United Kingdom total exports went to the sterling area, and only 24 per cent to the Continental OEEC countries. Between 1951 and 1955 the increase in the value of the trade of the OEEC countries had been 38 per cent; the increase in the value of trade of the rest of the sterling area had been only 8 per cent. The increase in world trade had been 22 per cent. Thus Britain was closely associated with *markets* that expanded less rapidly than the average. Western Germany, on the other hand, sold no less than 56 per cent of its total exports in the first half of 1956 to the Continental OEEC countries, the most rapidly expanding market.

Similarly British exports, compared with those of other exporting countries, have consisted too largely of textiles, a declining commodity in world trade. Between 1951 and 1955 world trade in textiles fell by 20 per cent. In 1951 16 per cent of United Kingdom exports were of textiles, and by 1955 this proportion had been reduced to 11 per cent.[11] By 1957 British textile exports had fallen to 9 per cent, but this compares with only 5 per cent for Western Germany in 1955 and 4 per cent in 1957.[12]

The importance of the structure of British exports by area and by commodity as an explanation of the falling share in world trade is, however, limited. As the Board of Trade pointed out:[13]

> The United Kingdom share of trade has fallen in every market except one ("other countries", which account for only about a tenth of her exports), and in every commodity group except metals and manufactures. This shows that the fall in her share of trade in all manufactures between 1951 and 1955 cannot be due mainly to the adverse effect of the pattern of her trade—in particular, her exceptionally heavy dependence on the Sterling Area, which expanded only slowly between 1951 and 1955, and the fairly high proportion of textiles in her exports.

Only about a quarter of the fall in Britain's share is calculated to be accounted for by the pattern of trade. The greater part of the fall has been due to a failure of British exports to hold their share in each commodity and market. Similarly, Western Germany in-

[11] Ibid., Table 4, p. 668.
[12] United Nations, *Yearbook of International Trade Statistics*, 1957, Vol. I, p. 238.
[13] Op. cit., p. 671.

creased its share in world trade with only slight assistance from the pattern of trade, and the share of Japan rose despite heavy dependence on exports of textiles. Of course, one-quarter of the fall in the British share in world exports represents a not inconsiderable amount. If world exports are about £20,000 million, and the British share has fallen by about 4 per cent of the world total since 1951, the value of exports in question is about 1 per cent of £20,000 million, or £200 million.

Adaptation of commodity structure

The Board of Trade carefully refrain from stating or implying that too great a rigidity of industrial and export structure has hindered Britain's export performance even to this extent. It is perhaps worthwhile to emphasise that a vast adaptation had already taken place in the commodity structure of British exports over the past hundred years. In 1850 exports of textiles represented no less than 63 per cent of total exports, in 1913 only 34 per cent, in 1937 24 per cent and in 1951 19 per cent. Over the same years exports of the metal and engineering industries rose from 18 per cent of total exports in 1850, to 27 per cent in 1913, 35 per cent in 1937, and 49 per cent in 1951.[14]

This adaptation of British industry has continued rapidly in the post-war years. Table 23 below compares the shares of the

TABLE 23

THE STRUCTURE OF EXPORTS

	UK	*Leading industrial countries*	*UK*	*Leading industrial countries*
	1938	1938	1955	1955
Machinery . .	15·4	19·9	22·4	24·5
Transport equipment	8·4	13·0	14·9	13·6
Chemicals . .	6·3	9·5	8·0	11·5
	30·1	42·4	45·3	49·6

In the declining group of textile manufactures the shares are as follows:

19·4	16·5	10·7	10·7

Sources: United Kingdom—*Annual Abstract of Statistics*, No. 93 (HMSO), 1956. Leading industrial countries—United Nations, *World Economic Survey*, 1956, p. 58.

[14] E. A. G. Robinson, "The Changing Structure of the British Economy" *Economic Journal*, September 1954, p. 453.

three main expanding groups of manufactures in the total exports of manufactures of leading industrial countries (Belgium, France, Germany, Italy, Luxembourg, Sweden, Switzerland, the United States and the United Kingdom) with their share in the total exports of manufactures of the United Kingdom in 1938 and in 1955–56.

So great an adaptation has taken place in the British industrial and export structure that there is now a more favourable structure of exports relatively to the other leading industrial countries, whereas before the war there was a relatively unfavourable structure.

The impression of these figures is confirmed by Sir Donald Macdougall:[15]

> It may be argued that the *United Kingdom* is badly placed structurally because of the commodity composition of her export trade and a slowness in developing new products. But while it is true that, *compared with the U.S.*, her exports of manufactures consist less of lines that are expanding rapidly in world trade and more of goods that are declining in importance, the pattern of her exports compares quite favourably with that of other industrial nations. . . . It can be calculated . . . that, in 1950, Britain had a substantially higher proportion of her exports of manufactures in the "expanding" group than the other nine main exporters (excluding the U.S.) taken together, a substantially smaller proportion in the "stable" group, and roughly the same proportion in the "declining" group.

Dependence on the sterling area

While the United Kingdom has adapted the commodity pattern of its exports to changing world trends, it has still not diverged very much from the traditional outlets for British exports, chiefly in the primary producing areas of the world. In 1956 the primary producing areas took 54 per cent of British exports, but only 33 per cent of the total exports of Western Europe as a whole.[16] The geographical distribution of United Kingdom exports has been slowly responding to the changing trends in world trade, but the process of adaptation has proceeded much faster in Western Germany, whose historic pattern of exports was in any case more suited to the newly emerging pattern of trade.

[15] *The World Dollar Problem* (Macmillan), 1957, pp. 354–5.
[16] ECE, *Economic Survey of Europe in 1957*, Ch. 4, p. 19, Table 13.

In 1938 the main sterling area importers of United Kingdom products[17] were taking 39 per cent of its total exports. In 1957 they were still taking as much as 34 per cent, and a large part of the fall in the share of these countries is accounted for by the fall in the share of exports to South Africa. Exports to the six countries of the European Economic Community were just over 13 per cent of total British exports in 1938, and their share was still less than 14 per cent in 1957. The proportion of total exports going to Switzerland and the Scandinavian countries, including Finland, increased only slightly from 9·4 per cent to 10·2 per cent between 1938 and 1957.[18]

It must be remembered, however, that Britain's main export outlets are also the most important sources of imports. Over a quarter of imports came from sterling area countries in 1957, and just under a quarter from Western Europe, whereas Western Germany took over 40 per cent of imports from Western Europe in 1957. The general pattern of origin of United Kingdom imports has hardly altered between 1938 and 1957 while that of Western Germany has moved significantly towards the North American and Western European sources.[19]

Thus, the structure of British export markets is very dependent on Britain's own import demand, on traditional sources of supply, outlets for British capital, and economic and political links with the Commonwealth.

Since over half of all exports are sent to the primary producing areas, the export trade of the United Kingdom is more dependent than that of any other European country on the prosperity and demand for imports of these areas. This dependence is accentuated by the different character of the markets for United Kingdom exports and imports. The demand for imports into the United Kingdom is relatively unaffected by changes in prices and incomes. (Just under half this country's total imports are of agricultural

[17] Australia, New Zealand, South Africa, Federation of Rhodesia and Nyasaland, India, Ireland, Malaya, Hong Kong, Ghana, Kenya-Uganda, and Nigeria.

[18] United Nations, *Yearbook of International Trade Statistics*, 1950, p. 162, and 1957, Vol. I, p. 589.

[19] United Nations, *Yearbook of International Trade Statistics*, 1957. Between 1936 and 1957, German imports from North America have risen from 6 to 20 per cent of total imports, and imports from the countries of the European Economic Community from 15 to 23 per cent of the total. In the same period German exports to North America have risen from 4 per cent to 8 per cent of total exports, and those to the EEC countries from 23 to 30 per cent.

produce.) But the demand of the primary producing countries for British exports is much more responsive to price and income movements. Thus, the demand for exports depends a great deal on the flow of foreign investment to these countries and on their internal prosperity.

In the period before the first world war when the United Kingdom occupied a dominant position in world markets, any increase in United Kingdom imports from the primary producing countries was largely self-financing. The increased incomes of the primary producing countries would be reflected in a corresponding increase in their imports from the United Kingdom. Today, however, the United Kingdom's importance in world markets, and in the markets in the primary producing areas, has declined, and consequently only a smaller proportion of the income expended abroad can be expected to return directly in the form of increased export orders.

Movements in the terms of trade between the primary producing and industrial countries have an important effect on United Kingdom exports. A movement in favour of the primary producing countries increases their incomes and therefore their capacity to import. Since the demand for primary commodities is relatively unaffected by changes in prices or incomes (though it does respond to changes in the level of employment) the demand for these imports is unlikely to fall very much as a result of higher prices, or of a reduction in export earnings of the United Kingdom. However, when the terms of trade move against the primary producing countries the fall in prices is unlikely to induce a rise in demand sufficient to offset the fall in revenue. Nor are the increased incomes of the exporters of manufactured goods likely to be devoted to a proportionate increase in imports of primary commodities. Thus, an adverse movement in the terms of trade of primary producing countries reduces the prices of their exports without a fully compensating movement in the demand for their exports. Therefore, exports from industrial countries to primary producing areas will be adversely affected by movements in the terms of trade against the primary producers. Because of the structure of export markets the United Kingdom will be more severely affected than the other countries of Western Europe.

The United Kingdom enjoys, however, a special relationship in the financing of trade with the primary producing countries of the overseas sterling area, and this appears to have operated so as to offset the harmful effects on United Kingdom exports of a movement of the terms of trade against the primary producing countries. The sterling balances, debts owed by Britain to these countries, provide a cushion to allow them to maintain their imports from the United Kingdom even at a time when their earnings from exports to the United Kingdom and elsewhere have been seriously diminished by adverse terms of trade.

The terms of trade moved against the primary producing countries after 1951, when the British index, taking 1938 as 100, was 139. During 1957 alone the index fell from 120 in the first quarter to 110 in the last quarter. This sharp fall was expected, after a short lag, to have serious consequences for British exports in 1958. Exports were indeed affected, but on the whole were remarkably well maintained, with the result that a record surplus was earned on the balance of payments for the year. The British share in world exports in fact showed a revival in 1958, while the share of other countries, those that had benefited most from trade with the most rapidly expanding markets, showed a decline. The conclusion is that while dependence on markets in the primary producing areas may have tended to slow down the growth of British exports in the post-war years, it also has the advantage, via the financial links, of helping this country to ride out the effects of a world recession of trade. The fear that dependence on these markets would make Britain particularly vulnerable to economic fluctuations, in addition to the long-term disadvantages, appears to have been ill-founded.

Conclusion

Britain's recent declining share in world trade in manufactures cannot be attributed mainly to the special circumstances of the post-war recovery of Germany and Japan, nor to the commodity and market structure of exports. This leaves the field open for the most general and the most pessimistic argument: that the falling British share in world trade shows that British exports are just not able to hold their ground against foreign competition. The Report of the Inter-Departmental Committee appears to be somewhat equivocal on this issue. First it says:

> ... to maintain or improve upon a particular share of world trade is not, of course, an end in itself. What matters is that exports should

> be high enough to pay for all the imports that the country wants, after other receipts, payments and commitments have been taken into account.

But then it proceeds to explain that: "... granted that a higher level of exports is required ... an examination of shares of trade ... gives some measure of the competitiveness of the United Kingdom's exports."[20]

When Britain's declining share in world trade is put in historical perspective, however, it does not seem valid to quote it as a sign of relative inefficiency. The British share in world total *production* of manufactures in 1870 was about 32 per cent, having already fallen from above 40 per cent in 1850. By 1900 it was down to about 20 per cent, and by 1913 to about 14 per cent. This decline in Britain's share in world *production* of manufactures was inevitable, and Britain's share of world *trade* in manufactures also fell: from 40 per cent in 1870, to 30 per cent in 1900, and 27 per cent in 1913.[21] The decline continued to 18 per cent in 1958.[22] It may be expected to continue so long as industries are growing faster in other countries, either through the process of industrialisation or through a more rapid population increase in economies that are already industrialised. In 1938 only 74 per cent of Britain's imports of goods and services were financed by exports of goods and services. In 1957 100 per cent were so financed. On this criterion it would seem that a great adaptation has taken place.

The decline in the British share would not matter if British exports enjoyed a declining share in *expanding* world markets, and if this share represented a volume of exports that is sufficient to purchase the imports needed to maintain a satisfactory rate of growth of the national product.

The increase in the volume of exports during the post-war period has been well in excess of the increase in the volume of imports. Between 1938 and 1957 the value of United Kingdom exports of goods and services increased by over 500 per cent while the value of imports rose by some 350 per cent. The significance of the increase in exports is more forcefully expressed by comparing the proportion of the national income which goes as

[20] *Board of Trade Journal*, 30 March 1957, p. 668.
[21] E. A. G. Robinson, "The Changing Structure of the British Economy".
[22] Treasury *Bulletin for Industry*, May 1959.

exports of goods and services with the proportion of imports of goods and services. Table 24 shows how exports and imports of goods and services have varied as percentages of the net national income from 1938 to 1948 and 1958.

TABLE 24

EXPORTS AND IMPORTS, 1938, 1948 AND 1958

	1938	1948	1958
		Current £ million	
Net national income at factor cost	4,816	9,556	18,235
Imports of goods and services	977	2,195	4,118
Exports of goods and services	723	1,992	4,377
		Percentages	
Imports as a percentage of net national income	20·3	23·0	22·6
Exports as a percentage of net national income	15·0	20·8	24·0
Imports not paid for by exports as a percentage of net national income	5·3	2·1	−1·4*

Source: National Income and Expenditure 1958 and *1959*, Tables 1 and 7.

* Excess of exports.

Yet apparently even this great improvement in the situation over the last twenty years has not been enough to put an end to worries about the balance of payments. Much has been done: but more is still needed.

OVERSEAS COMMITMENTS

A deficit on the balance of payments is the net result of a number of credits and debits, and the cure for any crisis may be found by increasing some or all of the credits or by decreasing the debits. The most positive and vigorous approach is no doubt to seek to increase exports, but a considerable effort has already been made in that direction. The debit items in the accounts are perhaps too often taken to be necessary and unavoidable liabilities (normally referred to in the *Economic Surveys* as "traditional", and rarely called in question), and an examination, at least as searching as that applied to the level of exports, of their relationship to the balance of payments is long overdue. In recent years increasing attention has been focused on the United Kingdom's commitments overseas and it has been questioned whether some of these may not reflect excessive international responsibilities and constitute unnecessarily heavy burdens on the economy.

One of the most forceful expositions of this view is to be found in *Britain's Economic Policy Since the War* by Andrew Shonfield. The total cost in terms of foreign currency of overseas military and political commitments was shown to be running at about £200 million in the mid-1950's. Of this £19 million is for grants and subsidies paid to Middle Eastern countries for political purposes, £27 million for grants to the Colonies, and £160 million for military expenditure abroad. This last item

> ... is just about equal to the average annual surplus on Britain's current balance of payments in recent years—after allowing for all expenditure on goods and services overseas including military expenditure ... if for instance we had been in the position of Germany and thus prevented from maintaining any troops overseas, then our average balance of payments surplus on current account would have been doubled to reach over £300 million. This is in fact more than the German average for this period.[23]

Another debit item which has grown since the last war is payments abroad in the form of interest on foreign loans. This item cost the United Kingdom £489 million in 1958, eight times as much as the 1938 total of £61 million. Property income received from abroad has in the same period increased only from £253 million to £758 million. So the net property income in 1958 was far below the 1938 level in real terms. A large part of the increase in interest payments abroad is due to the cost of servicing the sterling balances, which still total over £3,000 million.

These interest payments are unavoidable unless this country is to default on its obligations, and while their effect on the balance of payments may be duly noted there is little hope of relief from their reduction, except as the result of long years of repayment of capital, which would of course, while it lasted, constitute an even greater burden than the present interest charges, and require an even greater surplus on other accounts.[24] This leaves just one

[23] Andrew Shonfield, *British Economic Policy Since the War*, Penguin Special, 1958, pp. 104 and 105.

[24] The burden can also be reduced, of course, if interest rates can be kept low, but this is not always feasible.

major debit item which can reasonably be isolated as the final entry in the books that has over the years kept the accounts much nearer to the red than they need have been, and the reserves much more slender; namely long-term investment overseas.

It is commonly observed that Britain's balance of payments on current account has not been in deficit but has in fact earned a reasonable average annual surplus in the 1950's. However, a sum greater than the annual surplus has been debited to the balance of payments on account of Britain's exports of capital overseas. For this reason the gold and dollar reserves have not been built up, and crises have resulted in years of adverse payments conditions. This has led to a plea that Britain should cease to allow overseas investment. The case for such a change of policy is supported by other arguments besides the effect on the balance of payments. It has been variously argued that the encouragement of industrialisation abroad does not help British exports, that the capital is needed at home, and that the capital can be more profitably employed at home.

The fact that most of the overseas earnings of British companies are ploughed back into their overseas subsidiaries has been used to throw doubt on the profitability for the home country of these investments. Estimates of capital movements into and out of this country were published in *The Times* on 24 April 1958 in conjunction with two articles defending the practice of overseas capital investment.[25]

The analysis of direct capital investment in terms of investment by retention of profits and by fresh capital is important. Fresh capital exports ranged between £60 million and £69 million each year between 1954 and 1957, while profits retained abroad amounted to between £170 million and £210 million per annum. In fact, the fresh capital exported from this country amounted to little more than the total of foreign investment in the United Kingdom, and overseas investment out of retained profits of British companies almost entirely accounted for the net capital export shown in the balance of payments. The fact that this item includes as a capital export the profits retained overseas by subsidiaries of British companies is not always realised.

[25] John Wood and T. M. Rybczynski, "Should Britain Restrict Investment Abroad?", *The Times*, 24 and 25 April 1958.

TABLE 25

BRITAIN'S CAPITAL ACCOUNT

	1957	1956	1955	1954
	£ million			
I. Government				
1. Colonial grants . . .	−38	−27	−32	−29
2. Repayment by UK of loans from foreign governments . .	+59	−70	−48	−54
3. Foreign governments repayment of loans from UK . .	+30	+30	+28	+50
4. New loans from UK Government	−18	−11	−33	−16
TOTAL GOVERNMENT .	+33	−78	−85	−49
II. Financial facilities	+154	−41	+176	−7
III. Investment portfolio				
1. UK investment overseas . .	−50	+5	+42	−26
2. Foreign investment in UK .	Nil	+25	+5	+5
IV. Direct investment				
1. Foreign investment in UK by retentions	+45	+30	+46	+43
2. Foreign investment in UK by fresh capital	+15	+25	+12	+7
3. UK investment abroad by retentions	−210	−200	−190	−170
4. UK investment abroad by fresh capital	−60	−65	−65	−69
	−260	−180	−150	−210

− denotes expenditure. + denotes receipts.

It is of course still possible to argue that these profits should not be retained but remitted to the United Kingdom and no fresh capital sent out. Also, there is no particular validity in the off-setting of British investment abroad by foreign investment in this country. If the export of capital was abandoned, while foreigners continued to be encouraged to invest in Britain, the balance of payments would be improved and at the same time a more rapid rate of growth of domestic output could be achieved. But what is the scope for ceasing to export capital in the form of retained profits? Examination of the sources of the retained profits shows that the room for action is extremely limited. Wood and Rybczynski estimate that over half of the retained earnings were made by tin, copper, base metals, oil, rubber and tea companies. These still retain the traditional justification of British capital exports: that they facilitate supplies of products that might not otherwise be obtained. The remaining £100 million or so of retained profits are attributed to manufacturing or trading subsidiaries of British firms. Investment in trading subsidiaries may be essential to successful exporting, leaving for consideration only that fraction of the £100 million which goes to build up manufacturing overseas. Including the proportion of new capital exports that goes into manufacturing subsidiaries, the total at issue must be under £150 million, and probably is not more than £100 million per annum. From the point of view of the current balance of payments this sum is quite significant: in relation to Britain's domestic investment of over £3,400 million in 1957 it appears only marginal. But the strength of the argument cannot be judged by the amounts involved. The disposal of £100 million per annum is always worth considering. Why should this money not be invested at home rather than abroad?

Does overseas investment help exports?

Capital exports are frequently justified on the grounds that they are necessary for the maintenance or expansion of exports of goods from this country. Two arguments are involved. First, it is said that in particular instances markets will be closed to British exports by countries intent on industrialisation unless British firms co-operate by forming subsidiaries in the overseas country, and thus get inside the tariff barrier or other restrictions. The second argument is a more general one: that by assisting economic development overseas, this country will be sure of increasing supplies of materials, and also of a buoyant demand, if not for consumer goods, certainly for capital goods, in whose manufacture Britain has a comparative advantage over younger economies.

Neither of these arguments is particularly strong. The setting up of subsidiaries is of little direct assistance to British exports except where the manufacture is limited to assembly of goods manufactured in the United Kingdom. It is rarely so limited for very long, however, and the overseas subsidiary tends under the influence of economic nationalism as well as of the momentum of its own growth to take over the whole process of manufacture from the raw material to the finished product. Cars made by subsidiaries of British firms in Australia are Australian home-produced cars, not British exports. The foundation of the overseas subsidiary may assist the individual firm to find profitable outlets for its earnings and to expand its total output and profit, but from the point of view of the United Kingdom balance of payments it merely sets up a competing supplier of goods to overseas markets. This development may be inevitable anyway, if the overseas country is intent on industrialisation, but this is no reason why the process of displacing British exports should be supported and financed with scarce British capital.

The more general argument that Britain's best hope of increasing exports lies in a rapidly expanding world economy has more to commend it. If investment overseas can stimulate economic growth and thus lead to an increasing demand for British exports, particularly of capital goods, then it is to be encouraged. However, the connection between the export of capital from Britain and the expansion of export markets is no longer as clear as it was in the nineteenth century, when Britain held such a predominant position in the world economy that its own capital exports were the chief determinant of the economic development of areas that provided both the supplies of food and raw materials and the markets for the products of British industry. Britain's share of world industrial output and world trade is now much more modest, and British exports of capital have a much smaller influence on the growth of markets for British exports.

The justification of capital exports on grounds of immediate self-interest—that they help British exports of goods and services—is thus not easy.

Is overseas investment profitable?

The view that overseas investment is beneficial to this country, because it builds up a source of invisible earnings overseas that will be of value to this country in the future, has been severely attacked in recent years. The main arguments in support of this attack are that most of the profits of overseas subsidiaries of British firms are ploughed back into the subsidiary, and only a small proportion remitted to the United Kingdom. Thus, it is argued, even if the dividend yield on investment overseas is higher than the yield on the same capital if invested at home, the investment is still less profitable than if the money were invested at home.

However, if a higher rate of profit can be earned on investments overseas, it will in the long run pay the individual investor to invest overseas so long as some proportion of the overseas earnings is remitted each year, for the smaller the proportion of income remitted, the faster the build-up of assets overseas, so that eventually even a small proportion of earnings will be a large sum.[26]

It may be objected that the "long run" over which overseas investments may be profitable is so long that it is impracticable to base calculations on it. But Britain benefited considerably in the 1930's from the income in investments made before the first world war, and it is not inconceivable that such a source of overseas income would be welcome later this century.

Even accepting that a fair amount of profit will in fact accrue to the home country there is still another argument against overseas investments: that the overseas country will enjoy the benefits of the wages and other sums paid out in the course of production, and of the taxes paid on the profits of the enterprise. This is essentially an argument against the free movement of labour and capital, and like most protectionist arguments it is wrong. It would only be valid at a time when there was unemployment at home which could be cured by an extension of capital equipment. In a time of full employment at home it is possible to argue that the productivity of labour at home can be increased by more intensive use of capital. But the productivity of labour is not synonymous with efficiency, while if higher yields can be obtained on capital invested overseas, capital and labour *can* apparently be used more efficiently there than at home. Is there any particular virtue in keeping more labour and more

[26] The large amounts involved in dividend payments on account of foreign subsidiaries that have built up their earning power by self-financing is seen as a problem by the governments of industrialising countries. (See E. T. Penrose, "Foreign Investment and the Growth of the Firm", *Economic Journal*, June 1956, especially p. 221. In 1954 the dividend paid by the Australian General Motors-Holden subsidiary was equal to 8 per cent of Australia's total dollar receipts from exports in the year 1954–55.)

capital in the United Kingdom than can be employed there with at least equal efficiency to that which can be achieved elsewhere? This argument against overseas investment can be sustained on the basis of nationalistic aims that set the maintenance of a certain level of population and of military and political strength before the welfare of the individual. Or it may be supported on the ground that labour is not in fact very mobile. But populations have been increasing more rapidly in many of the countries to which British capital is exported than in Britain.

There is still a "best-of-both-worlds" argument for the curtailment of British capital exports. This argument runs as follows. The United Kingdom should seek to enjoy all the benefits of the foreign investment of *other* capital exporting countries, both through their developing overseas markets for British exports, and through their investment in the United Kingdom increasing British industrial capacity. At the same time the United Kingdom should keep all *its* capital resources at home so as to strengthen industry to the utmost. Of course, if everyone, meaning particularly the Americans, should follow this selfish example for the same reasons, the world would suffer from a slower rate of growth of production and trade. Britain, being so dependent on international trade, would then suffer more than most.

Finally, there can be no defence against those who attack overseas investment mainly on the grounds of the uncertainty of political conditions in the countries where the investment has taken place. It is only fair to point out, however, that the greater part of direct overseas investment, in the twentieth century as in the nineteenth, has taken place in countries opened up by immigration from Western Europe, which enjoy similar political, social, and economic traditions and attitudes, and are thus less liable to political upheaval.

Conclusion

When the export of capital from the United Kingdom is criticised, the sums involved are small in comparison with the total which is invested at home, and are mostly in the form of the ploughing back of profits made on earlier foreign investment. They may, however, be quite significant in relation to the balance of payments. Overseas investment may help British exports indirectly by assisting the growth of future markets for exports of goods, but its importance in this respect is now much less than in the nineteenth century. There is, however, little direct help to British exports arising out of the establishment of manufacturing subsidiaries overseas. Capital investment overseas is in the long run more profitable to the economy than investment at home (assuming that it was made in the first place on the basis of higher expected yields overseas) even though much of the profit is ploughed back into the overseas subsidiary. Arguments of a protectionist and nationalistic nature are historically ill-founded and do not apply unless it is thought that labour no longer does or should move between one country and another. Britain could still gain by curtailing exports of capital while other advanced countries continued to assist the process of industrialisation, but if all nations followed similar reasoning economic growth throughout the world would suffer.

The special arguments for reducing British long-term investment overseas do not then appear to be overwhelming. But this still leaves untouched the most immediate argument for the curtailment of this investment. This is simply that, however valuable overseas investment may be in the long run, it cannot be permitted to take place unless the country is earning a sufficient surplus on current account to finance it without running into payments crises. If the £200 million or so of overseas investment is precisely the marginal amount by which exports have failed to finance all the unavoidable current payments, then the investment should be sacrificed in the interests of sounder short-term international finances.

This is a powerful case, much more so than all the supporting arguments seeking to show that overseas investment anyway is not profitable for the country, but its weakness is similar to the weakness of the case against any marginal amount of non-consumption expenditure for "national" purposes. In this, as in every other example, it is possible to argue that this expenditure is superior to consumption expenditure, and that if anything is cut it should be consumption. Britain is a rich country by contrast with many of the countries that so urgently need capital for their development, rich in comparison with the Soviet Union, which yet manages to support a far greater defence burden per head of the population. While the struggle against inflation has not been won, it could be argued that to cut overseas investment would only have the effect of increasing the resources devoted to satisfying the home consumer, and that no lasting improvement in the balance of payments would result. And even if such a cut could succeed in its object, it would appear to be inferior to a restraint of consumption at home that made it possible for Britain to be solvent without giving up a valuable international role.

CHAPTER 8

INFLATION AND THE ALLOCATION OF RESOURCES[1]

STATEMENTS by the wartime Coalition Government have mostly passed into the limbo of achieved or conveniently forgotten aims. However, one declaration is indelibly imprinted on the economic mind of Britain: "The Government accept as one of their primary aims and responsibilities the maintenance of a high and stable level of employment after the war." In these terms the 1944 White Paper on Employment Policy[2] laid the foundations of Britain's post-war economy. There have, of course, been other aims of policy: a favourable balance of payments, price stability and a steady and sizeable rate of growth of national production and productivity. But in the fourteen years since the end of the war in Europe, only the first aim, full employment, has been achieved in its entirety. It has indeed had a success beyond the most sanguine aspirations of its founders. Lord Beveridge thought in terms of a maximum of 3 per cent unemployed, but the national average has in fact rarely exceeded 2 per cent since 1945.

Meanwhile, the other aims have met with less success. Chapter 2 has already expressed concern about the slow rate of increase of productivity in the United Kingdom compared with other countries, and price stability and the balance of payments have also not fared so well. Between 1946 and 1958 the retail price index rose by about 77 per cent. Only during three intervals, in 1948–49, in 1953 and in 1958–59 was there some semblance of stability. For the rest of the post-war period there has been a steady, and on occasion a fairly rapid, rise in the average level of prices. There have been few moments when the balance of Britain's international payments or the level of the gold and dollar reserves has not given cause for concern. Crisis has followed crisis, in 1947, 1949, 1951, 1955 and 1957.

Over the years the view has frequently been expressed that aims of policy of great value in themselves, and vital to Britain's

[1] This chapter is based on an earlier version published as a broadsheet, *The Price of Stability*, PLANNING No. 422 (P E P), 19 May 1958.

[2] Cmd. 6527 (HMSO).

economic future, have been sacrificed in the interests of one aim, full employment, which, though universally acclaimed, was not felt on all sides to contain in itself the sum total of economic value. After 1955 these opinions gained a new impetus, and since 1957 it has appeared that the Government are prepared to put price stability and the balance of payments at the head of the queue, even at some detriment to the high level of employment. The natural inflation of prices which inevitably followed the devaluation of 1949 had by 1957 run its course, and it was necessary to call a halt to a process that had become an accepted feature of the economy.

There may be controversy over methods, but there should be none about the principle that it is the primary aim of British economic policy to achieve a reasonably favourable balance of overseas payments over a period of years, and to maintain the gold and dollar reserves at a satisfactory level. This objective is a necessary pre-condition for the long-term maintenance of full employment and of economic growth; for the first requirement of any economy is solvency, and the balance of payments, and the level of the gold and dollar reserves in relation to the financial and trading activities they have to underwrite, are indications of the national solvency. Exactly what range of financial and trading activities Britain should undertake is a matter of some controversy.[3] It may indeed be a matter of choice, and therefore of controversy, whether to emphasise the value of the City and of the sterling area *per se*, or the role of physical exports based on buoyant production at home. But this issue does not affect the overall need of a nation that relies to the extent that Britain does on international trade to maintain an internationally acceptable currency, by whatever means may be necessary. If Britain fails in this all other economic aims are jeopardised.

Britain has indeed been failing in this respect. The gold reserves have remained quite inadequate since the war to support the burden of transactions that are carried out in sterling. With only a very small proportion of the world's foreign exchange reserves Britain has been attempting to finance a much larger share of the world's trade. The average net favourable balance of payments on current accounts in the years 1955 to 1958 was only £202 million per annum, including £24 million per annum of defence aid.

[3] See *The Debate on Sterling*, PLANNING No. 421 (P E P), 14 April 1958.

Over the same years an average of £217 million per annum was devoted to net long-term investment overseas, so the total result on the combined current and capital accounts was a deficit.[4]

Whether the annual favourable balance on current account should be sufficient to allow Britain to continue to provide long-term capital on a large scale for the Commonwealth and for underdeveloped countries outside the Commonwealth is a matter of debate. To some extent such exports of capital are unavoidable if the sterling area is to remain attractive to the members outside the United Kingdom and there is a strong case on moral and political grounds for devoting a larger share of the national income to raising living standards, especially in Asia and Africa. On the other hand, it can be argued that it is precisely this kind of effort to do things that Britain is no longer capable of doing that has resulted in the generally precarious balance of payments in the post-war years. When the favourable balance on current account averages only £202 million per annum, and the gold and dollar reserves stand dangerously low, overseas lending cannot be increased without prejudicing national solvency. Even if investment abroad is not increased, larger surpluses than have so far been earned on current account will be needed for several years in order to build a sound reserve position. If the Government decides it wants to, or has to, lend two or three or four hundred million pounds abroad each year, this sum must be earned in addition. The Radcliffe Report has recommended a current surplus on the balance of payments of £450 million a year to meet these needs.[5]

What does this prior condition of economic solvency, the maintenance of a favourable balance of payments, imply for the other aims of policy? It means that no more inflation of prices can be allowed than is proceeding at the same time in the economies of comparable industrial competitors, unless Britain is prepared to devalue the £ sterling from time to time. It is possible to maintain that a flexible exchange rate would enable the reconciliation of rising internal prices with a favourable balance of payments, but this cannot be accepted as a real alternative. It is difficult to see how such a policy could be fitted into the existing

[4] Balance of Payments White Papers.

[5] Report of the (Radcliffe) Committee on the Working of the Monetary System, August 1959, Cmnd. 827, para. 734.

international currency arrangements. It is even more difficult to see how a speeding up of the process of periodic devaluation could be avoided, since devaluation itself is a force making for inflation. Inflation at home would then proceed faster and faster, and the exchange rate become more and more flexible, downwards. If one could be sure of achieving flexibility both ways, there would be much to be said for it, but it seems all too likely that flexible exchange rates would move in only one direction, downwards.

Given a fixed exchange rate, if the British currency is inflated at a faster rate than the German or the American, or that of other competitors, as it was in the years 1955 to 1957, it becomes harder to sell exports, and more imports tend to be drawn in. The eventual impact on the balance of payments is such that speculation against the £ takes place whenever it is felt that inflation at home is getting out of hand. There are other reasons, of course, why inflation is undesirable. The harmful internal economic and social effects of inflation are well known—the expropriation of recipients of claims fixed in money terms, and the discouragement of effort, initiative, and flexibility. But inflation is also accepted by some sections of the community: some consider that it has helped the organised wage-earners to increase their share in the national income, others that it makes profits easy to earn, losses and bankruptcy rare. For these reasons, although few would openly support inflation, most of the remedies are finally regarded as worse than the disease, and have seldom been pursued beyond the point where they begin to hurt.

It may be that, internally, a mildly rising price level could be allowed; though many authorities, including the Cohen Council,[6] hold that it is essential to achieve absolute stability of prices. But the crucial point is that Britain cannot be solvent while inflation is proceeding faster than in competing countries. If the rest of the world were inflating, this country could allow a measure of inflation without harm to the balance of payments. If prices in the rest of the world are falling Britain cannot stand out as an "island of inflation". Indeed, if the need to ease the process of rebuilding the reserves is brought into the picture, it is possible to argue that for a number of years Britain ought to aim at less inflation than the rest of the world.

[6] Council on Prices, Productivity and Incomes, *First Report* (HMSO), 1958, Ch. IV.

It must be concluded that Britain certainly ought not to allow more inflation than is proceeding in the rest of the world. Without this condition other economic aims cannot be achieved.

SOLVENCY, GROWTH AND THE BALANCE OF PAYMENTS

The increase of productivity is itself one of the best ways in the long run of improving the balance of payments, but in the shorter period the need to avoid exchange difficulties has itself limited the growth of productivity. Because the expansion of industrial production usually needs increased imports, and may not always result in an equivalent increase in exports, it is difficult to maintain a reasonable balance of payments when the economy is growing rapidly, particularly if the available manpower is already fully employed and there is no prospect of increasing the labour force, or redeploying it to greater advantage.

Nevertheless, whatever the short-term difficulties, the ultimate gains from more rapidly increasing productivity present the most practicable approach to the related problems of strengthening the trade balance and at the same time avoiding inflation.

Steps should be taken, however, to ensure that at any given level of consumption there is a stronger inducement to invest than at present. The weakness of the present situation is that in order to stimulate investment it has been necessary to expand consumption greatly. By the time there is an induced expansion of investment, there is a tendency for the economy to become overloaded, endangering the balance of payments, giving rise to inflation and so leading to a check to expansion. That is what happened in 1955 and may well prove to have happened again in 1960.

Various measures were suggested earlier in this report, which were designed to make manufacturers more fully aware of the real cost of labour and, conversely, of the benefits of investment which will save labour. These measures are intended to secure an increased incentive to invest, and a greater disposition to get rid of surplus labour at a given level of consumption. The greater investment and the greater willingness to dispense with labour would provide the basis on which a more rapid rate of general expansion of the economy could take place without building up inflationary pressures by running into labour shortages so quickly. It would also not be necessary first to stimulate consumption in order to induce investment. Also, the greater productivity secured would improve the competitive position in relation to both imports and exports, with favourable effects on the balance of payments.

The structural aspect of the problem of reconciling a higher rate of growth with a favourable balance of payments has received considerable attention in recent years.[7] Following a favourable trend in world trade, Britain has come to rely heavily on the products of the metal and engineering industries to provide its exports. By 1958 some 56 per cent of British exports were in this category, and the greater part of the increase in the volume of exports over that of pre-war years was derived from these industries. But British industry relies largely on these same industries to provide for the replacement and expansion of its own capital. The need for greater exports from the metal-using industries, and for increased capital formation at home, can only be met by expanding the capacity of these industries. Economic growth can be reconciled with the maintenance of the satisfactory balance of payments only if the structure of the economy is constantly adapted and oriented towards exports. It must be recognised that British industry has already succeeded in adapting itself considerably to the need to pay for post-war imports almost entirely by physical exports instead of relying so heavily as in 1938 on income from overseas investments. The economic facts point, however, to a need for further effort in this direction.

Apart from all the doubts with regard to the adequacy of investment in Britain during the past few years, the distribution of investment is also open to criticism. Increased investment in the consumer goods industries is not beneficial if it takes place at the expense of investment in the investment goods industries themselves, including transport, particularly since it is recognised that the export of consumer goods by the metal and engineering industries is not capable of indefinite expansion. Comparison of British investment in manufacturing industry with the West German record since 1950[8] shows a heavier concentration by the Germans on the basic metal and engineering investment goods industries, and relatively less investment in consumer goods

[7] See, for example, R. Nurkse, "The Relation between Home Investment and External Balance in the Light of British Experience 1945–1955", *Review of Economics and Statistics*, Vol. XXXVIII, No. 2, May 1956.

[8] See Dr. T. Barna, "The Trend in Manufacturing Investment", *FBI Review*, October 1957.

industries. This may be related to their happier balance of payments history. Within a given total of gross investment in Britain more can be devoted to the investment goods industries only if a smaller share goes to the consumer goods industries. The share of public investment cannot be reduced because several sectors have already been starved of capital and need larger investments for many years ahead. Reduced capital expenditure in the consumer goods industries requires, not necessarily a cut, but certainly some restraint of increases of consumption of these goods.

The need to restrain consumption

The consumer is frequently blamed for economic troubles, on the grounds that "if only we would live within our income" all would be well. In recent years the popularity of theories of economic growth has made restraint of consumption in order to build for the future a well-understood element in a developing economy. If the underdeveloped countries can effect a cut in their abysmally low standards of living, in order to increase investment, surely Britain can impose on itself some measure of restraint in the increase of personal consumption so as to achieve a more rapid rise in the standard of living. Economic growth is cumulative, at compound rates of interest, and striking results are possible with the outlay of comparatively little effort for a wealthy nation with a low rate of population increase.

If the view is accepted that Government expenditure on defence and on the welfare services has been no more than necessary in view of the special priority given to these items, and that investment, both public and private, has certainly not been excessive, then the implication of the chronic excess of total demand is that consumers' expenditure, restrained though it may have been, has yet taken too high a proportion of the national income. It is clear that supplying the means to provide for defence and the Welfare State, and to attain a sufficient rate of investment, without overburdening the economy, involves further restraint in consumption. In the last war Britain succeeded in diverting resources from consumption to a far greater extent than would be needed to solve the peacetime economic problem, but in war many things are practicable that would not be tolerated in time of peace. Perhaps the principal characteristic of a time of war is the existence of an aim which enlists the enthusiasm of the whole population, and the re-creation of some part of this sense of purpose may be an essential ingredient of a peacetime economic policy that involves some immediate sacrifices or restraints.

Successive Governments have exhorted the people to save more, or to work harder, or to keep down wage claims and price increases, until everyone is weary of entreaty. A positive inducement was contained in Mr. Butler's "Invest in Success" slogan of 1954, but the promise of a doubling of the standard of living in twenty-five years was open to many interpretations, and rather far removed from the current aspirations of the individual. Plans for national superannuation would link present sacrifices specifically to real security in old age: the present savings under the scheme would provide funds for investment which would create the wealth needed to pay out the pensions in the future. However, most people discount the future so heavily that a hope of early benefit is probably needed. The diversion of a larger share of the annual increments in production to other purposes than personal consumption is likely to be achieved only if a clear promise can be made of benefits accruing in the form of increased personal consumption just a few years ahead.

Given sensible use, and timing, of the various measures available to the Government, it should be possible to check consumption rather than investment programmes if, in fact, the balance of payments problems recur. There is no objection to an increase in short-term interest rates as an immediate measure to safeguard the reserves. There is, however, great objection to increases in the long-term rate of interest and a cutting back of investment programmes as a means of dealing with exchange difficulties such as occurred in 1957. If the economy is overreaching itself, there are much more sensitive measures possible on the side of consumption. For example, an increase in hire purchase deposits, or other changes in the terms of hire purchase, works very quickly An alternative policy, which was suggested by the Coalition Government's White Paper on Employment Policy in 1944, is to increase the social service contribution by individuals. This policy might be more appropriate in the future, when contributions are to be proportionate to earnings, than it has been while contributions have been levied as an absolute amount. Fresh consideration might therefore be given to it. It is true that such an increase in contributions might stimulate wage claims. But it would probably not do so to the same extent as increases in purchase taxes, which increase the cost of living. Variations in the national insurance contributions would be a clear and direct way of dealing with a problem of too much consumption, and if the need for this could be well established in the public mind, it would at least be some time before the check to consumption was offset by higher wages. One advantage from the point of view of public opinion is that the extra contribution would be a form of compulsory saving and not a simple tax. The eventual pension of the individual would be increased according to his own extra contribution.

THE NEED FOR A NATIONAL WAGES POLICY

One condition of all policies which involve some sacrifice of consumption is that they should not be immediately offset by demands for compensatory wage increases. In conditions of full employment the trade unions have generally been able to secure wage increases to compensate for any deterioration in the purchasing power of their members' gross wages, whether deriving from taxes on income, from taxes on purchases, or from price increases, while for their part businessmen have been able to put up prices to cover increased costs, and profits have generally remained easy to earn. The Government has never had full control over the economy in terms of diverting purchasing power from consumers into investment or into improving the export balance.

Wages and prices have also shown themselves capable of rising independently of excess demand. Wages have risen not only because of the competing demands of firms for workers, and to compensate for price increases, but also in some industries on the grounds of productivity increases, in others in order to keep in step with these productivity inspired increases. To some extent they have risen because the wage bargaining system has developed a momentum of its own.

Full employment is an aim that should not take absolute precedence over the balance of payments and keeping British prices in line with prices in the rest of the world. It is questionable how far it should take precedence over economic growth. Yet the maintenance of full employment has affected the balance of payments, price stability, and the choice between consumption now and investment for the future. The problems that would arise were foreseen by Lord Beveridge in *Full Employment in a Free Society*,[9] where he endorsed the view that if complete freedom of wage bargaining by individual unions continued in a fully employed economy there would be a continuous upward pressure on money wage rates. In peacetime this problem might become chronic. He produced two suggestions for dealing with it. The first was that organised labour should evolve suitable machinery for a co-ordinated wages policy that would allow the claims of individual unions to be related to the economic situation. Secondly, he suggested the use of compulsory arbitration. Despite the widespread desire for a centralised national wages policy not only on the side of employers and the Government but among some leaders of the trade union movement, no such policy has come near to being achieved, except perhaps in the period of wage restraint under Sir Stafford Cripps. Arbitration, though it has probably helped to reduce industrial strife, has also come to be widely distrusted on both sides of industry. The employers complain that it tends to become an automatic mechanism whereby the unions always get a substantial proportion of what they first ask for, on the principle of finding the average position between their unrealistic initial demand, and the employers' unacceptable offer. The unions are alarmed by the way in which the Government appears to be able to influence decisions by pressing arbitrators to bear in mind the national interest.

The policy of the Government in the period from 1955 to 1958 was understood to mean a measure of disinflation which would reduce the pressure of demand and make it harder to obtain increases of prices or wages. It gave rise to keen discussion of technical questions about the effectiveness of changes in interest rates and credit restrictions.[10] The policy also encountered strong practical objections. It was argued that the effects of such deflation may at first be as harmful to the economy as the preceding inflation and that the anti-inflationary measures since 1955 have contributed to the slowing down of the rate of growth of industrial production. For at least three years while the Government pursued restrictive credit policies industrial output rose very little. What started as an attack on demand inflation continued as an

[9] (Allen and Unwin,) 1944.

[10] See the report of the (Radcliffe) Committee on the Working of the Monetary System.

attack on wage inflation into a period when several industries already had excess capacity. It was argued that deflation, by reducing the utilisation of capital equipment, and by encouraging short-time working and restrictive practices in industry, drove costs and prices up and not down.

However, the main doubts about the policy of deflation were felt by the unions. Deflation, whether or not it results in some increase in unemployment, must have the result of checking the power which the trade unions have enjoyed throughout a period of full employment if it is to succeed in stopping the rise in costs. In support of these policies, it was argued that they not only made it harder for workers to get wage increases, but also harder for businessmen to make profits, and, in general, prevented rises in costs from whatever source they derived. On the other hand the unions maintained that the policy of refusing to finance wage increases in those parts of the economy in which the Government is itself an employer threatened to destroy the whole structure of collective bargaining. As regards wage negotiations within private industry, the unions said that the Government incited the employers to a downright refusal to negotiate on any wage demand, a policy that could only lead to industrial strife. Some people took the view that no Government could allow its policy to be dictated by a particular interest group in the economy. The opposing point of view regarded the position of the unions as given data for the formulation of economic policy. Was there, in fact, any alternative policy that could cure inflation with the help, and not in the teeth, of the unions? This question is still important, despite the period of recession in 1958 and 1959, for it appears all too likely that the country will face again in the 1960's similar difficulties to those experienced in the years 1955 to 1958.

Much has been written and said since the war on the need for a national wages policy, yet none has ever come within the range of practical politics. Unions are as jealous of their freedom in wage bargaining as they are eager to see planning in the rest of the economy. A positive programme, based on the co-operation of employers, workers and Government, working towards not only a solution of problems but a real advance in economic and social welfare, is far more attractive than a negative "holding-the-ring" to contain potentially disruptive forces. But have such resounding proposals ever really got beyond the stage of ideals that will not stand up in face of the sacrifices that must go with them? Lord Cohen replied to critics of his Council's First Report:

> To those, then, who criticise our recommendations, we would say this: tell us how you would do it, and tell us in some detail. It is not enough vaguely to adumbrate alternative policies, using big portmanteau words like planning, or a national wages policy. We had to give our views on policies which are practicable here and now, in this country, not in some model economy from which all institutional difficulties and political intransigences have been removed. If you do not like the policies we commend, how would you stop the rise in prices?[11]

It is clear that, however difficult it may be, attempts must be continued to arrive at wages policies that are in the national interest. In this connection it is worthwhile to examine what is involved in such an aim. Mr. Harold Wilson explained the conditions on which the unions might agree to wage restraint in a series of articles in the *Manchester Guardian* in October 1957:[12]

> For a Labour Government, no less than for the Conservatives, success or failure in the battle against inflation would depend on its ability to secure an understanding with the Unions which would make wage restraint possible. In advance of the discussions which would be necessary it is impossible to lay down the kind of conditions required. But some or all of the following would need to be considered:
>
> (1) The unions and their members would need to be satisfied that a national system of planning and control—physical, budgetary and financial—would ensure that their contribution would not be lost through wasteful expenditure, capital or otherwise; they would have to be satisfied, too, that their future was safeguarded by an adequate rate of investment in industry;
>
> (2) They would need to be satisfied that the Government will play its full part in dealing with inflation and keep prices steady—an effective "plateau" policy. This may mean temporary price controls (whether voluntary or statutory), as well as rent controls and stiff action against monopolies;
>
> (3) Another requirement would be a socially just Budget. This by no means requires higher rates of tax; what is needed is a widening

[11] Lord Cohen speaking to a discussion group of London University economists, 27 March 1958.

[12] Harold Wilson, "Remedies for Inflation, III—What Labour would do", *Manchester Guardian*, 25 October 1957.

of the tax-base by attacking fiscal privilege—business expenses and perks, covenants and other avoidance devices—and ensuring that a substantial proportion of capital gains accrued to the community.

Mr. Wilson's demand for an adequate rate of investment in industry is in line with the conclusions of Chapter 3 of this report, and may be accepted without any difficulty. The other part of this first point, the need for more planning and co-ordination of investment, follows from the failure so far to reconcile economic growth with solvency. A great deal of co-ordination goes on already, through the Treasury and other departments for the public sector, and by the use of various economic controls and incentives for the private sector. No one wants a wide range of physical controls and targets, so what this suggestion amounts to is that there is room for improvement in the control of investment. Monetary policy encourages investment in those parts of the economy that can most easily find the funds, and pay the interest charges; that is, in the most profitable. Unfortunately these are not always the developments that will most strengthen the economy and help in the struggle towards solvency. There are great difficulties in deciding what would be the best distribution of investment, and many practical problems in bringing it about. This matter is discussed in Chapter 10.

The action proposed on prices is quite a fair requirement if wages are to be restrained, providing it is borne in mind that prices should reflect real costs and that flexibility should be maintained so that the economy can be adapted to changing circumstances. A price "plateau" may keep prices up, as well as down. There must always be room for price adjustments to correct, or prevent, wasteful distortions in the economy. Temporary controls or subsidies to offset the inflationary effects of a rise in import prices may be justified, so long as they are not allowed to become permanent. Alternatively, wages might be allowed to compensate for increases in costs of imports. A rise in import prices would lead to a rise in home prices, but some upward movement in British wage costs could be absorbed in a context of rising world prices. It could well be desirable to agree, as part of any wage policy, to a sliding scale relating wages to movements in the cost of living. This would be quite apart from any regular advance in wages to match the expected increase in national productivity. It may be better to let money incomes move in line with changes in the price level, rather than to anchor the price level in the hope of also anchoring money wages. Either policy would accord with Mr. Wilson's thesis that real wage levels should not be undermined by general price movements.

The attacking of fiscal privilege and the taxing of capital gains would secure sacrifices to match those of the workers. The economic effect would be small, and the psychological effect probably more important. Tax avoidance devices are encouraged by high rates of taxation. Though they are already subject to scrutiny by the Inland Revenue there is probably room for more severity.

The issue of a capital gains tax raises a more difficult problem. Where capital gains are the reflection of a general change in money values, there seems no reason to tax such adjustment in capital values. On the other hand there is a strong case for taxing capital gains where these involve the translation into income of a tax-free capital gain if this practice is significant in scale. The minority report to the Commission on Taxation advocated a capital gains tax with a reduction of other taxes on capital, notably the profits tax. It may well be that a re-thinking of the whole question of the appropriate taxation of capital might lead to a solution which would on the one hand give full encouragement to the creation of further wealth by investment, and, at the same time, would ensure that the community through taxation gets a fair share of this wealth.

A national wages policy would seem to involve a number of essential elements. First, provision for the maintenance of real wages even though there are changes in the cost of living. Second, provision for a general advance in real incomes of between 2 and 3 per cent a year in line with the productivity increase expected in the economy as a whole. Third, provision for flexibility in the wage system to allow for changes to reflect the reasonable rewards for special skill or to attract labour into new or expanding occupations.

Attempts have been made in other countries to regulate wage increases in the national interest, but it cannot be said that these have been widely successful in preventing inflation. Moreover, these countries have been able to make experiments with national wages policies because they already enjoyed a trade union structure better adapted to such a central determination of wages than that which exists in Britain. Given the present organisation and attitudes of trade unions in Britain, there is little hope at present of even the introduction, let alone the success, of a national wages policy.

In fact, economic policy in this respect is restricted by the political and social realities, and only when these have been altered is there any hope of pursuing the best economic policies. Meanwhile, it will be necessary to continue to rely on the use of fiscal and monetary policy and sometimes physical controls to keep the economy in balance and to prevent inflationary price increases. If these policies are carefully explained they may be assisted by varying degrees of co-operation from the different interests that are responsible for determining costs and prices.

There would be great gains to the population from an economic policy which combined a high level of employment and a high rate of growth, and therefore of real wages, as compared with a policy which endeavoured to moderate wage movements by the restriction of demand and the creation of unemployment. The difficulties of securing a wages policy which is genuinely favourable to the workers, as well as to the country generally, are undoubtedly very great and they certainly cannot be overcome quickly. Nevertheless, the gain would be so great that it should not be beyond the powers of a country with the political and economic experience of the United Kingdom to work towards a solution along the lines suggested.

CHAPTER 9

SOME INTERNATIONAL COMPARISONS

THE international comparisons in this chapter are taken from Western Germany and France, preceded by a brief note about the United States. Comparisons of particular features of these economies have already been made in various chapters. The aim now is to present a more systematic account of differences in economic conditions, organisation and policy and to bring out more clearly some of the conclusions for Britain.

THE UNITED STATES

The almost mesmeric attraction which the United States exerts over British and Continental economists probably derives in no small part from the superior wealth of that country. Some broad comparisons of the differences between the level of the national product and the growth of the national product in the present century in the United States and other countries, are set out in pages 27–31 of Chapter 2. But if the more immediately relevant facts of the post-war growth of the American economy are considered, the example of the United States appears to be not so significant as that of other countries. In the 1950's the gross national product per head in the United States grew no faster than that in the United Kingdom, and it is much more important to understand why the gross national product per head in the United Kingdom grew so much more slowly than it did in the OEEC countries as a whole, and in Western Germany and France in particular.[1] For most of the post-war period the superiority of the American economy has been taken for granted in Western Europe, but the apparent ending of the dollar shortage and even the novel experience of a weakness of the dollar on international exchange markets mean that this superiority may now be questioned. There is still no doubt that the American economy is far wealthier than that of any of the Western European countries. This greater wealth can be explained, as has been done in Chapter 2, by a variety of historical factors and, particularly, in the

[1] See Chapter 2, p. 31, Table 4.

present century by the less unfavourable effects on the American economy of the two world wars.

In looking for the reasons for the superior performance of the American economy, in the past at least, it is probable that observers in Britain have tended too much to be influenced by the best examples in American practice and have assumed that the American average was much nearer to the best than in fact it is. Misleading impressions can easily be given by the reports of productivity teams which, naturally enough, bring back a description of the best rather than submit a balanced appraisal. Perhaps the main drawback, however, to making comparisons with the United States is that the reasons for United States superiority appear to be so much the result of history, and therefore inevitable, that practical remedies for British inferiority are not easily envisaged. For example, the different social values in the United States, which have contributed so much to the country's economic progress, are primarily the result of abundant land and resources and of a hundred years of free immigration from every part of the world. How then can Britain hope to emulate this kind of social pattern which leads to economic growth?

Britain could of course copy much in detail from the United States. The educational system could be adapted to provide people well suited to become industrial managers, as the American educational system is so well designed to do. British experts can bring back a lot of useful information about American management techniques and their application, and the example of the profitable use of these techniques in the United States can be used as propaganda for their further extension in this country. British engineers in many industries have much to learn from American technology. In all these ways, American experience can give very real assistance to the British economy. But at the same time, it is likely that the really significant lessons for economic policy come not from the United States, but from countries in Western Europe whose economic problems are much nearer to our own.

WESTERN GERMANY

The economy of the German Federal Republic appeared to be so much more successful than that of the United Kingdom in the 1950's that comparison of German experience with British is inevitable when explanations are sought for the relatively slow growth of the British economy. It may be that in many ways Germany's economic experience since the war is not so comparable with that of Britain as is often assumed, and that many of the so-called "lessons" that have been derived from the German "miracle" have been greatly exaggerated. Even if this is so, however, the fact remains that Germany is the industrial nation most directly comparable with Britain and some of its economic experiences may have lessons to offer.

The West German economy is almost exactly the same size as the British: at the end of 1958 the West German population, including the Saar, was 51,453,000 against 51,870,000 in the United Kingdom.[2] The shares of the main sectors of the economy in the value of total output are very similar, and it can be seen from the table below that the two economies were even more alike in structure in 1955 than they had been before the war. The chief difference is that Germany still had a larger agriculture in relation to the size of industry than the United Kingdom.

TABLE 26

THE STRUCTURE OF THE BRITISH AND GERMAN ECONOMIES

(Commodity sectors as a percentage of total commodity output)

		Agriculture	*Mining and Quarrying*	*Manu-facturing*	*Electricity, Gas and Water*	*Construc-tion*
		%	%	%	%	%
United Kingdom	1937	9·3	8·9	63·7	2·5	15·6
	1949	11·2	6·9	66·9	3·8	11·2
	1955	9·6	5·6	70·6	4·3	9·9
Western Germany	1936	21·8	6·5*	60·1	2·4*	9·2
	1950	19·3	6·2*	60·7	4·1*	9·7
	1955	14·6	5·1*	66·1	4·3*	9·9

Source: ECE, *Economic Survey of Europe in 1956*, March 1957, Chapter VII, p. 13, Table 7.

* Estimate by ECE Secretariat

Between 1950 and 1958 industrial production in Western Germany increased by 111 per cent. In the United Kingdom in the same period it increased by only 21 per cent. For some years it was possible to assume that the Germans were still making up

[2] OEEC, *General Statistics*, 1959, No. 5, September, p. 48.

for the loss of output in the 1940's, but soon even the comparison with 1938 became unfavourable for the United Kingdom. It was still possible to excuse Britain's relatively slow expansion of output by reference to the rapid increase in the West German population in the 1950's. But estimates published by the Economic Commission for Europe in 1957[3] suggested that compared with pre-war years the United Kingdom and Western Germany by 1955 stood at about the same position as regards output per head in industry. German industrial productivity, which in 1950 had been well below the pre-war level, had by 1955 not only regained the pre-war level but had also caught up with the productivity increase in Britain. More recent estimates[4] have shown that after 1955 German industrial productivity went ahead rapidly each year, while British productivity showed little change, at least until 1959. Rough estimates on the basis of these figures suggest that in 1958 German industrial productivity was 50 per cent higher than it was before the war, while British industrial productivity was still little over 20 per cent above the pre-war level. It is true that in 1958 there was excess capacity in many industries in the United Kingdom, so that the year is not perhaps a very fair one for comparison. Even if allowance is made for this, however, and the potential British productivity, rather than the actual, for 1958 is used for the purposes of this comparison, Western Germany would still appear to have improved much more on its pre-war level of output per head than the United Kingdom. It probably did not matter that German productivity should have been rising much faster than the British between 1950 and 1955, if Germany was then merely making good more severe wartime and post-war losses. But the faster rise of German productivity after 1955 must be accounted a serious reflection on the British economy. The superiority of the German economy showed itself not only in a faster and continuing rise in productivity, but also in an important result of this—a growing strength in the balance of payments and freedom from foreign exchange crises.

In what respects has Western German experience since the war not been comparable with that of the United Kingdom? Apart from military occupation by the victorious powers the Germans

[3] ECE, *Economic Survey of Europe in 1956*, March 1957, Chapter VII, p. 18, Table 9.

[4] See Chapter 2, p. 32, Table 5.

had three great disadvantages in contrast with the United Kingdom. First, they had a vast number of refugees who had to be housed and fed and found employment. Second, their cities and their industry had been devastated. Third, their currency had become worthless and such production and trade as continued was carried on largely on the basis of barter.

Each of these disadvantages was to be transformed into an aid to economic growth and stability in the 1950's. The continuing flow of refugees became an important asset by its role in keeping down the pressure of wage demands, and delaying the emergence of a state of full employment such as was experienced most of the time in the rest of Western Europe. In rebuilding the industrial plants that had been destroyed the opportunity was taken to install the best and most up-to-date equipment. The discredited currency was replaced by a strong new currency, and, more important, by a determination at all costs to maintain the value of this new currency. One advantage which the Germans derived from their total defeat was with them from the beginning: they had no defence effort comparable with that which the British Government has undertaken since the war, though they paid occupation costs and in later years growing defence expenditures.

The policies that have combined with these advantages to produce the German recovery may be analysed under three heads: the currency reform and subsequent monetary policies, the provision of incentives to work and production, and the special encouragement of savings, capital investment, and exports. In addition the Government was aided by one outside factor of major importance: the restraint and moderation exercised by the trade union movement.

The social market economy

The philosophy of the "social market economy" has been at the centre of the German economic achievement, playing the major part in the expansion of production and in the maintenance of price stability. The emphasis has been placed on production first, and only afterwards on consumption. Nice questions about the distribution of the national product have not been allowed to distract attention from the drive towards economic recovery and expansion. As Dr. Erhard, the Federal Minister of Economics, has written:

> . . . how much more sensible it is to concentrate all available energies on increasing the nation's wealth rather than to squabble over the distribution of this wealth, and thus be side-tracked from the fruitful path of increasing the national income. It is considerably easier to allow everyone a larger slice out of a bigger cake than to gain anything by discussing the division of a smaller cake.[5]

In 1950 private consumption took 64 per cent of the national product, as compared with only 60 per cent in 1936. But by 1955 this proportion had been reduced to only 58 per cent. These proportions may be compared with the British: 76 per cent in 1938, 71 per cent in 1950, 67 per cent in 1955, and 65 per cent in 1957 and 1958.[6] The share of personal consumption in the national product had been reduced in the United Kingdom as in Western Germany from the pre-war level, and one of the achievements of the years 1955 to 1958 in the United Kingdom was to reduce its share by a further 2 per cent. Yet it was still taking, in 1958, a considerably higher proportion of the national product than in Germany. The low claim of personal consumption on resources enabled the Germans to keep up a high rate of investment, and to increase exports, without inflation.

TABLE 27

USE OF THE GERMAN NATIONAL PRODUCT

(Percentage of gross national product at market prices)

	1936	1950	1955	1957	1958
Private consumption . . .	60	64	58	59	58
Public consumption	21	15	14	13	13
Gross domestic fixed capital formation	14	19	23	22	22
Gross national product at market prices	100	100	100	100	100

Source: OEEC, *General Statistics*, 1959, No. 4, July, p. 102.

Public expenditure in Germany was also taking a progressively smaller share of total resources. The reduction in this figure from

[5] Ludwig Erhard, *Prosperity through Competition* (Thames and Hudson), 1958, pp. 3–4.

[6] OEEC, *General Statistics*, 1959, No. 4, July. The percentages for the United Kingdom have also been taken from the OEEC *General Statistics* in order that they shall be on a basis which is comparable with the percentages for Germany. There are, therefore, discrepancies between the percentages calculated on this basis and those calculated for the United Kingdom from *National Income and Expenditure* in Chapter 6.

21 per cent in 1936 to 15 per cent in 1950 reflects the absence of defence spending, though Germany did have to bear the burden of occupation costs in respect of Allied forces maintained on German soil. After 1950, the gradual expansion of Germany's own defence forces was offset by the reduction of occupation costs, so that in real terms defence expenditure of both types remained at the 1950 level. Thus, as the national product rose in the 1950's, the proportion going to defence fell, from 5 per cent in 1950 to only 3 per cent in 1958. Public expenditure for civil purposes took about the same proportion of the national product in 1957 as it had in 1950, 10 per cent, so that the net effect was that total Government expenditure took a declining share of the resources available each year between 1950 and 1957.

The restoration of incentives to work and production was a central feature of the moves to bring about economic recovery in 1948, and such incentives have continued to play a large part in the German economy. Dr. Lutz has asserted that "... it was the restoration of incentives which was responsible for the sudden rebirth of economic activity on the part of both business and labour", and that the series of tax reforms represented "... a gradual approach to a system of incentive taxation designed to stimulate work and enterprise, investment and savings".[7]

Price stability

In the fight for the stability of their currency the Germans were undoubtedly aided by the inflow of labour from the East. The total labour force in Western Germany rose from 21,700,000 in 1950 to 25,300,000 in 1957, an increase of 17 per cent in seven years. Some of these extra workers came from the gradual absorption of the unemployed, who numbered over one-and-a-half million in 1950. But the majority were immigrants from the East, and may therefore be counted a special advantage to the West German Government in preventing inflation. As B. C. Roberts commented:

> The refugees were at first looked upon as an economic burden, but they have, in fact, proved to be a tremendous windfall, enabling an investment boom to continue at an extraordinary pace without producing an inflation. Instead of the rising demand for labour

[7] F. A. Lutz, "Germany's Economic Resurgence", *Lloyds Bank Review*, January 1956, p. 18.

leading to wage increases which exceeded the rise in output, the pressure in the labour market was reduced by the continuous increase in the supply of workers.[8]

Nevertheless, as Dr. Erhard made clear in his account of German economic policies, the Germans did have to fight inflation, particularly in later years when the flow of labour from the East slowed down, and when unemployment had already been reduced to a low level. It is clear that in this struggle the Germans were aided by the determination to succeed born out of their earlier disastrous experiences of inflation. As Dr. Erhard expressed it:

> The Germans are perhaps more concerned about the success of these endeavours than anyone else. Within a single generation they experienced two periods of inflation that were more or less unprecedented in the economic history of the world.[9]

If a large part of the German "miracle" may be accounted for by sound economic policies pursued by the Government, it is also true that a vital part was played by the unions. Organised labour at least acquiesced in policies that paid little attention to fair shares and went all out to create a thriving capitalist economy. German exporters were aided by a progressively favourable development of their costs relatively to those of their competitors, due to the fact that in Germany wages did not advance much faster than productivity. Wage costs per unit of output rose by only 7 per cent between 1953 and 1958, whereas in the United Kingdom they rose by 26 per cent.[10] The German index of consumer prices, based on 1953=100, rose by 8 per cent between 1950 and 1951 and then remained virtually stationary till 1954. Between 1954 and 1958 it rose slowly by a further 10 per cent. This stability in prices may be contrasted with that in Britain, where the index of prices of consumer goods and services based on 1953=100 rose by 23 per cent between 1950 and 1953, and by a further 19 per cent between 1953 and 1958.[11]

That the German economic achievement did not cease with the

[8] B. C. Roberts, *National Wages Policy in War and Peace* (Allen and Unwin), 1958, p. 137.
[9] Ludwig Erhard, op. cit., p. xi.
[10] ECE, *Economic Survey of Europe in* 1958, Appendix A.8, Table VII.
[11] OEEC, *General Statistics*, 1959, No. 5, September, p. 104.

onset of problems of full employment similar to those that have faced other European countries is shown in more recent reports on the state of the German economy. For example, the following phrases in the opening paragraph of the OEEC 1957 report on *Economic Conditions in the Federal Republic of Germany*[12] read strangely to British ears accustomed to hearing a very different story. They are a useful indication of the continuing strength of the German economy.

> Throughout the past eighteen months the German authorities have been faced with growing export demand and increased consumers' expenditure The measures adopted to increase imports have not prevented a substantial increase in the foreign surplus.

Prices have since been rising more rapidly than productivity, and the growth of Government expenditure on defence and on the social services contributed to a change from budget surpluses to inflationary budget deficits. Yet the export position remained strong—in 1957 and 1958 exports continued to rise faster than imports—so that the export surplus was still the chief inflationary influence, and it was possible to cure the internal tendencies to inflation by measures that would reduce the surplus of exports.

Economic growth and strength is not necessarily the same thing as the material welfare of the mass of the people. Did the Germans sacrifice the interests of the consumer in the process of making their economy the strongest in Europe? The policy of seeking economic expansion at the expense of social reform certainly made everyone better off. The share of consumption in the national product may be low, but it was a much larger absolute amount than in 1950, or even 1936. Taxation policy and other measures may have biased the economy in favour of the rich rather than of the poor, but in so doing they made the poor much better off, and gave them better chances of further advancement than they would have had in an economy with a lower rate of investment and economic growth. Moreover, the social services have not been neglected in post-war Germany. The German housing shortage was much more acute than that of the United Kingdom, and more houses were regarded as vital for the mobility of labour. Over 500,000 houses were built per annum, compared with around 300,000 a year in recent years in Britain

[12] P. 5.

for a population of the same size. Other social services were also expanded.

Towards the end of the 1950's there were signs of increasing standards of consumption, in addition to the expansion of the social services. But this was consumption that could well be afforded. Any inflationary pressure resulting from it could be offset by measures to reduce the export surplus. The expansion of the social services, especially the extensive pensions scheme, meant that the more needy sections of the community were being put before the majority of moderately prosperous workers. The Germans may have appeared to sacrifice considerations of social justice in favour of a free-for-all capitalist economy, but their more paternalist economic policies may yet result in more real social justice, as well as a larger national income to share out, than has been achieved in Britain.

FRANCE

In the five years from 1953 to 1958 industrial production in France increased by roughly 10 per cent each year; investment increased both in absolute terms and as a proportion of the national product, and the French economy was the last in Europe to show signs of a recession of demand. In 1956 and 1957 the growth of output in France was much faster than in the United States or the United Kingdom, and probably slightly faster than that of Western Germany. The increase in production was achieved without any significant increase in the total civilian labour force, which means that higher productivity was chiefly responsible for the expansion of output. The French, like the West German, economy was a striking contrast with the semi-stagnation of the United Kingdom.

It should be noted that while the West German economy is similar to the British in area, population and industrial structure, the French economy is in many respects very different. The land area of France is almost twice that of Britain or Western Germany, and in 1957 26 per cent of the occupied population worked on the land, against only 4 per cent of the labour force in the United Kingdom.[13] On the other hand, manufacturing industry is less developed than in the United Kingdom or Germany.

[13] ECE, *Economic Survey of Europe in 1958*, Appendix A.10, Table VIII.

Between 1950 and 1953 industrial production stagnated, but after 1953 it advanced at a very rapid pace. Between 1953 and 1958 industrial production (mining, manufacturing and public utilities) rose by 54 per cent. The index runs as follows (1953=100)—1954: 110; 1955: 120; 1956: 133; 1957: 145; 1958: 154.[14] The increase was still running at about 10 per cent per annum up to the middle of 1958.

Explanations of the rise in output

This increase in production was achieved with a labour force that did not expand very rapidly. Additions to the labour force in the 1950's reflected the low birth-rate of the war and of the immediate pre-war years. On this restricted labour force, the military call-up made increasing demands. Nevertheless, there was some increase in the total man-hours of labour available. Immigration, particularly of Italians, assisted some industries, though France did not benefit from an inflow of foreign labour to anything like the extent that Western Germany did. Internal migration from the land into industry also allowed the industrial labour force to be expanded somewhat without any increase in the total labour force. With 26 per cent of France's population still employed in agriculture (in 1957) and limited scope for exporting agricultural surpluses, there is room for much more movement of labour from the land into industry, and this should make a significant contribution to the increase of industrial manpower in the future. As industrial production increased, the labour shortage was also solved to some extent by drawing women and retired workers into employment. In addition, the effectiveness of the increased labour force was improved by a steady rise in the number of hours worked per week. This was offset to some degree by the introduction of a third week's holiday with pay, but one hour's extra work per week is the equivalent of an extra week's holiday each year. The drawing of unemployed workers into employment was not an important factor, as it was in Germany, but, although the French statistics have usually shown France to have about the lowest rate of unemployment in Western Europe, there was not a chronic excess of vacancies over unemployed such as was experienced in Britain.

In all these relatively small ways the French were able to achieve

[14] Ibid., Appendix A.8, Table VII.

some addition to the number of man-hours worked per year in order to sustain their booming production. Yet the chief explanation of the rise in production has still to be sought in factors other than the expansion of the labour force. Two other explanations are possible: more effective use of the existing capital equipment, that is, a rise in the productivity of both labour and capital, and an expansion of the stock of capital equipment, that is, a rapid rate of investment.

French investment in the years after the war was more centrally planned than British investment. The State had to take over much more of the financing of private investment in the absence of sufficient small savings, and played a more important role in many industries, though whether investment was, as a result, greater than if the State had not played such a large part, is not entirely clear. The Monnet Plan for Modernisation was the first of three plans on which post-war investment policy was based. It concentrated upon the basic industries; fuel and power, transport, steel, cement, and agricultural equipment. It was successful in that by 1950 the supply of these basic goods and services had caught up with the demand. Indeed, there was some over-investment so that for example the engineering industries did not absorb all the capacity for steel making until 1955—which explains part of the increase in output that was achieved after 1953. The second plan covered the years 1952 to 1957, and switched attention to manufacturing industry, housing, and agriculture. The actual production targets set in this plan have been achieved with remarkable accuracy. For agriculture, an increase of 20 per cent was planned for 1957 over 1952: an increase of 18 per cent was achieved despite a series of bad harvests. For industrial production the target was 25–30 per cent increase: in fact 35 per cent was achieved. Investment increased by precisely the planned amount, 35 per cent. Real investment at constant prices increased by 38 per cent between 1954 and 1958, and its share of the national product rose from 16·2 per cent to 18·5 per cent.[15]

The French economic achievement after 1953 was therefore considerable but, before one can proceed to draw conclusions for British economic policy, it is necessary to mention a number of factors that, by putting this advance of production and investment in perspective, considerably reduce its impressiveness. The rise

[15] OEEC, *General Statistics*, 1959, No. 4, July, p. 101.

was from an extremely low level. The boom after 1953 was preceded by a period of relative stagnation between 1950 and 1953. This applies particularly to the boom in investment. Although investment in 1956 was taking a larger share of the national product than in 1953, it had only just recovered the same proportion as in 1949. During the years of stagnation investment suffered more than production as a whole and afterwards it was catching up. Looking even further back it should be noted that France had no stimulus to production in the war as so many other countries had, and that, of the inter-war years, 1929 was the year of peak industrial production. In fact, between 1929 and 1938 industrial production fell by 25 per cent. The first Monnet Plan for Modernisation was intended not only to repair war damage and to make up for the arrears of wartime, but also to catch up on the arrears of the 1930's. Looked at in this light, the rapid progress made after 1953 is not really remarkable, but only a belated attempt to recover from the economic failings of the past thirty years.

The following indices show the development of industrial production and of agricultural production from 1929 to 1958. They emphasise the importance of the spurt in industrial production since 1953, which can be seen to relieve an otherwise sad picture of stagnation since 1929.

The rapid increase of production after 1953 was to some extent achieved by making fuller use of the capacity already available in 1953. This was obviously a once-for-all aid to higher production and productivity, arising out of the previous stagnation, and therefore could not help the economy indefinitely. The capacity of French industry was stretched to the limit in the drive to increase output, and the fuller utilisation of capacity was an important explanation of the remarkable rise in productivity despite all the disadvantages of a labour force that was increasing only slowly. The interpretation of statistics of utilisation or capacity is doubtful, but together with other indications these statistics show that much of the rise in production was obtained by more intensive use of the existing industrial machinery and equipment. The stagnation of the French economy from 1950 to 1953, though it was accompanied by a fall in the rate of investment, left excess capacity which afterwards helped to make possible the extremely rapid rise in industrial production.

TABLE 28

FRENCH INDUSTRIAL AND AGRICULTURAL PRODUCTION, 1929–58

	Industrial production including building 1952=100	*Industrial production excluding building* 1952=100	*Agricultural production* 1934–38=100
1929 . .	92	86	103
1937 . .	76*	75*	96*
1938 . .	69	69	105
1949 . .	84	83	98
1950 . .	88	88	108
1951 . .	99	99	103
1952 . .	100	100	108
1953 . .	101	101	116
1954 . .	110	111	125
1955 . .	119	121	124
1956 . .	130	134	115
1957 . .	141	146	122
1958 . .	147	152	n.a.

Source: Ministére des Finances, Statistiques et Etudes Financiers, *Quatriéme Rapport du Fonds de Développement Économique et Social*, April 1959.

* 1937 figures taken from *Troisiéme Rapport*, February 1958.

The bid for industrial efficiency

In another sense also the French economy in the mid-1950's was "living on its fat". Up to 1955 the industrial expansion was, as in the United Kingdom, combined with an improvement in the balance of payments which actually provided a small positive balance of overseas payments in that year. The British inflationary and balance of payments crisis of 1955 was met by measures which, while ameliorating the immediate payments problem, had the effect of holding back production. The French on the other hand pursued the path of internal expansion at the expense of the balance of payments. Table 29 sets out the balance of exports and imports in the years 1951 to 1958.

TABLE 29

THE FRENCH EXPORT/IMPORT BALANCE IN 1951 TO 1958

(000 million of francs (old))

	Imports c.i.f.	*Exports f.o.b.*	*Percentage cover (Exports/imports)*
1951 . .	1,560	1,429	92
1952 . .	1,514	1,339	88
1953 . .	1,380	1,324	96
1954 . .	1,477	1,463	99
1955 . .	1,659	1,719	104
1956 . .	1,945	1,589	82
1957 . .	2,248	1,869	83
1958 . .	2,354	2,150	91

Source: United Nations, *Monthly Bulletin of Statistics*, May 1959, p. 116.

Inflation at home, caused by the high level of demand arising out of the industrial expansion superimposed on the burden of the Algerian war, brought French prices increasingly out of line with prices in other countries. Exports were discouraged, despite a variety of subsidies, and imports were attracted in increasing quantities to supply goods that the hard-pressed home economy needed. Some special factors, such as the bad harvests, contributed to this decline in the external position, but the insistence on industrial expansion was the chief cause. The gold and foreign exchange reserves, and to some extent France's borrowing powers abroad, were treated as a strategic reserve to back a bold throw for a dynamic and expanding economy. Of course in 1957 the pressure became too great and notice had to be taken of the payments crisis to the extent, in effect, of the devaluation of the franc, which helped to bring French prices back into line with prices in other countries and improved the balance of exports and imports in 1958. Further economic reforms followed the political changes of 1958. In explaining the reasons for their payments crisis to the Organisation for European Economic Co-operation in July 1957 the French Government[16] blamed: the burden of the large number of young people under working age; the large contribution to underdeveloped areas; and the need to "create an industrial potential to assure for France its competitive position

[16] Quoted in the *Financial Times*, 16 July 1957.

in the world". M. Ramadier, then Finance Minister, admitted in March 1957 that he had deliberately used the foreign exchange reserves in order to keep the expansion of output going, hoping for a reversal of the unfavourable factors. He stressed the importance of maintaining the expansion of production.

There is little doubt that the inception of the European Economic Community had a considerable influence in leading the French Government to give industrial expansion and modernisation priority over the short-term problem of the balance of payments. If France was to be opened to competition from its European neighbours, and forced to remove import restrictions and export subsidies, it was essential that every effort at industrial expansion and modernisation should be made so as to bring French costs nearer into line with those of competitors. It is ironic that this effort to prepare for the inception of the Common Market provisions was partly responsible for the withdrawal of trade liberalisation measures taken already under the auspices of OEEC.

Another factor which made the expansion and modernisation of industry in France of urgent importance was the prospect of a much larger intake of young workers each year in the 1960's. With the end of the war and the payment of generous family allowances as a measure of deliberate demographic policy, the French birth-rate in the late 1940's and the 1950's was much higher than in the 1930's and during the war. From 1961 onwards these larger generations of young people will be coming into industry, and it was essential that a greater industrial capacity should be built up to provide employment for them. Although this presented a problem to the French economy, at the same time it also offered a great opportunity, and the 1960's could be a period of great economic progress. The number of young people reaching the age of sixteen will rise from its lowest ebb of under 500,000 in 1957, reflecting the year of lowest number of births in 1941, to almost 600,000 in 1961, almost 800,000 in 1962, and over 800,000 in the years 1963 to 1966. The annual recruitment to the working age groups will remain over 750,000 to the end of the 1960's.[17] This improvement in the French labour situation is in marked contrast to an unfavourable demographic movement

[17] These estimates are based on the number of live births shown in the United Nations Demographic Year Books.

which is already affecting Western Germany. The number of young people reaching the age of sixteen has already fallen in Germany in the late 1950's and will reach its lowest ebb in 1961, reflecting the year of lowest birth-rate, 1945. There will be some recovery after 1961, but throughout the 1960's the annual additions to the population of working age will remain considerably lower than they have been in the 1950's.

The French ability to continue a policy of expansion much longer than the United Kingdom was able to do after 1955 is partly explained by the fact that France is in several ways less open to outside influences than the United Kingdom. The French currency is not so widely used in international trade: France is not so dependent as is the United Kingdom on imports for food and raw materials. In 1957 French imports amounted to 13 per cent of the gross national product: in the same year in the United Kingdom imports represented 21 per cent of the national product. And the French have a tradition of Government intervention and restrictive policies which make it easier than it is in the United Kingdom to impose import restrictions in case of need.

A fundamental problem of the French economy, which the recent expansion was attempting to solve, is the inefficiency of its industries compared with those of its competitors in Western Europe. This problem derives particularly from the small scale of French industry. In a wide range of manufacturing industries French firms are on the average smaller than their competitors in Western Germany or the United Kingdom. The OEEC Engineering Report revealed the following picture for the engineering industries of France, Western Germany, and the United Kingdom:

TABLE 30

NUMBER OF ESTABLISHMENTS

	Total number of establishments	of which:	*Number with 10–49 workers*	*Number with more than 1,000 workers*
France, 1956 . .	12,087*		8,750†	161
Western Germany, 1955	11,855*		6,821	362
United Kingdom, 1955	11,839		5,848	568

Source: OEEC, *The Engineering Industries in Europe*, May 1958, pp. 265, 266 and 275.

* Excluding establishments employing fewer than 10 workers.

† Number with 11–50 workers.

Therefore there is probably considerable scope in France for the development of larger and more efficient units.

Taxation is often made a scapegoat for the shortcomings of industry but in this case it does seem to have encouraged and accentuated the small size of firms in French manufacturing industry. The tax system has given special concessions to farmers and craftsmen. Moreover, tax evasion is easier in small firms and is in fact widespread. Altogether, therefore, small-scale operation is profitable from the tax point of view, even though it may be less efficient. Concessions and evasion erode so much of direct taxes that they contribute less than one-fifth of the total revenue. So four-fifths of the total revenue has to be obtained from indirect taxes, which bear heavily on particular products and require more concessions. The prevalence of import restrictions and export subsidies also served to enable French industry to operate in a protected market which gave no strong incentives to the formation of larger and more efficient units. Reforms set in motion since the inception of the Fifth Republic in 1958 have the aim of letting in many of the fresh breezes of competition to revive French industry.

CONCLUSION

Both Western Germany and France enjoyed in the 1950's a more rapid and a more continuous growth of production and of productivity than the United Kingdom. Yet they did so for very different reasons. The German example might be held to point to the need for more liberal economic policies in Britain and more decisive monetary measures when necessary to curb inflation. The French example, on the contrary, might be held to show that the United Kingdom should in future pay more attention to the planning of investment, and take more risks with the balance of payments in the interests of expanding production. But it really makes little sense to attempt any general conclusion as to which example this country might follow. The value of these international comparisons lies in the light which they throw on particular aspects of economic problems and policies.

These comparisons are perhaps most revealing on the subject of manpower. The West Germans enjoyed a great influx of labour, most of it young and able-bodied. This influx of labour clearly prevented such strong pressures towards inflation as were experienced in Britain after the war. The French achieved rapid increases in production without such an increase in the labour force. But they enjoyed changes in the structure of the economy and particularly a movement of workers from agriculture, which can be a substitute for an increase in the working population in providing more labour for industry. This is an aspect of the French policy of making labour dear and so driving it out of low output uses. Britain, with a more mature economy, and agriculture already employing only 4 per cent of the total occupied population, cannot easily compensate for an almost stationary working population by such large transfers of workers into the expanding industries. The lesson for this country is clear. The Government must give a high priority to measures which will encourage the release of workers in some industries and their rapid absorption by industries which must have more labour. This involves encouraging industrial research into labour-saving methods, expanding educational facilities for scientists and technologists, and assisting in the organisation of schemes for compensation for loss of employment which encourage the taking-up of new employment and overcome obstacles to movement between jobs, such as difficulty over housing, the cost of removal and the problem of re-training.

The effects of the radically different manpower situations in the three countries have been underlined by differences in the structure and strength of trade unions. Partly as a result of the high level of unemployment in Western Germany in the late 1940's and early 1950's, and partly from historical causes, trade unions in Western Germany were both weaker and more restrained in their demands than British unions. The rapid growth of production itself tended to maintain this moderation, and in any case a rapid rise in wages could be afforded without producing inflation when production was also rising rapidly. The widespread fear of inflation in all sections of German opinion also played a part in this moderation of wage claims and other union demands. In addition German trade union law, although it recognises the rights of unions, also circumscribes them more closely than do the parallel laws in the United Kingdom. In France the trade union movement was weakened by its tripartite division between Communist, Socialist and Catholic unions. The British trade union movement is by no means so monolithic as is sometimes feared by its opponents, but it is much stronger and has a greater freedom of action and more power to influence the course of the economy than the trade unions of France or Western Germany. The conclusion from this contrast is not that the trade union movement in this country should be weakened or its powers more closely limited, but that it needs to be more closely associated with the other organs of government and power in the attainment of the national economic objectives of full employment, price stability, a healthy balance of payments and last but not least, economic growth.

The significance and influence of the balance of international payments has varied considerably between Western Germany, France and the United Kingdom in the 1950's. In Western Germany it presented no problem, or rather the pleasant problem of surplus, and not the crisis that often results from deficit. This favourable situation arose from the great export potential of a country with rapidly rising production and an easy labour market. The French balance of payments problem was as chronic as the British. Nevertheless, imports are much less important in the French economy than they are in the British and France is considerably less susceptible to outside influences from its overseas financial and trading network than is the United Kingdom. This enabled the French to ignore mounting payments crises for quite a long period, and to press on with the expansion of production in a way which would have been quite impossible for the United Kingdom, given the greater dependence in this country on overseas trade and the network of British financial interests overseas. Up to 1955 the general development of the French economy was very similar to that of Britain. In both countries a period of relative stagnation of production was followed, after 1953, by an expansion of output. For two years this expansion was accompanied in both countries by a favourable development of the external balance and produced no great internal inflation. But in 1955 it became apparent in both Britain and France that resources were coming under severe pressure and that any further increase in demand would only lead to rising prices at home and increasing deficits in the balance of trade and payments. In these circumstances the British Government pursued policies that had the effect of curtailing the expansion of output in order to bring the inflation under control and to safeguard the foreign exchange reserves.

This policy was not carried out without considerable difficulty and certainly not without controversy, but it warded off the payments crisis at the expense of preventing any further increase of production. The French Government was able to pursue a bolder and more risky policy, deliberately sacrificing the foreign exchange reserves for the sake of expansion. As a result of a more orthodox approach to the financial crisis, productivity in Britain did not rise between 1955 and 1958. In France, on the contrary, productivity rose rapidly as industry squeezed the last unit of output out of plants already running at full capacity, and with little regard to the effect on the balance of payments. In 1958, of course, the French came to the point where this process could go on no longer and measures to correct the imbalance of payments were obligatory, and then production in both countries was affected by the general recession of economic activity. But the stagnation of industrial production in the United Kingdom in 1956, 1957 and 1958, while French industrial output was still expanding at a rate of about 10 per cent per annum, meant that in Britain resources were unemployed. Since capital investment continued to rise despite the stagnation of output, British industry by 1958, even before the effects of the recession were felt, was operating well below capacity. On the other hand, French industry was still operating full-out, and although this may not have been a particularly desirable condition or one that could be indefinitely prolonged, it did mean that productivity both of labour and of capital was able to be increased very rapidly.

What then are the lessons for Britain in the balance of payments histories of Western Germany and France? Obviously the best solution to Britain's problem is to organise the economy so as to obtain an export surplus as the Germans did. But this is easier said than done, and Germany had many advantages over Britain in achieving its export surplus. If it should prove impossible in the next few years to achieve an export surplus, should Britain turn to the French example and subordinate considerations of the balance of payments to the interests of economic growth? It would be foolish to take a simple comparison of rates of productivity increase as sufficient evidence in itself that Britain has pursued the wrong policies and the French have pursued the right policies in the last few years. A rapid increase of productivity was long overdue for the French and extremely urgent in view of their desire to enter the European Economic Community, and they still have a long way to go to bring their industry up to the levels of efficiency and competitiveness of British and West German industry. Their success in attaining this belated increase in production must be qualified by counting the cost of the sacrifice of price stability and a sound balance of payments. Whether the French did in fact make the most judicious choice among the economic possibilities that were open both to them and to this country in 1955 is a matter of some controversy. The Organisation for European Economic Co-operation has certainly been of the opinion that the effort to push the expansion of production beyond the limits of the available resources was bound to result in crisis and to lead to lower output in the long run. This view, that any attempt to give expansion priority over strengthening a weak balance of payments is bound to be self-defeating, is questionable in view of the British experience that safeguarding the value of the currency and the overseas balance has required the stagnation of output for three years.

In fact, however, Britain just could not have done what the French did after 1955 because of susceptibility to outside influences, and if possible Britain should certainly seek to provide more room for manoeuvre in meeting economic fluctuations by reducing the impact on the home economy of overseas events. This immunity could be achieved by having an export surplus based on greater efficiency at home or by measures which will limit any British role in overseas financial and capital transactions, which leaves the economy more at the mercy of overseas events. It is sometimes pointed out, for example, that the exports of capital from the United Kingdom in the 1950's have been, in fact, as great as the foreign surplus which the West Germans have earned in the same period. The crisis of the autumn of 1957 is, of course, the prime post-war example of internal restrictions as the result of a balance of payments crisis which was largely of overseas origin. The ability to limit British commitments overseas has been examined in Chapter 7, pages 172–81, where the conclusion was that the scope for reducing commitments is limited. But economic policy is often a matter not so much of radical and immediate changes as of gradually influencing the course of future events over a long period, and it would certainly be wise to assess very carefully the implications of future overseas commitments.

It is on the subject of economic planning that the comparisons with Western Germany and France are most contradictory at first sight. It would be incorrect to assume that Western Germany relied entirely on the advantages of a free economy for its economic recovery. The social market economy, though not in any sense a planned economy, is one with a clear direction laid down by the State in the way of monetary policy and incentives to savings, investment and exports. With fully employed resources, the French laid down a series of plans for investment and economic growth, and this "dirigiste" method of running the economy was as successful as the German social market economy, judging by the results since 1953. Perhaps the lesson for Britain is that either the German or the French method could have been more successful than the rather aimless economic policies which were in fact pursued in this country. The question is of sufficient importance to be treated separately in a chapter of its own. Chapter 10 discusses the planning of investment in the United Kingdom, and pages 220–22 in particular refer to French methods.

CHAPTER 10

PLANNING FOR ECONOMIC GROWTH

THE evidence of preceding chapters suggests that one explanation for the failure of the British economy to grow as fast as that of other countries may be that it has not been organised to do so. In the language of Chapter 8, economic growth has appeared to come low in the order of priorities: at various times the maintenance of full employment, the avoidance of inflation, and the averting of crises in foreign payments, have received greater emphasis in the formulation of policy. It would be difficult to deny that such priorities have often been the right ones, given the circumstances of the time when they were applied, but too little attention has, perhaps, been paid to the long-term aim of achieving and maintaining a high level of investment, and to the other measures that might be necessary to ensure that such investment could be effective. The desire for expansion has, of course, influenced policies, but it has not been allowed to exert the systematic pressure on decisions that it would have done if the Government had been committed to a national objective for economic growth.

INVESTMENT PLANNING IN FRANCE

It is sometimes suggested, therefore, that what Britain needs is a system of investment plans similar to those adopted in France since the second world war. The first of these plans covered the four years up to 1950, and its objectives were not only to make good the destruction of the war but also to regain the ground that had been lost by the French economy after 1929. This plan did not attempt detailed regulation of investment throughout the economy, but concentrated on the basic resources of coal, electricity, steel, cement, agricultural machinery and transport. The second plan covered the years 1952 to 1957, and switched attention to manufacturing industry, housing, and agriculture. The targets for output which it established were achieved with a remarkable degree of accuracy. A third plan has been adopted which covers the years up to 1961.

The key organisation in the post-war planning of investment in France has been the *Commissariat du Plan de Modernisation et d'Equipement*, first appointed, with M. Monnet as *Commissaire General*, in January 1946, with the limited aim of producing a reconstruction plan for the years 1946 to 1950. The *Commissaire General* was the delegate of the *President du Conseil* (Prime Minister), and as such had power to obtain the co-operation of the various ministries involved. The plan was drawn up during 1946 with the help of eighteen Modernisation Commissions, composed of civil servants, industrialists, trade unionists and experts. The Commissariat was then given permanent status and made responsible for seeing that the plan was put into effect, drawing up annual programmes within the framework of the long-term programme. It was not given powers equal to those of the normal departments, but it was to work through the other departments, bringing to the notice of the Government any factors that might prevent the implementation of the plan. The officials responsible for carrying out the plan were to take important decisions only in agreement with the Commissariat and after a joint study of the problems.

Perhaps the most important aspect of the arrangements was that the planning of investments was removed from the confusion of current politics, and the desire for economic development was allowed to assert itself. The plans have indeed had to compete with other calls on resources, and some compromises have been accepted; but there has always been a powerful representative of the long-term needs of the economy to ensure that they were not neglected under the pressure of more urgent short-term considerations.

It should be noted that the plan was not in any sense total and systematic: the Commissariat itself has never had a large staff. It has operated by working through existing institutions, and not by usurping their functions. This has enabled a high degree of flexibility to be combined with a firm general intention. The plans have been adapted as necessary to meet changing circumstances from year to year, but at the same time the final objective has been maintained.

For nationalised industries the plan was obligatory. Once it had been approved by the *Conseil du Plan* it became an order to the departments concerned. They had, of course, played a large part in drawing up the plan which they now had to carry out. In the private sector the method was for the State to enter into contracts and arrangements with firms, who agreed to carry out their part of the plan in return for allocation of the necessary materials and finance. For industries widely dispersed throughout the whole country, such as agriculture and building, these contracts were arranged through regional organisations. The State had no power to force the plan on private industry, but it did have considerable influence, in the early stages, through these allocations of materials, and later through the provision of finance. Representatives of private industry had themselves been partly responsible for drawing up the plan and this may have facilitated its acceptance.

When the Monnet Plan was first published in 1946, *The Economist* saw lessons for Britain in the French experiment. On 14 December 1946 it commented as follows:

> It is the first time that a democratic state has ever given itself a set of authoritative signposts to guide its economic policy making. Several times, in the course of the exposition, Britain is held up to the French reader as an example to be copied. But the British reader will find himself wishing that his country had as comprehensive a guide to follow over the next few years.

Comparing the Modernisation Commissions with the British Working Parties, *The Economist* pointed out that the Modernisation Commissions

> . . . were given a definite part to play in forming a consistent policy to embrace all of them. The parts consequently fit together into a whole, and M. Monnet has an industrial policy where Sir Stafford Cripps will have, at best, only a collection of unrelated expedients.

CENTRAL PLANNING OF INVESTMENT IN BRITAIN

In one sense economic planning in Britain is much more centralised than in other Western nations: the Treasury is the only department concerned with broad national economic and financial policies. Whereas other countries have their Minister for Economic Affairs as well as their Finance Minister, in the United Kingdom these two functions are performed under one roof in Great George Street. Only for a few months in 1947 was there a Ministry for Economic Affairs, but this lapsed when Sir Stafford

Cripps succeeded Dr. Dalton as Chancellor in November 1947, and took his Economic Affairs staff over to the Treasury with him. But despite this centralisation, the degree of planning and co-ordination of investment has in fact probably been less than in France. The Treasury has never been a super-Ministry in any positive sense, just as, at the political level, the Chancellor is only a member, albeit a powerful member, of a Cabinet who are collectively responsible for all decisions.

The British system of economic planning has been described by Professor Beer in his *Treasury Control*.[1] He begins by noting the recognition after the war of the need for a greater degree of co-ordination of policy than had existed before the war:

> Above all, if the shape of the economy, of its future structure as well as its present operations of production and distribution, are to be controlled by governmental decisions, a single centre with the power to direct and command in accord with a unified and consistent system of plans may well seem indispensable.[2]

But such a strong centralist solution was not adopted, partly perhaps because public opinion was opposed to much regimentation, but also because of the nature of British government and administration, particularly the system of "cabinet democracy". No super-minister was able to emerge as a supreme arbiter of investment plans. In this respect even Sir Stafford Cripps does not appear to have been in a very strong position. The initiative in investment planning, even in the nationalised industries, has always been taken by each industry, with more or less intervention by the relevant Minister. The boards of nationalised industries are statutorily required to accept directions from the Minister about reorganisation or development plans, but the Minister only acts after consultation with the Board, Commission or Authority in each case. In private industry, the "sponsoring" department has been able occasionally to exercise some influence on investment plans, but again the chief initiative lies in the hands of the industry, or the firms, themselves.

How are the decisions of the individual departments co-ordinated? The answer is, by the traditional system of Treasury control. Investment planning in Britain has been absorbed into the

[1] S. H. Beer, *Treasury Control* (Clarendon Press), 1956. See especially Chapter 3.
[2] Ibid., p. 75.

method whereby the Treasury controls expenditure of all kinds. In the autumn each department concerned with investment forwards to the Treasury its estimates, and these are subject to review. But the Treasury has never exercised the same degree of control over investment as over supply. Nationalised industries have sufficient financial freedom to make them more independent of Treasury control than any supply department can hope to be.[3] Professor Beer has also pointed this out:

> . . . one might at certain times have found real similarities between the annual review of estimates of expenditure and the review of investment programmes or of import programmes. On the other hand, while the Treasury has kept in frequent touch with the economic activities of departments, there are no procedures in the realm of economic co-ordination comparable to those flowing from the requirement of prior approval. With regard to such activities, indeed, the Treasury has at no time had that complete control which it traditionally has enjoyed over activities with a financial aspect.

In any case

> . . . the Treasury does not itself commonly take the initiative, dictating to departments what they shall undertake in order to fulfil government policy or plans. Rather it shapes the initiative already taken by departments, by a criticism which is mainly negative bringing that initiative into accord with policy.[4]

This negative aspect of the Treasury's part in investment as in financial planning implies that the total of the individual plans submitted by the Ministries is too great for the resources available, and therefore the plans have to be pruned. But the Treasury has no power to institute or increase investment schemes where these are not forthcoming or are inadequate. Possibly in an inflationary period pruning has been the most relevant form of control by the Treasury, although it still begs the question of co-ordination. Some principles must guide the Treasury in applying priorities when making the necessary cuts in the plans put forward by the departments. In Beer's view, the plans submitted by the individual departments are reviewed by the Treasury in the light of priorities laid down by the Government. But how is the Government guided in determining these priorities, and by whom? Beer

[3] See S. Please, "Government Control of the Capital Expenditure of the Nationalised Industries", *Public Administration*, Spring 1955.

[4] Op. cit., p. 77.

appears to be referring only to priorities determined in the light of inflationary situations and shortages of materials, and not by any long-term plan for investment. Despite recent developments, there is little published evidence that any co-ordinated view is taken of a future more than a year or so ahead.[5]

The only real Treasury control, and therefore the only real co-ordination of long-term investment policy, takes place at the time when the boards of nationalised industries submit their long-term investment programmes, which are subject to a three-cornered discussion between the industry, the sponsoring ministry, and the Treasury.[6]

One of the principles of British planning has been that the persons responsible for carrying out decisions to invest should be involved in the making of those decisions, on the ground that there is then much more likelihood of decisions being satisfactorily implemented. While this is a sound principle it is necessary to safeguard against the danger that investment policy may then be determined according to which industry has the strongest advocates. Mr. D. N. Chester[7] has suggested that Professor Beer may perhaps be too sympathetic to the existing method of Treasury control which operates very much on the basis of close contact between a relatively limited number of important people who do some of their best work informally. Chester goes on to observe:

> . . . what he is in effect saying is that given the present kind of economic policy and planning the Treasury is the best home for it because it so resembles the traditional Treasury job, or, alternatively, having placed economic co-ordination in the Treasury this is the kind of approach and arrangement that fits so readily the Treasury pattern.[8]

This is really as much as to say that there is little long-term investment planning in Britain.

The nationalised industries

In comparing the British arrangements for co-ordinating investment with those in France it is interesting to note that much of

[5] A notable exception is the steel industry, where not only the investment and production targets, but also the economic reasoning that lies behind them, are published. See below.

[6] See *Report from the Select Committee on Nationalised Industries*, Minutes of Evidence taken in February 1957 (HMSO), October 1957.

[7] D. N. Chester, "The Treasury, 1956", *Public Administration*, Spring 1957.

[8] Ibid., p. 17.

the French plans was concerned with organising investment in industries the British counterparts of which are nationalised, and nationalisation might have been expected to do for them what the plans did for France. But the experience of investment planning in the British nationalised industries does not suggest that it has succeeded in this respect.

The discussion now moves on from the general statements of the preceding paragraphs to some more specific comments on two of these industries: transport and fuel and power. These will be followed by some further comments on the desirability, or otherwise, of extending some form of planning to cover a larger part of private industry and by some brief comments on the manner in which investment is planned in the iron and steel industry.

The traffic problems of road and rail are closely related. On one hand, road congestion creates serious difficulties for road transport, and deprives road users of the quality of service a road system is capable of providing, and, on the other hand, the decline in rail freight traffics aggravates financial crises on the railways and deprives the remaining rail freight traffics of the lower costs they would enjoy if the system were being more fully utilised. Yet investment planning goes on largely as though the two sectors were isolated and independent, instead of part-complementary and part-competing transport industries. The road programme is for four years, the railway modernisation plan for fifteen. Road investment is being belatedly undertaken in order to catch up with a volume of road transport far in excess of the capacity of existing roads, and current plans cater for only a fraction of the leeway yet to be made up. Rail investment, also undertaken belatedly, is designed to reverse the trend of falling traffics and to provide internal economies which will help to reduce the annual deficits and eventually eliminate them. But if traffic continues to decline, and road transport expands still further at the expense of existing levels of rail traffic, it is possible that the new installations and equipment will not be utilised sufficiently to yield these economies.

The rapid expansion of road transport has been achieved despite a considerable burden of taxation. In the financial year ended March 1959 total receipts from the motor fuel tax were £294 million and receipts from vehicle and licence duties totalled £105 million. If the estimated receipt of £165 million from purchase tax on motor vehicles is included, this makes a total burden of taxation on road transport of £564 million in one year.[9] In the year ending 31 March 1958 this total burden of taxation was just over £500 million and expenditure on roads by the central government and by local authorities was estimated at £133 million.[10] Even if the cost of police, hospitals, and other services to the motorist and his victims are added to this total, the burden of taxation on road transport probably outweighs the cost of current public services to it.

The railways make no direct contribution to the national revenue in the way of taxation, and receive no services from the central government except the financing of loans for capital expenditure and, in recent years, loans for covering revenue deficits, which are, however, subject to normal interest payments. Revenues have, however, been depleted by what might be called "payments in kind" instead of taxes. The railways have been operating a policy which has been strongly influenced by recognition of public and "national" obligations, both as regards the level of charges and fares and the maintenance of services, or frequency of services, in areas where they are not commercially justified and may be losing money.

These public obligations have probably constituted a burden on railway operations at least as great as that borne by road transport through taxation. But it is impossible to put a figure on them and one of the first needs is to make them explicit so that they can be estimated as the basis for future planning of transport.

What is certain, however, is that, while the volume of rail freight transport and also the current balances of the British Transport Commission have been deteriorating under the impact of these social burdens and the competition from road transport, a very rapid expansion in the volume of road transport has been taking place in spite of the heavy taxation on the industry. Under these conditions either the distribution of transport which is emerging should be accepted and investment plans adjusted to provide for considerable expansion of road transport and contraction of rail transport, or, if this distribution is not considered to be really economic, a transport policy should be designed which will produce a better allocation. The planning of road and rail

[9] British Road Federation, *Basic Road Statistics 1959*, p. 40.
[10] Ibid., p. 40.

investment should go hand in hand with forecasts of the country's total transport requirements and a conception of the best distribution of transport between road and rail.

The results of some of the modernisation schemes that have already been completed on the railways show that some of the services that have been modernised nevertheless continue to operate at a loss. It is not enough that a modernisation scheme should reduce costs and/or increase revenues. If it is to be fully justified it must also enable the service in question at least to cover its costs. If it cannot, then either the service should be abandoned and alternative road services developed, or a specific subsidy should be provided for that service if there are good grounds for it. The continuation of losses on some of the services which have been modernised is a salutary example of the result of going ahead with a major investment programme without having a clear idea of the relative functions of road and rail services in meeting the transport needs of the country. This is not to say that the present level of investment in the railways is too great. Indeed, one of the most urgent needs is to improve the quality of the services. The money will only be properly spent, however, if it can be concentrated on efficiently providing the services which the railways are best suited to, and not squandered over the maintenance, in the face of keen competition from road services, of services that the roads can more efficiently provide.

Nowhere is there a clearer need to co-ordinate investment policies than in the fuel and power industries, nor is there a better example of the dangers that beset attempts at co-ordination. The allocation of the market among the different forms of energy has never since the war been entirely determined by free market forces, for this has been a period characterised by a scarcity of total energy supplies and also of foreign currencies needed to pay for imported fuel. It is suggested that with the new competition between coal and oil, the time has now come when market forces can at last determine the allocation of the market. But vital decisions about future energy supplies have already been made on the basis of considerations that have little to do with the current commercial position of the different fuels. The programme for nuclear power was based on a long-term forecast of the need for energy in the late 1960's and the 1970's and later this century. It was implemented as a matter of some urgency even though electricity generated in nuclear power stations was not competitive with that generated by modern stations burning coal or oil. It was hoped that atomic power would be competitive in price soon after the first stations in the programme had been completed, but more recent estimates of the cost of nuclear electricity have been less sanguine and fears of a future physical shortage of other kinds of fuel appear to have been exaggerated. In fact, the programme for nuclear power is a good example of what happens when investment is planned on the basis of forecasts that are later falsified by events. It is now too late to reverse entirely the plans drawn up on the basis of forecasts made in the mid-1950's, although they have been revised and construction of new nuclear stations delayed. In these circumstances it is somewhat unfair to insist that the coal industry must accept its fate in a competitive market.

On the other hand, advocates of a planned allocation of the market among the various sources of energy often appear in the position merely of supporting the existing allocation. They do not wish to see a change which will be detrimental to the vested interests of the miners in having a large and prosperous coal industry, and the call for a national fuel policy becomes in some mouths merely a euphemism for the age-old protectionist plea. The country needs a fuel policy, but not one which implies the ossification of the existing structure of fuel and power supplies.

Like the transport industries, the fuel industries are part-competing and part-complementary, and basic to the economy. A completely free commercial solution to the problem of their relative roles in the supply of energy is not feasible because too many considerations that have no connection with the current competitive positions of these industries are involved. Nor can a rational decision about fuel policy be taken on the basis that the existing size of each industry must at all costs be maintained.

Private industry

In the basic nationalised industries consumers' demand is relatively easily forecast,[11] since it usually follows general trends in the economy. But much of the private sector consists of consumer goods industries where the demand is more unpredictable. These industries tend to grow at varying rates in response to the choice

[11] Although even here the difficulties of forecasting are such that investment plans in the coal industry, and in nuclear power, have run into trouble.

exercised by consumers in freely making their purchases, and this freedom of consumers is bound to make future sales of any product somewhat uncertain, and therefore to raise doubts about investment programmes. Further difficulty arises from the variations in overseas demand for British exports. There is no way of avoiding such risks but it is reasonable to say that those who bear them should have the right to determine whether the investment shall be made.

The planning of investment would be facilitated if the Government were to decide what should be produced, and adjust prices in order to ensure that what had been produced could be sold. The Government would have to purchase the planned output of each firm, and dispose of it to the consumer through central marketing agencies. In placing these contracts the Government might make errors of forecasting just as private firms might do. Thus, it might overestimate the demand for a product and stocks might begin to accumulate, but it would then be possible for the central marketing agency to reduce its price and clear the market. The reverse procedure would be followed if supplies were scarce. The crux of the matter is that prices received by producers might be divorced, by means of socialised distribution, from prices paid by consumers. The fact that two different sets of prices were thus employed would allow the decisions of the planners to be insulated in some measure from private preferences, although the planners could try, if they wished, to accommodate their decisions to what they believed those preferences to be. (Russian planning relies on a procedure of this kind.) Thus, the plans of the central authority can be enforced without involving financial embarrassment. But it can be done only at the risk of what may be very serious interference with consumers' preferences. Moreover, the whole procedure may become more difficult even in Russia as real income rises and variety increases. Politically, socialised distribution would clearly not be acceptable in the West.

In the absence of State purchasing, individual producers would be left with the problem how to dispose of their output, and would continue to compete against each other for sales. In this event centralised forecasts of future demand, and the setting of industry-wide objectives for investment, would be of limited value. Many firms already make their own forecasts of the size of the total market for the produce of their industry, and there is no reason to believe that these individual forecasts achieve wildly different results. What is more significant for investment programmes, and for their outcome, is the share of the total market that each firm thinks it will be able to obtain. Examples are not unknown in some industries of individual competing firms making plans that add up to a total production substantially larger than can possibly be sold. For industries where units are small and productive capacity easily switched to other purposes this may not be as wasteful as it sounds, but it does present a barrier to the success of any system of plans for investment.

It seems probable that businessmen, although they may from time to time express a desire for more guidance from the Government in making their investment plans, would yet fail to accept the implications of such guidance. For a purely advisory body would be ineffective in providing the kind of guarantee of the future that firms would like to have. The publication of a national objective for the major industries would have meaning only on two conditions. First, the firms whose plans went to make up this national objective would have had to sort out in advance the problem of shares in the final market; that is, competition as it is at present known in many industries would have to be sacrificed. Secondly, the individual firms would have to commit themselves to carry out the intentions expressed in their contribution to the plan. Such national investment planning would not necessarily mean that the Government would dictate the tasks of each industry, but it would involve the Government acting as arbiter in cases where firms failed to agree or made plans obviously inconsistent with other parts of the objective, and it would involve individual firms giving up their freedom of action once the plan had been completed and published.

In fact, such a proposal appears to be in conflict with the present organisation and ethos of private industry in this country, so that little optimism is possible about its immediate practicability as a means of achieving a rapid and steady increase of investment and production.

The most thorough existing co-ordination of investment in the private sector is to be found in the steel industry. Under State or private ownership, under Labour or Conservative Governments, the industry has been guided in the public interest. A method has been arrived at for achieving five-year plans for investment which aim at harmonising the schemes of individual, and often competing, private firms with the national interest. The national interest has been able to influence the policy of the private firms through the Iron and Steel Board and by discussion with Government departments and particularly with the Treasury.

Steel is fundamental to the economy. It is just as vital to have sufficient steel available to supply a reasonable rate of growth of industrial production over the next decade as it is to have enough electricity, and the order of magnitude of the required increase in the capacity of the industry is comparable with that needed in the electricity industry. By 1962 the capacity of the steel industry is expected to be about 75 per cent larger than it was in 1952. The Iron and Steel Board, to whom powers of supervision were entrusted by the Act of 1953, pointed out in their Special Report, *Development in the Iron and Steel Industry*,[12] in 1957 that capital expenditure on major development schemes during the five years of this second development plan, 1957 to 1962, would amount to roughly twice the £300 million at 1957 prices spent in the preceding five years, representing a rise from about £60 million a year in 1955 to about £120 million a year.

The only possible basis for an investment plan of this kind is a forecast of demand for five years ahead, and the chief factor affecting demand for steel is the general rate of growth of industrial production. It was assumed that industrial production would increase by 3¾ per cent per annum between 1954 and 1962, a rate of growth about equal to that between 1948 and 1956. Higher rates of growth of industrial output were ruled out as involving such a high rate of increase of imports that exports were unlikely to rise sufficiently to prevent a balance of payments deficit.[13]

The Iron and Steel Board planning had an influence on particular schemes as well as on the total rate of expansion. This is illustrated by the Board's emphasis in the 1957 Plan on the need for a fourth wide strip mill by 1962. The industry took a contrary view. Nevertheless the Board was successful in securing the building of a strip mill at Newport scheduled to be in operation

[12] (HMSO), 1957, paras. 199–200.

[13] This was an official Treasury view, and is a good example of the way in which not only current investments, but also longer-term plans, are ruled by the needs of the balance of payments. See the Special Report, 1957, paras. 61–3.

early in 1962, and indeed, with some prompting from the Government, a fifth strip mill is planned to be completed in Scotland at almost the same time. On the negative side the Board turned down a proposal from the Steel Company of Wales to build a sixth strip mill by about the same date on the grounds that this would involve a wasteful expansion of capacity and an overloading of the plant makers, who could to greater advantage be concentrating on other constructional work both for export and for other sections of the steel industry in this country.

These remarks on planning in the steel industry must not, of course, be taken to imply that it constitutes a model which other industries should strive to imitate. Not only may needs and possibilities differ elsewhere but it must be recorded that there has been criticism of the system operated by the Iron and Steel Board, both from those who would like to see more freedom of decision left to the individual firms and from those who object to the influence of the private firms on the planning of future capacity and output. The fact remains that this attempt to plan investment is an interesting one and may contain some lessons for other industries.

Why should the steel industry have such detailed and carefully considered plans for its development while the motor industry and the machine tool industry, for example, have no such plans? The historical, organisational, and political reasons may be plain enough, but the economic reasons for these differences in the determination of investment between one industry and another are not so obvious. Some intervention by the State to plan investment in other private industries would not necessarily be opposed by all private businessmen, and might be preferred to the alternative of periodic credit restrictions and other attacks on investment at times when private and public plans for expenditure, taken together, add up to more than can be accommodated without inflation. At least one industrialist has asked for some national plan or set of objectives within which to organise future development. Sir Ivan Stedeford, Chairman of Tube Investments, in his annual statement in 1957 was reported in *The Economist* as follows:

> Referring to present restrictions on the growth of capital investment in industry, he said that this was a grave step, when there was so much leeway to make up. Ways must be found of according

> industrial capital investment a high national priority like that given to housing after the war. Was it impracticable to give some broad forward assurances on which to plan, such as agriculture received? There was room for a central organisation, which could try to forecast a few years ahead the capital needs of the nation and then issue warnings in good time when plans incompatible with the economy were being shaped by public or private sectors. Something like an advisory national investment committee seemed at least as important as the new advisory body for wages and prices.[14]

What is under discussion here is not the type of detailed controls that were perhaps necessary, but certainly frustrating, in the early post-war years. It is suggested that broad objectives and a plan for investment could, perhaps, help to moderate cyclical fluctuations in investment, while giving it a priority in the economy that it has not enjoyed in the post-war period. Something may be worth attempting on the lines of the French *Plans de Modernisation*, which brought together private interests and the civil servants and gave investment an impetus and a priority that it could not otherwise have achieved, in an economy working under strain.

It is not only in the preparation of investment programmes and production targets in individual industries that a national objective would help to give a priority and an impetus to economic growth such as it could not otherwise attain. Other chapters of this report have revealed examples of policies which operate to discourage growth or at least do nothing positively to encourage it. If all these policies had to be judged against a statement of national objectives stipulating a certain rate of growth, as well as against all the other criteria, such as their effect on the balance of payments or on the political situation, then there is reason to believe that they would tend to be adjusted to promote growth, or at least that the need for growth would have some influence on them. If Britain had had a M. Monnet to complain whenever any policy appeared to be adverse to the expansion of production, the rate of growth might have been somewhat faster than it has been.

It would seem that, whatever may take place inside the Treasury, the plans for the public sector as published do not adequately provide objectives for economic growth. There is little doubt that a more consistent series of published plans covering the public sector would go a long way towards providing private firms

[14] *The Economist*, 16 November 1957, p. 630.

with the kind of assurances they need about the future growth of the economy. It has to be recognised, however, that any proposal for improving the degree of certainty about the future, especially on the need for investment, runs into fundamental difficulties in the private sector as a result of the exercise of free choice by consumers and free competition between producers. Nevertheless, there is no doubt that on the whole the economy would benefit from the Government exercising a more, rather than a less, positive influence over the investment planning of the private sector.

CHAPTER II

CONCLUSIONS

A GENERAL survey of economic problems and policies such as this has been cannot hope to arrive at specific recommendations for policy. Each aspect of the economic problem requires much more detailed consideration than it has been possible to give in the compass of a short report. The aim has been not so much to arrive at conclusions and recommendations as to present a balanced, though necessarily somewhat selective, account of the nature of the British post-war economic problem and of the relevance of policies to it. The following paragraphs should therefore be regarded not as calls for action but as a summary of the areas of policy to which attention should be directed.

1. In view of the low rate of increase of productivity, and the evidence that a relatively low proportion of the national product has been invested, the rate of growth of productivity could be improved by stepping up the amount of investment. The years since 1954 have already seen an improvement over earlier post-war years in this respect, but investment in Britain still does not appear to be in line with that achieved in other countries. If the need for a higher proportion of investment is held in mind there is an opportunity to lift the economy on to a higher plane of investment in the 1960's without repeating the errors of the mid-1950's.

2. It is important that, within the general aim of increasing the level of investment, priority should be given to encouraging labour-saving investments. As the expansion of the economy proceeds in the 1960's it will be limited by renewed shortage of labour before all the surplus industrial capacity built up in the years of high investment since 1955 has been fully utilised. Emphasis on further widening investments would merely aggravate eventually the danger of surplus capacity, and the long-standing shortage of labour and inflationary pressure of the 1950's. Several basic industries whose most urgent task in the 1950's was to expand output by any means possible are now operating in competitive markets where they can only maintain their position by investing in greater efficiency of production. This gives them an oppor-

tunity to release labour for other industries that are still expanding.

3. One of the disadvantages of full employment is that the labour force tends to be inefficiently used. Although the labour supply may be eased in the early 1960's by the larger number of young people leaving school each year, it will still be important to make the best use of the labour force, and this implies that attention must be devoted to increasing the mobility of labour, particularly between declining and expanding industries. Whether work should be taken to the areas with a surplus of labour, as in distribution of industry policy, or whether the emphasis should be placed on inducing workers to move, by providing assistance such as transfer and resettlement grants and by increasing housing in areas of expanding industries, is a matter of some controversy. But, in any case, it will clearly remain essential to achieve the maximum flexibility in the labour force if a high level of investment is to produce the desired improvement in output per head.

4. The special shortage of skilled manpower of all kinds is likely to continue as industry expands, and priority must continue to be given to the programme for technical education. Shortage of teachers is likely to be as great a problem as lack of buildings, and one that cannot so easily be solved just by spending money. The total supply of skilled workers and scientists will only gradually be increased even with a large immediate expansion of the numbers passing through the technical colleges.

5. Apart from the special consideration of the need to expand technical education, it is clear that general education, at all levels, is essential to economic progress. The achievement of higher productivity requires an intelligent and well-educated labour force. Unless the level of education in the schools is also improved, the technical colleges will find their standards falling as they expand in numbers. The expansion of teachers' training colleges has been neglected in the 1950's, despite the fact that an adequate supply of good teachers is probably more important than the building of new schools. Now that school building has at the lower ages at any rate caught up with the "bulge", priority must be given to increasing the supply of teachers, and raising the standard of their training. Social investment is often dismissed as being economically "unproductive", but investment in education, apart altogether from its social value, can also make as great a contribution to production as other forms of investment.

6. In order to achieve the correct distribution of resources between various industries, and, in particular, to prevent wasteful use of capital, pricing policies in the public sector must be designed to reflect the real costs of production wherever possible. In several nationalised industries this need has been overlooked in the drive to increase output, and on other occasions the adoption of realistic policies has been prevented by Government intervention to avoid price increases. Now that investment in efficiency is more essential than investment to increase production in some of these industries, it becomes even more important than in the past that prices should be determined according to correct principles and not on the basis of expediency.

7. A special misdirection of pricing policies is involved in holding down prices to the consumer while industrial prices have had to rise to carry the burden of increasing costs. Discrimination in favour of the consumer aggravates shortages in industry in times of scarcity, and encourages consumption. Since these industries are especially heavy users of capital, the growth of the economy is restricted by the diversion of capital to satisfy the resulting artificially high consumer demand for these products. It also leads to an underpricing of labour and reduces the pressure to increase productivity. The public sector must therefore cease to be so sensitive to consumer hostility to price increases where these are necessary.

8. Prices in the public sector should not include hidden subsidies to particular types of consumers or users. If it is desired to give a special subsidy, for example to maintain uneconomic rail services in rural areas, this should be made explicit and met by a grant from the Treasury. Giving the subsidy in this way will avoid obscuring the true financial position of the nationalised industries, and prevent harmful repercussions on their efficiency and morale. In addition, the fact that the subsidy is brought out into the open will make rational discussion of its purpose and necessity possible.

9. So far as is consistent with other objectives of the taxation system, taxes should be designed so as to minimise the disincentives, and where possible to provide positive incentives, to investment and enterprise. Many taxes are already adjusted for this purpose, and others that are much criticised are in fact used for the purpose of economic control, so that criticism of them, as

taxes, is irrelevant. But sometimes, and especially in the case of death duties, there is room for further action.

10. One particular form of Government expenditure, the provision of social services and insurance, is financed very differently in the United Kingdom from the method employed in other European countries. The majority of the revenue in Britain comes from general taxation, and the direct contributions of employers and employees are only a small proportion of the total expenditure. The employment of labour is in this way made less expensive, and taxes on capital use more, than if most of the revenue were raised from specific charges on employers related to the wage bill. In this way part of the real cost of employing labour is hidden, and the ratio of capital to labour costs weighted in favour of the use of more labour. In view of the need to encourage the use of more capital, and the saving of labour, this method of financing the social services should be reviewed in the light of practice on the Continent.

11. It is essential that in future regard must be had to the economic consequences of any increase in defence spending. Should another international crisis occur, requiring outlays on armaments of the same scale as the Korean war, it will be necessary to ensure that the military strengthening of the country is not counterbalanced, as it was in the early 1950's, by economic weakness resulting in part from the strain of defence expenditure. If consumption can be reduced to an equivalent degree (but only on this condition), then any defence expenditure that is felt to be required cannot be criticised on economic grounds. But if investment or the balance of payments or both are to suffer, the expansion of defence spending needs to be limited. It may be appropriate to cut down investment for a while, if this is done deliberately and with a clear acceptance of the consequences, for military defence has priority over the expansion of the economy. When solvency is threatened, however, extra defence expenditure is of questionable value.

12. Since the contrary has sometimes been maintained in the past, it is necessary to state that there is no evidence that spending on the social services has contributed significantly to Britain's economic problems since the war. Many forms of social service expenditure, and particularly that on education, have a great contribution to make to raising productivity by their role in

maintaining and improving the efficiency of the "human factor of production". Social service capital expenditure should therefore continue to have a high priority, especially in those areas, for instance, hospital building, where it has been neglected.

13. Britain is wealthy enough to maintain an important role in world economic affairs, and a defeatist attitude towards this question is no more permissible than it is towards that of defence spending. Some overseas commitments appear to have survived out of regard for tradition, or for the sake of pure prestige, and their economic value to this country is doubtful. These should obviously be curtailed. There is another category of overseas expenditure which brings no benefits, at least no immediate benefits, to this country: investment in underdeveloped countries. This expenditure has a strong moral claim on the resources of a nation as wealthy as Britain. But help to other countries is self-defeating if it results in the continuing weakness of the home economy. Policies pursued at home must make resources available on a sufficient scale to meet these demands for capital overseas, when this type of commitment is pursued. Capital must not be allowed to go overseas when the outflow results in difficulties with the balance of payments.

14. The export performance of the economy since the war has been considerable, but in view of the failure to build up an adequate reserve of gold and foreign currencies, or to reduce the sterling balances, it must be concluded that exports have been inadequate to meet the demand for foreign exchange. The possibilities of doing something to limit the spending of money overseas are limited, so the solution is to increase exports still further. This will be made possible by increasing Britain's competitive efficiency. The creation of the European Free Trade Association, tariff reductions through the General Agreement on Tariffs and Trade and possibly some form of association with the Common Market, may all increase the competitive forces playing on the British economy.

15. Inflation has so far only been checked by measures of control that have had the effect of halting the expansion of the economy. Often the effect of counter-inflationary policies has been to cut back an already inadequate level of capital investment. In the years since 1955 investment has been well maintained, though not expanded, but production has been checked so that there has

been excess capacity in many industries over several years. In the political and institutional conditions of the 1950's these policies have probably been the only ones available to meet a danger that was immediate. Yet great harm is being done to the economy by the failure to find a solution to the problem of inflation that does not have these unfortunate consequences. An attempt must be made to find a cure for inflation that allows expansion to continue at a satisfactory rate. This is a long-term policy, that should be set in motion at once if it is to have any effect in the foreseeable future.

16. Such a cure for inflation implies radical changes in political and social attitudes, and reforms to the organisation of many economic institutions. Co-operation is required between the Government, employers and the trade unions in a wages policy that will ensure that the annual percentage rise in wages does not exceed the percentage rise in productivity available to pay the increased wages. The prospects of such an agreement in the near future are remote, and it is likely that many years of a gradual evolution of policy in this direction will be needed. But because something is difficult and will take a long time is no reason for not starting to try to do it. Inflation has persisted in the past because of the lack of co-operation between Government, employers and the trade unions, and only a removal of the conflict and of the squabbles of these partners in the economic system can bring about a satisfactory solution.

17. Investment in the public sector must be controlled, and in the private sector guided, according to published programmes for the growth of the most important industries. This will help to correct the relative neglect of long-term aims and the tendency which has been continuous since the war to solve immediate crises by means which can only weaken the economy in the future. People who know where they are going are much more likely to get there. It will give managers and workers a much-needed sense of purpose, and provide a basis for co-operation in industry. It is not enough to state that a certain rate of growth of the national income can and should be achieved over the years ahead. It is necessary to specify what contribution towards this aim is expected at least from each of the major industries.

APPENDIX A

MANPOWER

TABLE A1 shows changes in manpower between mid-1939 and the end of 1948, and between the end of 1948 and the end of 1958. The first comparison is based on the old Ministry of Labour series. The new series from June 1948 covers the working population more comprehensively, and the industry classification is different in some respects. Between 1939 and 1948 the total working population, including the armed forces and the unemployed, rose by less than 600,000, a matter of only 3 per cent. The armed forces took 350,000 more than in 1939, but the total labour force actually engaged in civil employment increased by 1,150,000 through the absorption into employment of over 900,000 of those who had been unemployed in 1939. Thus, the greatest influence on total civil employment was the reduction of unemployment, and not the increase in the total working population. In the period between 1948 and 1958, the picture is very different. Of an increase of 864,000 in the total of civil employment, 806,000 was attributable to an increase in the total working population, and 236,000 to a reduction in the armed forces, offset by an increase of unemployment by 170,000.[1]

The total in civil employment rose by 6 per cent between 1939 and 1948 and by only 4 per cent between 1948 and 1958, but the second part of the table shows how the distribution of civil employment has changed so that some sectors have been able to expand fairly rapidly while others have released labour to them. Nevertheless, between 1948 and 1958, 1,500,000 workers were added to the labour force in the sectors that gained labour and of these 864,000 came from the increase in the total of civil employment and only 643,000 from the sectors which lost labour. The sectors which lost labour over the period 1948–58 were: agriculture, forestry and fishing—304,000; transport and communications—129,000; national and local government services—173,000; and building and contracting—12,000. The sector to

[1] This increase was temporary, and a comparison between 1948 and 1955, for example, would show a rather different picture.

TABLE A1

MANPOWER IN GREAT BRITAIN, 1938–48 : 1948–58

	OLD SERIES				NEW SERIES			
			Change, 1938–48				*Change*, 1948–58	
	Mid-1939 (000's)	*End* 1948 (000's)	*No.* (000's)	%	*End* 1948 (000's)	*End* 1958 (000's)	*No.* (000's)	%
Total working population	19,750	20,327	+577	+3	23,185	23,991	+806	+3
Less Armed forces*	480	826	+346	+72	826	590	−236	+29
Less Unemployed	1,270	348	−922	−73	348	520 †	+172	+50
Equals Total in civil employment	18,000	19,153	+1,153	+6	22,011	22,875	+864	+4
Distribution of civil manpower								
Agriculture, forestry and fishing	950	1,126	+176	+19	1,271	967	−304	−24
Mining and quarrying	873	840	−33	−4	870	845	−25	−3
Building and contracting	1,310	1,357	+47	+4	1,480	1,468	−12	−1
Gas, electricity and water‡	242	279	+37	+15	301	376	+75	+25
Transport and communications§	1,233	1,461	+228	+18	1,803	1,674	−129	−7
Distributive trades	2,887	2,406	−481	−17	2,739	2,965	+226	+8
National and local government service	1,465	2,230	+765	+52	1,470	1,297	−173	−12
Professional, financial and misc. services	2,225	2,110	−115	−5	3,876	4,217	+341	+9
Manufacturing industry	6,815	7,344	+529	+8	8,201	9,066	+865	+10
Distribution of manpower in manufacturing industry								
Chemicals	266	343	+77	+29	433	535	+102	+24
Building materials‖	567	585	+18	+3	—	—	—	—
Metals, engineering and vehicles	2,267	2,908	+641	+28	3,921	4,562	+641	+16
Textiles	798	690	−108	−14	971	854	−117	−12
Clothing	1,005	839	−166	−17	716	633	−83	−12
Food, drink and tobacco	654	642	−12	−2	738	911	+173	+23
Other manufactures	1,258	1,337	+79	+6	1,422	1,571	+149	+10

Sources: Old Series: *Ministry of Labour Gazette*, February 1949. New Series: *Ministry of Labour Gazette*, September 1949 and February 1959.

* Including those on release leave.
† This figure does not include 60,000 workers temporarily stopped.
‡ Figures for the Old Series are "Public Utilities".
§ Figures for Old Series are "Transport and Shipping".
‖ Not given separately in the New Series.

increase its labour force most was manufacturing, which gained 865,000; the distributive trades recovered 226,000 of the workers that they had lost during the war; professional, financial and miscellaneous services gained 341,000; and gas, electricity and water supply gained 75,000. The shifts in employment cannot be regarded as striking. The largest increase was only 25 per cent and several of the changes were largely a restoration of the pre-war manpower in industries that had lost labour during the war.

The third part of the table shows the changes in manpower in the major branches of manufacturing industry. Between 1939 and 1948 textiles and clothing lost labour, while engineering and vehicles and chemicals gained over 700,000 between them. The significant feature of the comparison between 1948 and 1958 is that none of the major manufacturing industries lost labour, although the period does hide some swings in employment, for example, in the textile industry, which gained labour up to 1951 and then lost it rapidly. The fastest growing industries over the period as a whole were chemicals, 24 per cent, and food, drink and tobacco with an increase of 23 per cent, followed by the metals, engineering and vehicles group with an increase of 16 per cent. This group also had the largest increase in terms of numbers, gaining 641,000 workers.

The supply of labour in the post-war period has also been slightly increased by a small rise in hours of work. In 1948 average hours worked each week in all the industries included in the Ministry of Labour Enquiry was 45·3; by April 1955 it had risen to 46·9, and in April 1958 it had fallen back slightly to 46·2. Thus, over the whole period there was a 2 per cent increase in hours of work, and between 1948 and 1955 an increase of 3·5 per cent. The industries where the hours of labour increased most were building and contracting, engineering, ship-building and electrical goods, and transport and communications.

APPENDIX B

UNFILLED VACANCIES

THE statistics for unfilled vacancies are not very reliable indicators even of the existence of the excess demand for labour, for they reflect only very imperfectly the demand for labour in different industries, or in the whole economy, between one year and another. The figures are affected by the various orders regulating labour vacancies in the post-war period, and by different degrees of usage where this has been optional. The general Control of Engagements Order was in force between 1947 and 1950, and the Notification of Vacancies Order between 1952 and 1956, but there was no control in other years since the war. Agriculture and coal mining were at one stage protected from conscription for national service, but this exemption was removed in 1950. There is evidence, for example, that the big rise in the number of unfilled vacancies notified in agriculture in the mid-1950's did not result from any real change in the labour situation in agriculture, but was chiefly the result of a change in the practice as regards notification.

TABLE BI

UNFILLED VACANCIES IN SELECTED INDUSTRY GROUPS AS A PERCENTAGE OF THOSE EMPLOYED

	July 1952	*July* 1955	*July* 1958
Agriculture, forestry and fishing	0·7	2·0	2·3
Treatment of non-metalliferous mining products (excluding coal)	1·5	2·5	0·9
Chemicals and allied trades	1·1	1·7	0·7
Metal manufacturing	1·4	1·6	0·4
Engineering, ship-building and electrical goods	1·8	2·2	0·8
Vehicles	1·8	2·1	0·7
Metal goods, not elsewhere specified	1·4	2·6	0·8
Textiles	1·1	2·2	0·9
Clothing	3·3	4·4	2·0
Food, drink and tobacco	1·0	1·9	0·7
Paper and printing	0·8	1·7	0·7
Building and contracting	2·4	2·9	1·3
Distributive trades	1·7	2·7	1·1

Source: Ministry of Labour Gazette, September 1952, 1955, 1958.

The number of unfilled vacancies in mid-1948 was just under 500,000 or about 2·6 per cent of the number of people in civil employment. The number fell in 1949 and in 1950, but rose again with the renewal of inflation in mid-1951 to over half a million. The disinflationary measures of 1952 reduced the total to 300,000 and reviving demand in the years 1953 to 1955 carried the total back to just below 500,000. Since 1955 the number of vacancies has been falling and in July 1958 there were only just over 200,000, the lowest figure in the whole post-war period. Looking to the distribution of unfilled vacancies between industrial sectors, there are two general conclusions. First, despite the existence of a generally high level of demand for the products of all industries, unfilled vacancies are not spread evenly over all industries. Second, it is not the industries that have been expanding most rapidly that have been most short of labour, but rather industries which have been stagnant or even declining. British industry was very considerably helped by the fact that the industries that had to take the greatest share of the export burden after the war, namely the engineering industries, had already expanded both their capital equipment and their labour force during the war and therefore were well placed in 1945. Other trades which lost labour during the war have had very high levels of unfilled vacancies throughout the post-war period. In 1952, 1955 and 1958 the clothing industry had the highest number of unfilled vacancies, in relation to its existing labour force, followed by building and contracting, and leather, leather goods and fur. The distributive trades suffered a loss of labour during the war, which they have since been making up, and their percentage of unfilled vacancies has been high. The textile industry has had severe shortages, again because it lost labour during the war, and despite the recession of 1952 unfilled vacancies have continued at a high level in relation to the total labour force. In fact, the analysis suggests that the shortage of labour has been most seriously felt in the low wage industries, which is a reasonable indication that the expanding industries have been able to bid up wages sufficiently to attract some labour away from those sectors which have had low productivity.

APPENDIX C

THE NORWEGIAN EXAMPLE

THE following table shows how, in the view of the Norwegian statisticians, the increase of employment has an equally important part to play with the increase in the proportion of net investment, in raising the national product.

TABLE CI

POSSIBLE RATES OF GROWTH OF NATIONAL PRODUCT AND OF NATIONAL PRODUCT PER HEAD*

(Percentage per annum)

Net invest-ment ratio	*Percentage yield on net investment* (1) *incl. the technical factor*	*Percentage yield on net investment* (2) *excl. the technical factor*	*Employment increase, per cent, per annum* 0 *National product*	0 *Per head*	0·5 *National product*	0·5 *Per head*	1·0 *National product*	1·0 *Per head*	1·5 *National product*	1·5 *Per head*
0			1·8	1·8	2·2	1·7	2·6	1·6	3·0	1·5
10	24	6	2·4	2·4	2·8	2·3	3·2	2·2	3·5	2·0
15	18	6	2·7	2·7	3·1	2·6	3·5	2·5	3·8	2·3
20	15	6	3·0	3·0	3·4	2·9	3·7	2·7	4·1	2·6
30	12	6	3·6	3·6	4·0	3·5	4·3	3·3	4·7	3·2

Source: Odd Aukrust and Juul Bjerke, "Real Capital in Norway, 1900–1956", *Income aud Wealth,* Series VII, International Association for Research in Income and Wealth.

* The columns showing national product per head have been inserted into the original table by PEP by subtracting the percentage increase in employment from the figures for the growth of national product. The percentage yields have also been inserted.

It can be seen that the assumption of a 1·8 per cent per annum growth of the national product arising out of the technical factor, that is, out of replacement investment and improvements that do not require any investment for their realisation, radically reduces the valuation of the effectiveness of net investment in raising the national product. If the technical factor is included in the return from net investment the yield on a net investment of 10 per cent of the national product is 24 per cent. But on the assumption that the national product would increase by 1·8 per cent per annum even with zero net investment, the yield is reduced to 6 per cent. It may be suspected that this kind of approach, which takes account of the almost automatic increase in the national product arising out of the large stock of capital built up in the past, may be more relevant to an industrialised country like Britain than the simpler approach which attributes all the gain in output to additional net investment.[1] The table also suggests that, even with higher rates of increase of employment, the growth of output per head remains virtually unchanged for a given rate of investment. For example, with 10 per cent net investment, the growth in output per head is 2·4 per cent per annum if employment is stationary, and is still 2·0 per cent per annum if employment is increasing at the rapid rate of 1·5 per cent per annum. On the other hand, if employment remains constant, or continues to expand at the same rate, large amounts of net investment make little difference to the rate of growth of national product and national product per head. For example, with no growth of population, doubling the rate of net investment from 10 per cent to 20 per cent only raises the rate of growth of the national product from 2·4 per cent to 3·0 per cent. The relatively small change in the rate of growth is due to the assumption of a normal growth of 1·8 per cent per annum due to the technical factor even with zero net investment and a low yield on net investment.

It is perhaps worthwhile to quote from the conclusions of the Norwegian study:

> It is immediately seen that the rate of growth of the national product is affected comparatively little by the size of the investments. Without any increase in employment it is necessary to have as high investment ratio as 20 per cent in the next years to accomplish a 3 per cent growth per annum in the national product. If we reckon with an employment increase of for example 0·5 per cent per annum, a net investment ratio of 15 per cent (somewhat lower than the average in Norway in the last years) will give a growth in the national product of approximately 3·1 per cent per annum. To raise the rate of growth to 4 per cent would—if our computations are realistic—require a net investment ratio of no less than 30 per cent.
>
> In light of the above, it appears that the rate of growth which can be attained in a society like the Norwegian to a much smaller extent than hitherto believed depends on the investment policy followed. Whether investments within reasonable limits are high or low, the national product with constant employment will rise by 2–3 per cent per annum, largely because the technical factor alone

[1] This simpler model may of course be more appropriate for underdeveloped countries.

automatically warrants a growth which here has been estimated at roughly 1·8 per cent per annum. The pace can be increased somewhat beyond this by maintaining a high investment level, but not very much.

If this is correct, it has obvious economic policy implications. A stringent economic policy designed to maintain a high investment level becomes much harder to justify. One question which naturally arises in this connection is whether the trend factor here termed "technique" in itself is an invariable or whether it can be influenced, for example by placing more emphasis on the education of efficient management, technicians and workers. In view of the results derived it is natural to ask whether some of the resources which at present are devoted to investment projects could not with advantage be released for a greater effort within education and research.

It has been noted in Chapter 2 that there is reason to believe that rapid population growth may have certain advantages for the growth of productivity, and that these may be such as to offset the more apparent disadvantage that a rising population requires more investment to maintain the existing level of capital per head. If a suitable amendment were made to Table C1 to take account of the positive contribution of an expanding working population to the growth of total output, for example by increasing the "technical factor" by 0·2 per cent for every 0·5 per cent increase in employment, then the table would show a rising national product per head with faster rates of population increase. For example, half the increase achieved by a rate of net investment of 10 per cent, with stationary employment, could be achieved by an increase in employment of 1·5 per cent. This particular model breaks down at this point because part of the effect of the increase in employment is through its influence on investment. The two cannot be kept separate and there is no simple way of showing their interaction. But it can be seen that the significance of investment *in itself*, already depreciated by the assumption of a "technical factor", is still further diminished if one considers the influence of the growth of employment on productivity.

INDEX

Major References are given in bold type

S

T

U

W